SABOTAGE

IN THE AMERICAN WORKPLACE

ANECDOTES OF DISSATISFACTION, MISCHIEF AND REVENGE

EDITED BY MARTIN SPROUSE

PRESSURE DROP PRESS • AK PRESS

I have seen the blacksmith at work before the open flame of his forge. His hands were soiled and he was as dirty as a crocodile.

The various workers who handle the chisel — do they enjoy more leisure than the peasant? Their field is the wood they carve, and they work well after the day is ended and even at night if there is light in their houses.

The mason works the hardest stones. When he has finished carrying out the orders received and his hands are tired, does he perhaps, take a rest? He must be back at the yard at sunrise though his knees and back are at breaking point.

The barber works at his trade well into the night. For a mouthful of bread he must run from house to house in search of his customers.

Why such toil hardly to fill one's belly?

And the dyer of cloth? His hands stink; they smell of putrid fish. His eyes droop with sleep, but his hands never rest from preparing finely-colored robes. He hates cloth, every kind of cloth.

The cobbler is very unhappy and is always complaining he has nothing to chew but his leather.

They work, they all work — but it is as with honey, the gatherer alone eats it.
— Egypt, 14th century B.C.

Copyright © Pressure Drop Press 1992 except where otherwise credited.
All illustrations including front cover © Tracy Cox 1992

First edition, May 1992

Pressure Drop Press, POB 460754, San Francisco, CA 94146

Library of Congress Cataloging-in-Publication data:

Sabotage in the American workplace: anecdotes of dissatisfaction, revenge and mischief / edited by Martin Sprouse. – 1st ed. p.   cm.
  Includes bibliographical references.
  ISBN 0-9627091-3-1 (US) : $12.00
    1. Employee crimes–United States. 2. Computer crimes–United States.
3. Machinery in industry–Sabotage–United States.
I. Sprouse, Martin, 1966-
HF 5549.5.E43S23 1992
331.25-dc20
                                                                92-4236
                                                                  CIP

AK Press, 3 Balmoral Place, Stirling, Scotland FK8 2RD, U.K.

British Library Cataloging-in-Publication Data

Sabotage in the American workplace: anecdotes of dissatisfaction, revenge and mischief
  I. Sprouse, Martin
  306.3
  ISBN 1-873176-65-1 (UK)

Editor: Martin Sprouse
Assistant Editor: Lydia Ely
Illustrations and cover art: Tracy Cox

Copy editing, proofreading, research and lots of help that made this book possible: Rory Cox, Cynthia Connolly, Rikki Sender, Steve Spinali, Jennifer Cobb, Karra Bikson, Star Seifert, Alice Nutter, Emily Soares and Tim Yohannan.

Thanks: Ramsey Kanaan, Jason Traeger, Betty and Jerry Sprouse, Bob Beyerle, Peter Plate, John Yates, Simon Dumenco, Anjali Sundaram, Melissa Mann, Chris Carlsson, Cammie Toloui, Jeff Ditz, Harry Sherrill, Carin Adams, Dave Stevenson, Hilary Binder, Patrick Hughes, Tom Alder, Walter Glaser, Chas Bufe, Don Paul, Kate Rosenberger, Michelle Haunold, Katja Gussman, Steven Perkins, Spencer Reynolds, Caroline Ely, Anna Chapman, Russell Left Bank, Phil Sanchez, Steve Tupper, Lawrence Livermore, The MRR staff, The Coalition on Homelessness, Jon Reproman, Dick Ellington, Erin Cullin, and Ann Japenga.

ALL TYPOS AND MISTAKES
IN THIS BOOK ARE DUE TO
EMPLOYEE SABOTAGE.

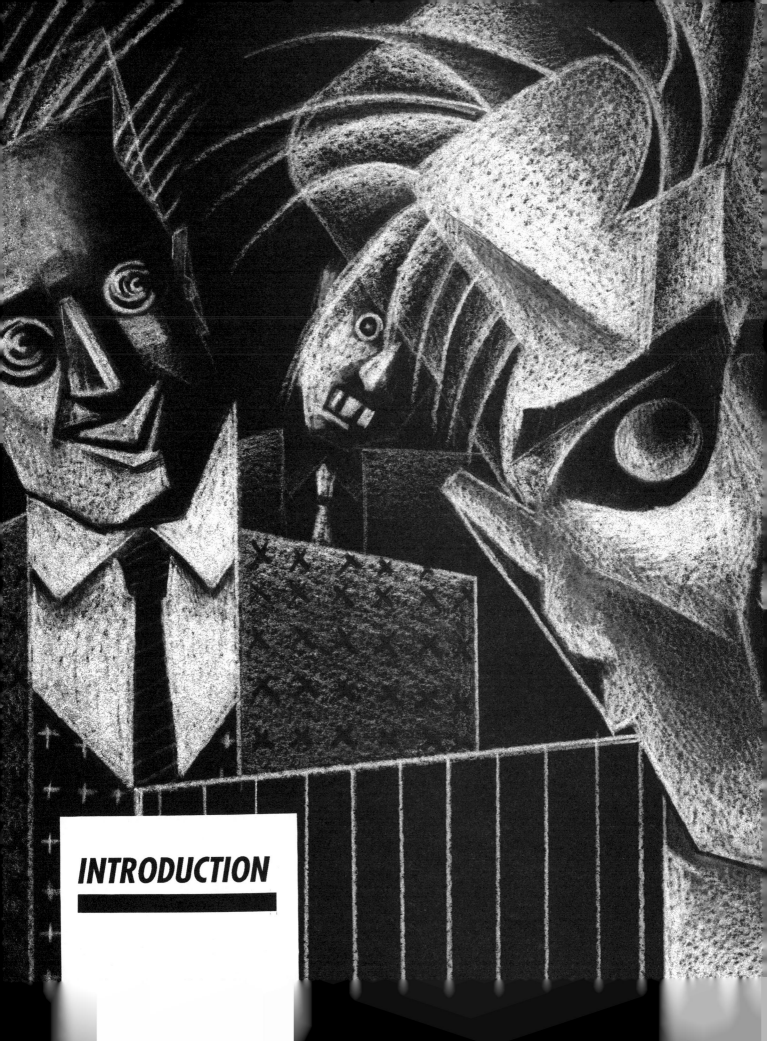

INTRODUCTION

In 1987, I applied for a mailroom job at a San Francisco financial magazine. Since licking envelopes requires little experience and I was first in line, I got the job. The interview with the office supervisor was just a formality. Our only conversation was about my starting pay, $4.75 an hour, which was barely a living wage. It was never acknowledged, but the supervisor and I both knew there were twenty others who would have taken the job if I didn't. Like a lot of other people, I was desperate for work, so I accepted the offer. The supervisor gave me a copy of the employee rules manual, shook my hand, and said, "Welcome to the team." I knew I was in trouble.

The company was growing fast, changing and expanding. New departments were constantly set up and old ones phased out. Even at its calmest, the office was chaotic. Although the company rarely gave out raises or promotions, and demanded a lot from the employees, they didn't think twice about firing them. Staff turnover was high, making it impossible to keep track of who was in and who was out. I never saw anyone quit. Most people needed work and any job was better than nothing.

The mailroom was, appropriately, located in the basement. The four people I worked with quickly taught me that the mailroom staff were at the bottom of the company totem pole. We were there to do the mail, but if an executive needed his desk moved or if an overflowing toilet had to be fixed, we were expected to do it. On the few occasions where everyone got bonuses, the mailroom staff got a pizza.

Our commitment to the company was minimal. We were there to collect our paychecks, and that was it. Gradually I realized that all the departments had the same attitude. Dissatisfaction started with us in the basement and rose all the way up to the desk where the CEO's secretary worked.

Discontent was matched by an equal amount of sabotage. The company postage machine, long distance telephone lines and expense accounts were considered public domain. Office supplies couldn't be kept in stock for more than a few days, and furniture, as well as a couple of computers, vanished. People took long lunches and slacked off whenever possible. Some employees found more unusual ways of expressing their dissatisfaction. The morning after word got out about possible pay cuts, the staff were greeted by an office fountain spiked with bubble bath. It flooded the reception area with white suds, and most of us struggled to restrain our laughter as the office managers stared in disbelief. As usual, the mailroom staff were called in to clean up the mess.

My two years with this company provided the initial inspiration for this book. There I was in a typical American office, witnessing sabotage done by almost every level of staff. It was a clear reflection of how they felt toward the company and it made their jobs more tolerable. Sabotage was part of most employees' daily routines, and so widespread that it was barely noticeable. I doubt that even the most observant of managers had a clue about what was going on.

The basic idea behind the book — to document reactions to the day-to-day frustrations and conflicts of earning a living in America — hasn't changed. I knew what I'd seen at the magazine job wasn't unusual. In fact, almost anyone who has worked knows that dissatisfaction is a part of a great number of American jobs.

Because I wanted the book to include a wide range of anecdotes — encompassing different types of sabotage, people and jobs — I chose to define "sabotage" loosely, as *anything that you do at work that you're not supposed to do*. Even though the bubble bath prank at the magazine makes for a great sabotage story, I was just as intrigued by the straight-laced data processor who always added extra hours to her time card, or the graphic designer who regularly came down to the mailroom and talked when he should have been behind his desk. Then there was the quiet, middle-aged accountant who had me send his Christmas gifts at company expense. Did he do it because he knew he could get away with it, or because he felt the company owed him something?

These aren't the kinds of people that come to mind when sabotage is mentioned, but these are the people who were yelled at when the boss was in a bad mood. Considered expendable by the managers, they were the first to have their salaries cut. I wanted to listen to their stories, find out where they drew their personal line of tolerance, and hear how they defined sabotage.

I wasn't sure what I was getting myself into, or what sort of response to expect, but I was optimistic when I began the project. I made flyers soliciting stories and handed them out and posted them up wherever I could. Few stories materialized this way, so I tried a more direct approach. I spent several afternoons in San Francisco's financial district trying to interview people on their lunch hour. As you might expect, I got more suspicious looks than stories. They must have thought that I worked for their boss doing a company security check. I quickly realized that getting stories was going to be a lot harder than I had first anticipated.

It was obvious that I was going have to find and pursue my own leads. On the suggestion of a mutual friend, I interviewed Steve, who told a story about working as a dishwasher in Olympia, Washington. I met Jane several years ago when she moved here from the East Coast where she had worked as a prostitute. Jane put me in contact with her friend Peggy, a former casino poker dealer. A.J., an army mechanic stationed in Germany, sat in on my interview in a coffee shop with Harry, the utility file clerk. As soon as I told A.J. what the book was about, we started talking, and our conversation turned into an interview.

As word got out, people started coming to me with stories. A computer disc arrived bearing a story from Dexter, a computer technical writer. In a letter, Bruce described a phone prank he did at his job as senior officer for a branch of the government. Robin, a former hotel security guard, heard about the book through a friend and eagerly filled a cassette tape with his story. Rita, a flight attendant of twenty years, and the cab driver, who called himself Axel, responded to an ad I placed in a local paper. Flyers were still circulating; Frances, a paralegal, found one in her office cafeteria when, coincidentally, she was feeling frustrated by her bosses. I interviewed her over the phone on her company's time.

After reading about them in the newspaper, I tracked down Ron, the Florida toy store manager, and Louie, the bus driver from the Midwest. Finding them was worth the effort; they both had me laughing when they told me their stories.

I knew most people would be more comfortable telling their stories if they did it anonymously. Each person decided how much detail they were going to provide. In some cases, people who had severely broken the law were wary of letting me record their stories. Others reacted the same way at the thought of admitting they had taken long lunches behind their boss' back.

The people I interviewed have backgrounds as varied as their stories. Some could barely survive, living paycheck to paycheck; others made $60,000 a year. Their ages range from twelve to sixty-five. Their stories are set all over America, from Los Angeles to remote Alaskan coastal towns, from Wall Street to the North Dakota wheat fields.

Pedro, a plumber in Southern California, had a wife and kids. He had never been interviewed before and was somewhat hesitant, but became relaxed after a couple of beers and some conversation. Alejandro was originally from Mexico; when he couldn't find employment in America, he got a job with an American company in the Middle East as a graphic designer. I spent an afternoon talking to a nurse who introduced himself to me as Ed. He amazed me with his knowledge of medicine and his insights on the routine sabotage done by hospital nurses.

As I did more interviews, I began to see that each person's choice of sabotage and reasons for using it were as much a reflection of their character as of their jobs. The motives behind the acts covered the spectrum between altruism and revenge.

Terry worked on a speeding assemblyline packing pickles in jars. He knew that his co-workers, most of them young kids, were being forced to work too fast, so he shut down the line, giving everyone in the factory an unexpected break. Jeff gave his all to the roofing company he worked for, but he never got the promotion he had been promised. His sabotage cost his boss $80,000. Barbara enjoyed being a physician relations manager but wasn't able to do her job because her supervisor, threatened by her presence, gave her useless work to do. Barbara decided to read books instead of work. Tico, a former disc jockey, was a troublemaker and prankster. At the station where he worked, he tried to get away with as much as possible without getting fired. While working at a conservative think tank, Reggie realized he disagreed with his bosses' politics, so he used his position as mail clerk to sabotage their fundraising efforts. Alan and his co-workers at the copy shop felt they were being underpaid so they gave themselves daily cash bonuses from the register.

Along with the highly dramatic, I've included several stories of quiet sabotage. There's Brian, the car mechanic from Rochester who didn't like his boss overbilling the customers. Brian took control of the situation and made it work the way he wanted. Afterwards, he felt better about his job and the customers got a fair deal. Although his sabotage might be considered fairly minor, it had a noticeable impact. Alice, a secretary, used the term "perks" to describe her padded time card and extra discounts on company merchandise. She was a bit shocked when I suggested that her actions could be considered theft. As far as she was concerned, she had never stolen anything in her life. She felt completely justified in her actions. The sabotage was not unique, and I found her rationalization of it to be common.

There's no doubt that certain kinds of sabotage affect consumers. Depending on the act, the customer either benefits or gets a bad deal. Marc was a clerk at a convenience store where products were sold for higher than the standard retail price. Using his pricing gun, Marc gave customers what he thought were fair discounts. Eugene worked in a Detroit factory where he and his co-workers produced thousands of faulty carburetors. He was convinced that if a consumer bought a lemon, they would never buy another vehicle from the company that he hated with a passion. Eugene's probably right. Carol has been a waitress most of her life. While working at one restaurant, she and other waitresses let food spoil before serving it to customers. Most people will probably see her story as one of the most extreme in the book (Tracy Cox was horrified by it as you can tell from his illustration accompanying it). Carol told her story matter-of-factly; to her, what she did was no big deal. In her eyes, the food poisoning was just a way for her and her co-workers to give the restaurant a bad reputation and get even with their boss, who had refused to give them a raise.

I interviewed a number of people who didn't have any sabotage stories. Some had no complaints about their jobs; others took any form of abuse that came their way. I talked to a sales representative for specialty food companies who claimed to have no criticisms of her job, mainly because of the autonomy she had in her daily routine. After an hour of discussion, I called it quits. I did get her to admit that once in a while she took a long lunch — but always made the time up the next day. Fair enough. I heard detailed stories from a former San Francisco police officer, a fertilizer chemist and an appraiser for an exclusive auction house. Each of them had gripes about their jobs but chose to wait the problems out. Although they didn't have stories for the book, what they told me gave me more perspective on sabotage.

Six months into the project, Lydia Ely had become assistant editor. Together we researched the subject of sabotage. We found few books that provided a contemporary view. Some of the earliest accounts describe American slaves who made sabotage a way of life to protest their ultimate degradation. The slaves deceived their owners by feigning stupidity, incompetence, and slowness — actions which, at the very least, caused the owners irritation and expense.

American labor history books generally focus on struggles from the early 20th century and frequently refer to strikes and walkouts, with little discussion of sabotage. When sabotage is mentioned it's usually linked to the Industrial Workers of the World, or Wobblies. They were the most notable union to officially advocate — or at least consistently threaten — the use of sabotage. Eventually, due to legal harassment and internal disagreement, the Wobblies disassociated themselves from wholesale support of sabotage.

Studs Terkel's *Working* was one of the few books where Americans described work-related frustrations in their own words. Although there have been significant changes in the notion of work since when the book was first published, in the mid-seventies, the attitudes and conflicts that it documents are eternal and will always be as much a part of work as the time clock.

Accompanying the interviews are excerpts from newspaper and magazine articles, management manuals, quotes, poems, proverbs, lyrics and statistics that relate to work and sabotage. Some of these items are opinions, facts, or have historical value, while others are included because of their absurdity. The statistics are rarely factual and are the result of guesswork by consulting firms who profit from producing and selling such information.

During the time that I was working on the book, I was interviewed about sabotage on a radio talk show. The interviewer asked what I thought could be done to solve the problem of sabotage. I told him I didn't see sabotage as a problem, but as a necessary and valid reaction to dissatisfaction caused by work. Since it's not a problem, there's no solution — a point that I hope this book illustrates.

If the cause of discontent in the workplace is obvious, sabotage can be used to improve working conditions and give people greater control of their jobs, as in the instance where bicycle messengers used it to change an idiotic company policy. When resentment springs from general attitudes toward work, there are no simple answers. Very few of the people in this book liked being told what to do by their boss or supervisor and most were acutely aware of the countless differences between those who gave the orders and those who actually did the work. Several people explained that they felt trapped by meaningless work, while others made it clear they didn't like working for other people. These conflicts might be commonplace but they are also the most basic reasons for sabotage.

As long as people feel cheated, bored, harassed, endangered, or betrayed at work, sabotage will be used as a direct method of achieving job satisfaction — the kind that never has to get the bosses' approval.

— Martin Sprouse, February 1992

1 YOU CAN'T GET THERE FROM HERE

Transportation

BUS DRIVER • PREACHER

I started working for the Chicago Transit Authority as a bus operator when I was twenty-seven. Later, due to my expert driving ability, I became a line instructor, which meant I continued to drive the bus but I broke in new students on my line. This was a prerequisite to becoming a management supervisor. I worked until I was fifty, but I never made management.

We had threadless, bald-headed tires on those vehicles. I once asked how the vehicles had any traction. They said, "You have double wheels on the rear and the airspace on the two tires provides traction." I don't know how they got away with it. We had a sign-in sheet; at the end of every day, we signed in our opinion of the run and how the bus was going. I would regularly write "bald-headed tires," or whatever the complaint was. I was called into the office about that. They said, "If you want to be a supervisor, see nothing, hear nothing, say nothing," which I wouldn't do. When I became a line instructor they said, "Preacher, keep your mouth shut." If I wanted to be a management supervisor, I would have to be a "company man."

Our depot served twelve routes. The routes that entered into the white neighborhoods got the nicer, newer coaches. The routes that entered the black neighborhoods got the worst, stinking, ten to twenty-year-old buses they had, where the windows wouldn't open in the summer and the heat wouldn't come on in the winter. When they got brand new air-conditioned coaches, they put them on the white lines. I had one shift where I got a brand new coach because the route extended into a white neighborhood off Lake Shore Drive, where Hugh Hefner lives. In other words, six of 100 buses were elite buses.

In the buses, there was a button which dropped a slug into the engine and automatically shut it off. It was for emergency purposes only, like overheating or malfunction. When we got a "raggedy coach" — leaning to one side, with fumes in it, or with poor brakes or poor shocks — some drivers would go to the end of the route where the passengers wouldn't be inconvenienced and take the layover time (when you get to rest ten to fifteen minutes) and drop that slug into the engine, grind it and run the battery down. The mechanic would come and want to know why they did it. The driver would say they didn't know how the slug went down.

"Dragging the street" is when you slow the line down on purpose. One day, it was ten below zero, baldheaded tires, 100 people trying to get home in a snowstorm, Preacher doing the best he can, never had a chargeable accident in the entire time I was with the company. I'm going ten miles an hour, trying to make a stop as best I can on streets that may or may not have salt over the ice. After you made a full stop, if someone in the back of the bus shifted their weight, those baldheaded tires would slide across the ice and I'd slam into a parked car. I was told in the depot, "You're driving too fast for the conditions." So the next day I slowed down from ten miles an hour to five miles an hour. The supervisor's scanning the area to find out why all these buses are late. "There goes Preacher and a few other guys dragging the street again!" So

Workers have been known to boast of "soldiering" or purposely slowing down on a job. Actually, the time lost by workers and not paid for directly is paid for indirectly by the company because the day or piece rates must be higher to provide the expected weekly wage. "Soldiering" may react on both the management and the worker through increasing labor costs that cannot be passed along to the buyer in higher prices, thus creating avoidable losses which may curtail plant activity.

— Organized Labor and Production, Morris L. Cooke and Philip Murray [1]

Like workers on an assembly line that has been speeded up, flight attendants have been asked to hand out commercial love at an ever faster rate, to more people in the same amount of time.

Unable to keep up, attendants have countered with a slowdown. They could not slow down their actual physical labor — they had to serve meals in the flight time allotted — but they could slow down their emotional labor. And, in a way not quite articulated, that is what they have been doing. Passengers no longer get the steady good hearted cheer promised ever more boldly by smiling young women in ads.

— "Smile Wars," Mother Jones [2]

you're damned if you do, damned if you don't! It got to the point where I didn't care if I went three miles an hour. If you and your momma and your daughter are on the bus, I'm not going to endanger your lives. I'm going to go as slow as it takes for me to operate that bus without hurting anyone.

When a driver retired, they'd retire his run with him. So you had fewer runs on the same route, with more and more volume. A bunch of drivers got together and said, "Fuck this schedule! We don't want to drive defensively" (which means over and above quota). That was our Catch-22; if we went any faster and tried to maintain schedule, we'd be driving in a reckless manner. We would drag down entire streets that way.

When they first got blacks in the position, it seemed as if they had to be super sharp and super clean. The whites only had to get off the buses and into supervision. All they had to do was have a cousin or a relative or a priest or any other form of nepotism. Don't get me wrong — there were black supervisors that were impeccable in their performance, never kissed ass. But the majority of them, if they wanted to be a supervisor, had to skin and grin up to the man's face, more so than anybody else had to. It's like when I see a black pilot flying a 747 — he's so much more superior to the co-pilot than a white pilot would have to be. They want you to be Little Lord Fauntleroy.

I could do my job. They could have my labor. But they couldn't have my soul.

FLIGHT ATTENDANT • RITA

I had fun when I first started. My expectations were that I would jump on an airplane, get off in another city and party. I was going to have a great, carefree time. It never occurred to me that there would be some problems down the road.

When I started flying in 1967, flight attendants couldn't be married. I also had to agree to quit at the age of thirty-five. These things, of course, have since been struck down by employee discrimination legislation. Back then we were seen as party girls, young and single, with no worries at home. A lot changed when flight attendants were allowed to get married, but in many ways we're still perceived as carefree girls. There's still this expectation that we're going to be outgoing; passengers assume I'm going to tell them personal stuff willfully and gladly. Early on, I began thinking differently about what passengers really expected of me. They wanted to pick my brain and they wanted me to be friendly and talkative and constantly available for them.

The company has a set of rules that say we're supposed to make ourselves available and let other people hear our conversations. They want us to give the impression that we are outgoing and loquacious. They want us to speak in complete sentences. It never occurred to me in training that the days would be long, or that I was going to have to deal with people who were rude, dirty, drunk and obnoxious.

When I start to get tired on a flight, I avoid the passengers. I have a friend who has a name tag that says "Oh, Miss." If I hear somebody saying "Oh, Miss," I don't even look back at them. I don't hear that little plaintive voice calling me. I avoid eye contact. I do the same thing in the boarding area. Passengers come over to me and want to talk and ask questions about the flight. I don't hear them talking. I look away. I walk away. I consider that on-the-job avoidance. It's not important to me to let the passengers know what I'm all about. I'll do these things when there are a ton of people on a flight and I'm feeling overloaded, when I just can't take one more request from a passenger.

The whole airline business is based on emotional labor — being nice when you don't want to be. I think anybody in a service position does this, but we do it a lot. The company wants us to sell a smile, but giving it really takes its toll. The company doesn't recognize it, my union doesn't recognize it, but those who do the job realize it all too clearly.

I can't say I hate the job. There are some things about it that I enjoy. I like the people I work with. I like the fact that I don't have a supervisor, that I have a different schedule each month, and that I can pick and choose the days and times I work. I get good vacations. I don't think I'm going to find all of these things in that many other jobs. But for these pluses, there are some real minuses.

My outlook has evolved over the years. Instead of trying to do backflips to turn the situation around, I just stop putting out and it's better for me. I've got to do what I can to stay sane. It's not enough to come home and not talk about my job. I need to do something on the job to keep my emotions fairly healthy. I know I was hired because they thought I was going to do things their way, but I can't anymore. There's a saying that we have at work: "The company knows the price of everything and the value of nothing." That pretty much sums it up.

GAS STATION ATTENDANT • KEITH

My boss was a racist bitch who had a severe chip on her shoulder. Most of the people who got jobs there either quit or got fired within three days. I worked for her at this gas station/mini-mart on and off for about a year, and I saw her go through no less than 100 employees. Pretty much everybody I knew in town had worked there at one point or another.

She did inventory once a month. Since I was constantly planning to quit, I usually saved my bigger thefts until right after inventory was taken, so it wouldn't get figured out until a month later. By then, she'd have gone through ten employees who she could conveniently blame for the crime. She never even suspected I was robbing her blind. I was always very nice to her and I cleaned the place spotless every night. I was never short more than a few cents at the end of my shift and the cigarette count never came up short. I was a model employee who could always be counted on and only called in sick once.

Mostly, I stuck to soda, ice cream, beef jerky and that kind of thing. I made sure to swipe plenty of oil, transmission fluid and whatnot. One kid working there would program the pumps so that the price per gallon was one cent, and all his friends would come in and fill up for free.

I pulled little scams that were impossible to pin on me. On

weekend nights, if I was getting a lot of obnoxious suburban drunks in, I'd just turn out the outside lights, put up a closed sign, and watch TV. If I didn't feel like dealing with someone's shit, I'd just pretend I didn't hear them. I'd just keep on going "What? What?" until they got sick of me and left. We also sold instant lottery tickets at the station and I'd entertain myself by snatching five or ten and try to win big money. I'd usually win enough to pay for the tickets I took and turn a slight profit — although once I did win 200 bucks right before Christmas.

SHUTTLE DRIVER • ANTONIO

I drive passenger shuttles between the airport and San Francisco. I am an independent contractor: I pay $75 a day rent — "gate" — for the use of a van that seats eight people including the driver, and my gas which is now $25 a day.

I do many things to rip off the company. I don't pay the gas, or I claim to have transported fewer passengers than I did and say I'm unable to pay the full gate. Sometimes I drive people who don't pay cash, but give me vouchers which are paid by airlines, hotels or travel agencies. I turn in fake vouchers. Some of them are not marked with the number of passengers or the distance or their destination. I can make up the information, depending on the time I called in last. This means I don't have to pay the gate at all.

When I steal time, I try to make it up later to make more money. If I'm late in the morning, my shift is shorter than ten hours, but I still have to pay the full "gate." If my shift starts at 6:30 am, I have to be out at 4:30 pm. Between 11:00 am and 4:30 pm I don't make much money, so I need more time. To convince the office that I need the van longer, I say that I had a "10-6," which is the code for a mechanical problem. The van overheated; it got a flat; it stalled. They ask me if I need a tow. Usually I say, "Oh, I'll let it cool down," or "I'll do my best; I'll be coming in really slow."

When I want to go short shift, I pour water in the gas tank, which makes the van stall. Sometimes they'll bring me a van, but most of the time there aren't any, so I go short shift and don't pay my gate. I can get a flat by punching the tire into a curb. I can break the radio by disconnecting the wires, and someone has to come fix it. Other times at the end of my shift, I put myself in a huge traffic jam. I know where the traffic is; drivers are always calling where the jams are on the radio. I say that I'm in a particular jam. They can't track me, and among drivers there is that kind of camaraderie and cooperation. Even if someone sees me, nobody will tell the office where I am or what I'm doing. I can be talking with the office, saying I'm downtown in traffic when instead I'm at the airport, picking up and dropping off people. Everybody sees me at the airport and hears me saying on the radio that I'm downtown, but no one will tell.

I do these things for self-defense, because the job is stressful and my pay doesn't match the service I furnish. If I didn't do it, I would have to work seven days a week and still be able to barely pay my bills. Everyone is underpaid except the owners, who are very powerful and get money from the state and city. Because everyone is an independent contractor, there is no way to struggle against them. Employees burn out very fast.

Sometimes I feel bad about it because I've had other jobs where I was a professional with a work ethic. I'm an immigrant; I have an accent; I have many problems getting work. But I have to make money. This job is not a way to live, it's a way to waste my life. But what can I do? Starve?

CAB DRIVER • AXEL

I was at loose ends as Christmas approached. A friend of mine drove cabs and said I could make an okay living at it. At first I was uncertain because I didn't know what the hell went on being a cab driver. As it got closer and closer to Christmas, I was afraid I wouldn't be able to buy any toys for my kid, so I thought I'd give it a try.

I've been driving for four years now and I still enjoy my job. I'm a talker and I talk with people from all walks of life. I find that about ninety-five percent of the people I pick up are prepared to start chatting with me. I'm great for five, six minutes of conversation and people enjoy the hell out of me. When I'm behind the wheel, I'm the master of my little domain. I don't have a supervisor looking over my shoulder, but like any other job, there's management.

I think cab management is just a little less ethical than drug dealing. When I tell this to non-drivers they're surprised at the harshness of my words, but when I say it to drivers, they say, "So?" because they know how it is. The way the cab business is set up, there is no incentive for management to make it work better for the drivers or the customers. Management gets their money from cab rental fees paid by the driver, not from the customer. So when a customer calls for a cab, it doesn't matter whether a driver gets to that customer or not.

When we're given an order and it's ten blocks away, we're expected to go pick it up. But we don't know how old that order is, we just know someone has called for a cab. The problem is, many times people will call a cab then go out to the street and flag one down. We'll drive up a minute later, ring the doorbell trying to find the person, but no response. It's company policy to try every possible way to locate the person who called the cab, but if the order's an hour old, that person is gone.

It's clear to most drivers that the more you're in motion and the more fares you pick up, the more money you make. When we go off to get an order, someone will usually flag us down on our way there. But if we pick the flag up, the dispatcher is going to yell. So we have to concoct a lie, which is something every driver quickly learns to do. We tell them the original order needs a second cab because they had two people going separate directions, when in fact we had never made it there in the first place. When you first start driving, you pass up flags; then you soon try to find out how many you can get away with picking up.

Our fear is that if the company finds out we're doing this, they'll can us. But if we're completely loyal to the company and follow their rules, we'll be perfect cab drivers but won't make any money.

I guess what I do is like survival. They're making rules to our detriment, so we need to break them to make a living.

BUS DRIVER • LOUIE

It's a city-owned bus utility, so it's heavily financed by the government. It's in a college town so drugs are considered part of the lifestyle. Marijuana use is a common thing among the people who live here.

A group of drivers and mechanics got concerned after we got federal orders that all bus utility workers employed by a company getting Urban Mass Transit Administration money would have to be drug tested. People were just saying, "This sucks! The government doesn't have any right to tell us what to do." We wanted to know why we had to jeopardize our jobs for having a joint on the weekend.

First, someone xeroxed a brochure on how to flush your system out. So I started copying that and giving it out. Then a couple of people got information from the American Civil Liberties Union on what our rights were. And interestingly enough, our union, which wasn't a very active union, started getting involved.

When something really hits home, people start to get more involved. We started gathering information which spread around the shop. The level of interest increased as we got closer to the date the random tests were supposed to begin. Some people stopped using their drug of choice until they could figure out what was going on.

The weekend before the drug testing was to begin, we had an "After-Holidays Party." Somebody — nobody knows who it was, though someone in management thought they knew — brought in a pan of brownies laced with marijuana. Obviously, the purpose was so innocent people would test positive in the drug test, and the results would have to be thrown out.

Once people heard about it they crossed their fingers. The brownies became the hit of the party. The tension grew every time an unsuspecting dispatcher or supervisor ate one of the brownies. Unfortunately, the general manager didn't eat any. Nobody realized what had happened until it was too late. All they knew was that the pan of brownies had been eaten. Management was completely flustered. They had absolutely no idea of what to do.

A couple of weeks later a federal court ruling came down that knocked down the testing requirement because of some technicality. The Urban Mass Transit Administration had to rewrite the rule, so we have a year reprieve. In the meantime, we're trying to get new language in our contract. The federal government can tell you to have random drug testing but it can't mandate discipline. If we don't succeed, I know at next year's party, people are going to look at the brownies and ask themselves, "Do I want to eat these?"

2 HARVESTING THE FIELDS OF PLENTY

Food Processing

Furthermore, there is no need to destroy machinery completely in order to stop it from working: just as the sabotaging of one key machine can cause general disruption, so the sabotaging of one key component of a machine can cause it to come to a standstill.
— Sabotage in Industry, Pierre Dubois [1]

Around the turn of the century, management destroyed the old craft unions in the steel, oil, and chemical industries and reorganized factories according to Frederick Taylor's principles of "scientific management." The essence of those principles was that management should itself determine the best method of performing the job, then prescribe precisely how workers should proceed. As a result of this reorganization, it is claimed, workers in automated plants are effectively docile servants dominated by management in highly "Taylorized" settings.
— America's Working Man, David Halle [2]

PINEAPPLE PACKER • LANCE

In Honolulu, most people start working at Dole Pineapple right out of high school. They usually end up staying there for the rest of their lives like my grandparents did. If you don't have a good education, it's hard to find any other job in Hawaii. I'd have to say that for most people, it was just a shitty job. The work was hard and the factory was noisy and hot. No one liked it. The managers were incredibly abusive; in order to avoid promoting people, they switched us around a lot so we never got skilled at any one job.

I worked at the Janacka machine, which cuts the hides and skin off the pineapple. I also worked where they seal the tops of the cans, and then I worked inspection, where they weigh random samplings of cans to make sure they have the right amount of juice and everything.

The Janacka machine was probably the best. We usually worked a straight ten-hour shift, so a lot of people would just burn out. The biggest problem was people falling asleep and getting their hands caught in the machine. To combat that, people would try to get more breaks — we were only allowed two breaks a shift. To do this, they would send a pineapple down the wrong direction, or send a glove down, and it would break the whole machine. If the Janacka machine shuts down, you can't cut the pineapple, and if you can't cut the pineapple, the line can't go on. The whole production line shuts down. It takes at least three hours to fix, so you're getting paid for three hours at least for just sitting around.

There was only one manager for the people who sealed cans, and it's such a huge place that they couldn't check on us more than once an hour. We could easily switch the wrong button and the juice would go into the wrong container, or we could change the levels so that everything overflowed. They'd have to shut down the machine to figure out what went wrong.

There were about five of us working at the inspection place in different shifts. We would collect the pineapple for samples, go into the back room, hang out, listen to the radio for a couple of hours, and then throw all the samples away. It was a pretty common practice.

We never got caught and I don't know anyone who's ever been fired from Dole. First off, it's incredibly cheap labor and, overall, they're making a hell of a lot of money from our ten hour shifts. It was so easy to make a mistake that they'd never know when we did it on purpose. Everyone who worked there knew that people did it. They welcomed the break — they'd be stupid not to, and be ostracized by everyone else.

PALLETIZER • PATRICK

I worked in a food production factory that made thousands of bottles of warm goo a day. I stood at the end of a conveyer belt where boxes with a dozen bottles of this warm crap came whizzing down to me, about one per second. I would stack them on pallets and the forklift driver would take them away. Occasionally, when we got a major shipment of boxes with plastic bottles for the front end of the assembly line, the foreman would take me and a few others off the line and send us upstairs to the old wooden storeroom. The boxes would come up on a conveyor belt to us, where we would stack them on the floor.

One day we were called to unload a major shipment. The boxes were coming at us at an alarming rate. Me and two co-workers were running like fools, arms stretched wide, grasping these boxes. We would have to run them over to where they were being stacked on the far side of the wall. It was sweltering hot up in the attic storeroom of this antiquated old factory. We were sweating and running with these boxes, squeezing tight so the middle ones wouldn't fall out. The conveyor belt was crammed with boxes. The foreman, a despicable Marine sergeant type, sat on a stack of boxes and picked his teeth, chiding us to go faster. If one of us fell behind the others, he'd call us "pussy" or some other insult sure to drive us into a working frenzy.

There was no let-up in boxes, and with sweat dripping into our eyes and cardboard dust irritating our skin, the three of us exploded into open revolt. Tim punched a box off the conveyor belt, and in a matter of seconds, we were punching them all off the belt. Boxes and plastic bottles were flying all over the floor. As the boxes kept coming from below, we kept punching them off. One after the other in a wild, deliriously happy frenzy. We ran to the stacks of boxes and started pulling them down with a dull crash onto the old wooden floor. The foreman was grabbing at our arms, trying to stop us, hollering as loud as he could over the din of the boxes and conveyor motor.

Finally, with big sheepish grins on our faces, we stopped. The boxes had stopped. The foreman told us to take the day off, to go home. The next day we came to work as if nothing had happened. I took my place on the line. The boxes of warm crap came whizzing down to me, about one per second...

FISH CANNER • DAVID

I worked in Alaska at a cannery in a very remote, isolated location. The place was pretty terrible. The living conditions were at best a step above camping. The plumbing didn't work, and there was no hot water. We were well-fed, but beyond that, the company's attitude was pretty oppressive. Generally, the idea was that we were making a big chunk of money, and that's where the company's concern for us stopped. "You're paid well. You can't make this kind of money in the lower forty-eight, so beyond just giving you this paycheck, we don't really care what happens to you." A lot of the workers were sorta young, so they had the ability to let it slide off of them.

It was very much of a Christian bible camp atmosphere. The Sunday services were always well-attended. I wouldn't say that I was in the total minority in the sense that I didn't attend, but it was strongly recommended that you make your pilgrimage every Sunday to the prayer service.

The first job I had there was in the can shop, which was the beginning point of the assembly line for canning the fish. In some ways the can shop was easy because it wasn't very physical. But the

Trying to get a worker to do what is an unreasonable amount of work can backfire. Work goals, to be effective as productivity incentive, have to be in the range of what a good worker can be expected to achieve. Unrealistic goals tend to slow the pace of productivity.
— Supervisor's Factomatic, Jack Horn [3]

The supervisor is the first line of defense against the saboteur. If employees know that management is watching, those most inclined to do damage will think twice.
— Supervisory Management Magazine [4]

By his very success in inventing labor-saving devices, modern man has manufactured an abyss of boredom that only the privileged classes in earlier civilizations have ever fathomed.
— Lewis Mumford

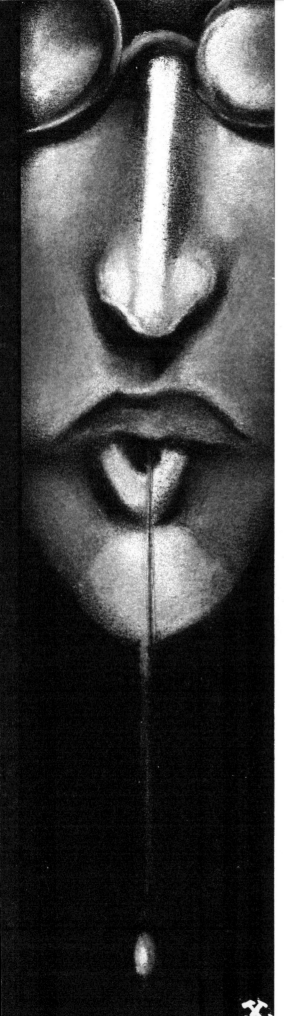

noise and the heat and the mindlessness of it were really punishing. Essentially, the cans were assembled first by stamping machines and then they went down the line and were filled with fish. Then they were sealed and stacked in a warehouse. I was at the beginning of that line. In any given line there were fifty people. I had to take big stacks of can lids that I pulled out of these boxes and shove them into the line a handful at a time. Once I had the can lids on top, I'd push the spring down vertically and somehow some part of the conveyor belt came along and grabbed the can lids.

It was a union job so there was the standard fifteen minute break every four hours, but if you spread that over a fifteen hour day, that's four breaks. We were given a lunch and a dinner but it was still pretty monotonous and horrible.

It became clear after a while that the system would just break down. More often than not, it would break down in the can shop itself. Even if just one can lid was put in upside down, the entire system would jam. They would have to send mechanics in, open up the system and pull out this errant can lid. That would give us about a fifteen minute break.

This happened all the time. After having a few of these breaks and sort of milling around talking with people, we found that most of what was happening was being done on purpose. It became this accepted thing that the line would be shut down to give people a break. It was pretty ridiculous because it wasn't very difficult to get the lids in right to begin with. They came in a stack, in the right position, and the only way to get them turned around was to physically put your hand in the stack, take one, and flip it over.

I don't know what the management was thinking. I guess that it had been like that for so many years that they accepted it. As long as it didn't repeatedly come from the same line, it was accepted that it was a part of the process.

Every time we shut down the line we got some satisfaction out of the fact that we were spitting back at management in some way. The whole thing just seemed so alienating that I could justify doing practically anything. It was probably one of the most miserable experiences of my life, and somehow what I did helped make it a little more livable.

DATE PITTER • SUSAN

I used to be a pitter for Land of Plenty Dates. I probably still would be if I hadn't been fired for incompetence, or rather, competence.

I took the job on a dare. I had just graduated from high school. All my girlfriends were humming the wedding march. My parents were beginning to wonder when I would start to date. Then I saw the ad: "Wanted: m-f date specialist — pits." I applied immediately. The interviewer was afraid I was overeducated, but I quickly disabused him of this illusion. I asked if the process was painful for the dates.

My first week at the job was uneventful. A machine did most of the work. I just had to oversee the operation: regulate the flow, make sure the contraption didn't jam, and help out the boxer,

Maggie. She looked strong enough to take on Mohammed Ali. As the dates plunged at her, she would make up little poems about them. She must have answered the wrong ad.

After the second week, I began to get a little ... fruity. Maggie's ditties about dropping crates of dates down grates and spitting pits were driving me up a date tree. Finally, when I was about to walk into the office and tell everyone where their dates would fit, I hit upon the ideal solution. A pitted date has a hole in it, right? An empty space. Why couldn't I roll up little pieces of paper and stuff them inside? They would be like Chinese fortune cookies! I could write all sorts of messages and send them throughout the fifty states plus Japan — our market area.

My first message was very innocuous: "Hi, I'm your pitter. Do you want to pitter-patter with me?" I didn't get an acceptance, but I didn't get a rejection either. I sent out about a thousand more of these date surprises. Then I laid low. Three weeks later, I started inserting my name and phone number. I thought of adding my measurements, but 31-28-37 doesn't excite many people. Maggie had been replaced by Hubert. He polished each date before boxing it. I didn't see a bright future for him at Land of Plenty.

Six weeks went by and I still hadn't heard anything from my note receivers. In despair, I switched tactics, cramming "Stuff it!" into the ugly little monsters. I was busily working away when I heard through the partially open office door "Aaaggghhh!!!" What had happened? No one ever ate the dates. They all knew better.

"Miss Dudley!"

So I'm back in my bedroom reading help wanted ads. All my girlfriends have been married and divorced since last June. Hubie is taking me out tonight. I guess I couldn't have been all that incompetent if I ended up with what I was really after.

PICKLE PACKER • TERRY

In the part of Michigan where I lived, if young people were desperate for a summer job they worked at Aunt Jane's Pickle factory. For many of them it was their first job, so they were sincere, full of energy and worked hard. The company took advantage of this. They knew that children could be subdued fairly easy and wouldn't complain with force like adults do. This place was a sweat shop where the working conditions were poor; it was non-union so the people that worked there had no rights. The foremen made sure everyone looked straight ahead and didn't socialize. Profit was more important than anything else.

Most people worked on the assembly line, the worst of the jobs there, packing pickles in jars as fast as they could until their arms were aching. I studied that factory well. There were seven main conveyor belts that brought pickles into the factories from the trucks. The belts brought pickles to other belts that brought the pickles to the different packing stations. I found the controls for the belts and slowed down the belt for the packers and sped it up from the trucks. So I was overloading the main belt with more pickles than could be packed. Every day I would increase the speed a little bit more. I noticed that the bearings on the belt were worn, and the speed-ups only put them under more stress. I started throwing pickles under the belt to add to the stress of those bearings. Finally the belt started ripping and I threw more pickles under it and then the belt snapped in two. Everything came to a halt.

After the belt was fixed during lunch break, I took a whole case of jars and threw them into the tumbler. The jars would go through this first, which would put pickles in the jars at random, as the packers on the lines finished the packing. Lo and behold, when production started up, the jars in the tumbler were smashed. There was so much noise in the factory that you couldn't hear a thing. Consequently, glass ended up in the jars. It took a while until someone noticed, but by that time it was too late. The foreman in charge of our line shut everything down for three days in order to clean out the tumbler. The company had to throw away three complete pallets of packed pickles to be sure that no glass was sent out to the public. The foreman took us off the line, put us against a wall and asked, "Which one of you son of a bitches did this?" Nobody knew except me how it happened and of course I denied everything. So, no one got blamed and the company lost thousands and thousands of dollars.

During the time that I worked there, the line that I was working on lost a significant amount of money because of the machines being broken, parts that had to be replaced and the amount of jars and pickles that had to be thrown away. The beauty of it all was that I was a clean cut young man that looked forward when the foreman told me not to socialize. When he told me to be a robot, I was a robot. But I was a thinking robot.

One cannot walk through a mass-production factory and not feel that one is in hell.

— W.H. Auden

3 TERMINAL BLUES

Computer

PROGRAMMER • LAZLO

I worked on Bank of America's payroll program, interfacing a clumsy old in-house system. It was one of the worst designed systems that I had ever seen. It was using a wasteful amount of computer time and had a very bad user interface. It made me ashamed to be a programmer. I thought, "Look at this piece of shit." It insulted me that I was supposed to make the system work better, but I wasn't allowed to make any fundamental changes. I could only patch things up.

Because I was restricted in the amount of work I was allowed to do, I was having a lot of problems implementing the system. It was a real pain in the ass. Bank of America started being pushy because I wasn't getting the work done as fast as they wanted me to. When the higher-ups in the bank wanted to know what was going on, the computer supervisors said I was incapable of doing the job. They put all of the blame on me because they didn't want the bosses to know how shitty their computer system really was. They made me look really bad, then went a step further and stopped paying me. I got so pissed off at them that I planted a logic bomb in the system, a kind of electronic "Fuck you!"

I had all the passwords that I needed to do it just right. I got into the payroll program and wrote a new program that would delete it. The next time the payroll program started running, it slowly started disappearing. Once it started failing, all the other programs started deleting themselves. The logic bomb had a chain reaction effect. It started out small, but then all of a sudden the entire system was corrupted.

On payday, nobody got paid in Northern California's PayNet system. Granted, I fucked with the workers, but I really ruined Bank of America's credibility. A couple of the supervisors got fired. Heads rolled and that's all that mattered to me. They knew I did it; I even admitted it, but this was before there were laws against these types of things. Technically, I didn't commit a crime. All I did was destroy data. I didn't steal anything.

TECHNICIAN • CONRAD

It was a new computer company, and I was one of the original twenty-five employees. I was hired as a field technician, which meant that I installed computers, trained customers how to use them, and integrated different hardware and software.

I had never done any actual maintenance or repair on computers. I hadn't even taken a computer apart before. I only knew them from the operational point of view. I had been hired expecting to be trained, but I didn't get any training at all. I was just thrown right into it.

The first time I was sent to a customer's office, I was supposed to figure out what the problem was with their IBM mainframe and fix it. I had no idea of what to do. I was under a lot of pressure and had to act like I knew what I was doing. I had to do this complete charade while the customer was standing there looking over my shoulder. I knew I was going to have to open it up. I noticed the

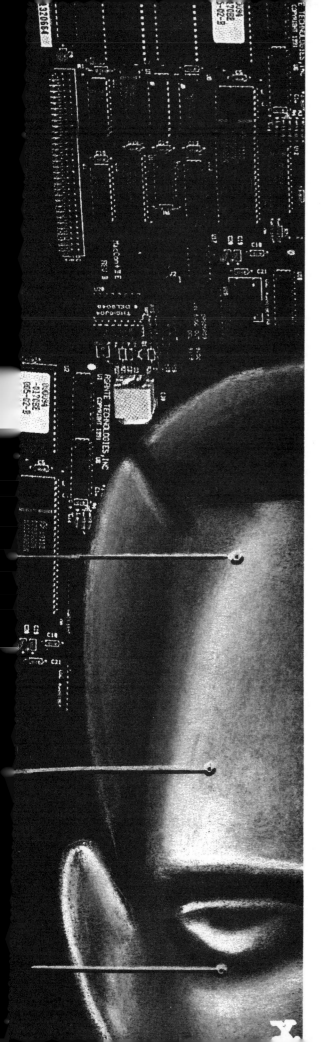

sticker on the back: "To be opened by qualified service personnel only or warranty is invalid." I mentioned this to my boss and he handed me a screwdriver and said, "Now you're qualified." But I did it. I'm a smart guy and I figured out what the problem was. The point is, the entire company was a sham.

At some point, I realized that the efforts of all twenty-five people in this company were funneling through me as the one who actually ended up executing the deals. They had five or six salespeople whose job it was to make wild promises of what I was capable of doing. These people had no technical experience and made promises that were impossible to keep. If I was successful, either I was extremely lucky or stayed up all night poring over manuals. I would be put in situations where I'd be driving to a site with a manual on my lap trying to read it and drive at the same time, so I'd have a chance of knowing what to do when I got there.

Everybody was led to believe that if they helped get the company off the ground they would be rewarded with remarkable opportunities in the company's future. We thought this was our chance to make it in the world. The company kept asking us to give more and more. We were all killing ourselves for this company. I literally worked thirty-six hour shifts without sleep in order to fulfill the salesmen's absurd promises. The raises and opportunities never came and that's when we started to realize we had been used. One by one all the original employees felt they were just going to die if they worked another day for the company.

I wanted to get fired so I could collect unemployment. I started coming in at noon instead of 8:00 am. They yelled and got upset, but they didn't fire me. I started to constantly contradict the salespeople. They would tell the customer something ridiculous about how a certain computer system could do more than it actually could. I would go to the customer and tell them not to buy it because the company wouldn't be able to live up to its promises. Most of the customers took my advice. This would get back to the boss, but they still wouldn't fire me because they were absolutely dependent on me.

For years they had twisted things around so I felt that I was dependent on them. I thought I had to stress out over every little thing or I'd lose the job of a lifetime.

The company is still there, bigger than ever, but I know that their growth was achieved on the backs of hundreds of people.

TECHNICAL WRITER • DEXTER

I'm at my place of employment right now as I type this into my Macintosh. I could be working. At least it looks like I'm working. Since I'm a technical writer, it's only natural that I'd be filling up my screen with words. However, for the last four years, I have spent only one-third of my time at work filling the screen with work-related words.

At my job, I write, edit and format all manner of technical documents including user documentation, service manuals and advanced development specifications. To accomplish this, I regularly communicate with engineers for hardware and software, physicists and marketing people. The people and the technology are interesting, and I really do enjoy technical communications. But I am quick to find ways to not work. I have mastered many writing, communications, and desktop publishing skills, and this mastery usually allows me to do a week's worth of work in about two days. In two days' time — spread out across the week, of course — I can do whatever they expect to be done and even a little more sometimes, since it pays to seem industrious.

My philosophy is this: I'm a generalist, a person with diverse interests which multiply daily. Left alone and well-financed, I would produce voluminous amounts of creative stuff in a variety of media. But alas, society doesn't cater to such capricious and irresponsible thinkers. So I circumvent society's shortcomings, and still pay the bills, by doing my techno-artistic projects at work, on company time. In the last four years, I have written a novella, a workbook for a major publishing company's science textbook, two travel narratives, and countless smaller things. I have explored computer music, art, and animation at work and have even written a computer game. I have spent at least a couple thousand hours of company time on my projects, and at a pretty good salary.

Most of my company work involves text and graphics, but so do my projects. Most of the time, my co-workers think I am working for the company. I'm never too cautious. Over-caution leads to paranoia, and paranoia dampens the hedonistic spirit. The co-workers who catch me have mixed reactions. Some of them subscribe to the old ethic and think you should devote all your work time to work. Others wish they could find the time at work to do non-work-related stuff like I do. My various bosses have never caught on. So my co-workers tolerate or admire me. They are usually too caught up in their own activities to pay direct attention to mine. And my bosses are content that my productivity is up to or beyond par.

My situation is a by-product of the company environment. I will try to get away with whatever I can for the sake of creativity. The company is benefiting the whole planet by subsidizing my creative efforts without even knowing it. Sort of unconscious philanthropy.

SYSTEMS DESIGNER • STAN

I beat "the system" by helping to foul up a computer system for the largest bank in the United States. I did it, well, sort of accidentally. I've always felt ill-at-ease with the intentional stuff.

I started working for a savings and loan several years back, in the systems department. Frank, the resident computer expert there, was six feet tall and impeccably groomed — the very image of conservatism. He was the one who taught me the art of corporate sabotage.

Whenever there was a bug in the system, he took me to the computer room on the fourth floor. Most big corporations have their computer rooms protected by guards, pass-keys and special ID devices. Not this place. We just asked the old, revered receptionist to give us the key. She kept it in the unlocked top drawer of her desk. Once in the computer room, Frank and I would find five huge consoles blinking and whirring. When we — or rather, he — figured out which console had the problem, we would switch it off

and on really fast. This erased loan data from all over California. But at least the computer system was working again.

Ironically, Frank left the company to become a consultant. Now it was my job to take care of the company's computer hardware. It wasn't too long before the system went down again. I trudged to the fourth floor and asked the old, revered receptionist for the keys, which she surrendered gleefully. But I had a problem. I'd long since forgotten the procedure for figuring out which computers worked and which didn't. I could think of only one solution. I turned them all off and on really fast. I reminded myself to take a look at the list of company job offerings on the way to my desk.

A few minutes later, a co-worker told me that everything was now working fine. He congratulated me for having absorbed so much during my short tenure in the systems department.

One of the things I learned from all this is that the less you care about your job, the easier it is to indulge in sabotage. But there's a paradox to it. If you're doing something you really hate, why in the hell are you doing it?

SCIENTIST • ROGER

I'm in the Civil Service for the U.S. Army. Civil Service means that I work for a branch of the government but I'm not in the military. Military personnel run our facility but most of the people I work with are civilians like myself.

I'm a computer programmer. I design software for various weapons systems and see that it gets developed and installed into computers in very remote locations. I've been doing this for about twenty years.

I get reasonable pay. It's not as good as what I can earn on the outside because the benefits aren't as good as in the private sector. Sometimes I think about working for a private company, particularly when friends have left and gotten twenty-five percent pay raises. It makes me think, but I choose to stay because I enjoy my work.

I travel in my job, and for certain projects I travel an awful lot. In the eighties there was a period of time where we were required to keep track of all of our meal expenses. It was a pain in the butt to keep track of what I spent for breakfast, lunch and dinner. It was much easier to just claim standard amounts of money even though I actually spent less. I learned that if I put down a certain dollar amount I got reimbursed without any questions, because it was within the maximum that the government would pay. No matter what, I would always spend the maximum.

It's hard to say what would happen if they found out. It would be difficult to prove that there was some discrepancy of what I recorded and what I actually spent. I could claim that it was a record-keeping error. It was a system based on honesty, but it really was just a convenience to the government. I don't think I was taking advantage but it sure made my record-keeping easier. Technically, I was doing something wrong, because I was supposed to sign the log sheet and say that I spent the exact amount I said I did, but I don't see it that way.

SUPERVISOR • BRIAN

I worked in Los Angeles at the world headquarters of Carnation Company, the milk people. I worked on computers in the insurance department. I was the one who knew the ins and outs of the computer system. I did overnight — running reports, doing checks on the computer printer, and cleaning up the garbage that had been retained on the computer during the day. I had to run it at night because everyone else had to be off the computers.

The company installed a Muzak system to keep the employees brightened up, to keep them going. In the morning they played Muzak that woke everyone up without being too upbeat. Just before lunch it got a little smoother. After lunch, when everyone was getting narcoleptic, it was real upbeat, like, "Tie a Yellow Ribbon Around the Old Oak Tree."

The Muzak was played twenty-four hours a day. When people were in the office, the Muzak was just background noise but when there was no one in the office, it was horrible. It would be louder and brighter than usual. I couldn't concentrate on my work while listening to this shit. I thought about asking my supervisors to turn it down, then I thought about what would happen if they said no. I would be fucked. So, I climbed on top of a desk, pushed up a section of the acoustic tile ceiling, and with a pair of scissors, snipped the wires to the entire Muzak system.

Everyone came in the next day and no one noticed the Muzak was gone. That was the amazing part. It wasn't discovered until my bosses realized they had missed a couple of the retirement parties which had been announced over the building's speaker system.

I immediately became a suspect. I got called into the top guy's office. He asked me if I knew anything about it. I said, "No, I don't know anything about it. There was some construction going on at one point. Maybe one of those guys accidentally did it." The boss had a good idea that I did it, but knew he couldn't prove anything. He just gave me this look like he was going to watch me really closely from then on.

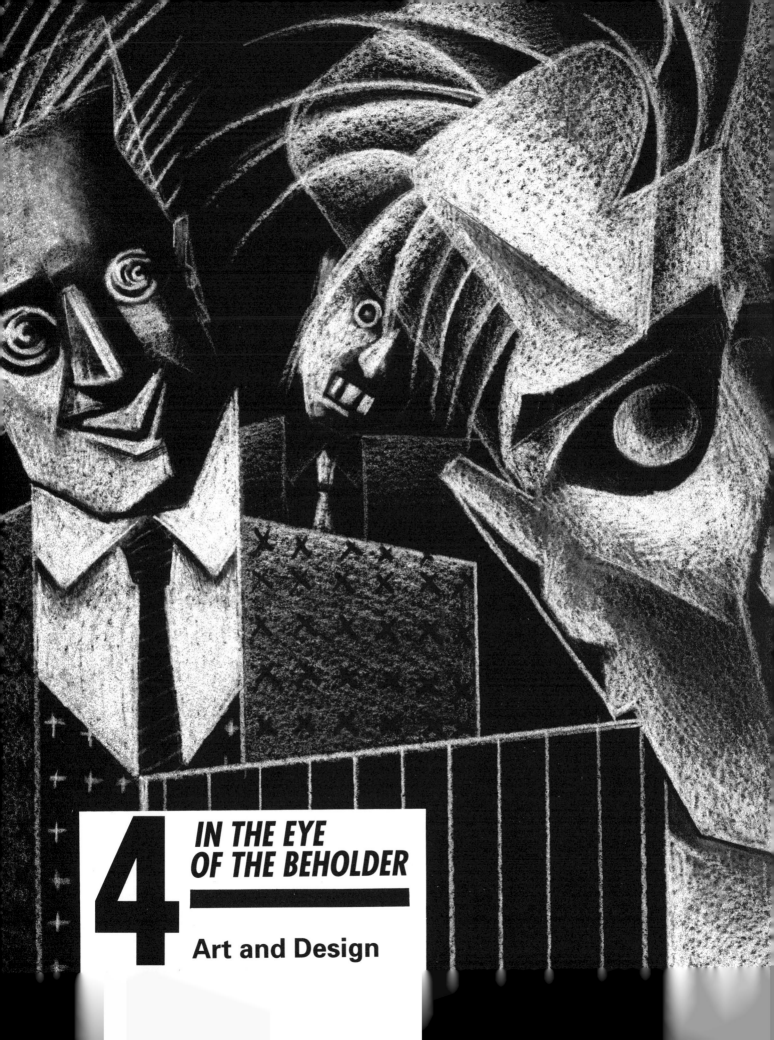

4 IN THE EYE OF THE BEHOLDER

Art and Design

MURAL PAINTER • HARVEY

I work for a company that produces custom murals and decorative paintings. We do a lot of work for cruise ships, hotels, restaurants and casinos in Vegas and Atlantic City. As far as I know, there aren't many companies that do what we do. Art consultants bring us jobs from all over the world.

We mainly do pictorial murals. We don't do anything abstract. My bosses have a real chip on their shoulders against anything conceptual whatsoever; the more vapid the subject, the more they like it. In fact, they try to keep human figures out of the compositions as much as possible because the human figure can be a very controversial thing. If the painting is in a public space and it contains a group of figures, you're almost guaranteed to offend someone. The piece we're working on right now has absolutely no figures in it at all. It's a big architectural painting of classic Greek columns with a landscape in the background. It has a couple of animals in it. It's impressive to someone who doesn't want to think about an image and just wants to be struck by its surface as they glide past. It's made to sit against the wall as a whisper instead of a shout.

I do my best not to focus on the down side of my job but I'm not a hopeless optimist either. I have to watch it while I'm working there because if I let my cynicism be known I'll just fuck myself out of a job. It's more important that I keep this veneer of calmness and satisfaction.

Since I'm able to do more than just paint, I don't really fall into a monotonous routine. I think the frustration with my job comes more from the fact that what I consider to be worthy and beautiful art is opposed to my bosses' opinions. They put a lot more emphasis on money and let their artistic standards be dictated by it. I'd like to think that mine are associated with something other than cash. True, it's a business, but they love to pose as artists. My bosses' notion of what good painting is really annoys me. It's all fluff. All false. We have to pump up the colors in the paintings to these absurdly tacky proportions. I can have this twisted grin on my face, just wallow in the cheesiness of it and really run with it, and my boss will think that I'm really into it. In reality I'm mocking it. I play the role and ape my boss. Then it ceases to be fun, and it becomes dreary and I have to look for other ways to keep myself amused.

Recently we did a job for the Walt Disney Corporation. They specifically requested the Great Gatsby as the theme, which basically is about rich people in the good old days. The idea was to make the people look happy and create the ideal that people off the streets should strive to get a white suit, Panama hat and a croquet mallet. One of my favorite scenes was a hotel scene where people were seated at tables. In the background there was this balcony where I painted this little SS Stormtrooper. It was my little comment on what was happening in the rest of the world while the Great Gatsbys were whittling away their hours with cocktails. My boss noticed it and said that it looked like a soldier, but I convinced him it was a security guard. He dropped it at that. All of the people that I worked with noticed it was a Nazi right away.

I changed some of the pictures as I worked my way down the panel. The scene had framed pictures hanging on the background wall which I changed to paintings by Francis Bacon: weird-shaped monsters with pear-shaped bodies sitting on a wobbly table with claws hanging over their heads. My boss didn't say anything about those either. There were some very large figures of two men and two women in the foreground which I improved by adding a psychological element. I made it look like the two men were ready to fight it out in sort of a territorial mating battle over the women. There were fifteen people painted into the middleground who were all looking very alarmed, shocked and dismayed. The foreground had the two men about to fight, the middleground had these shocked onlookers, and the background had Francis Bacon paintings and a Nazi. My bosses repainted the foreground figures but never fixed anything else. It's now installed in a hotel. That gave me a lot of satisfaction. It's pretty minor but it did make me feel better.

I did a series of reproductions of Pompeii wall frescoes for an Italian restaurant in Vegas. I changed figures in that too. I painted one guy with cloven hooves instead of feet, and put a knife in his hand. I painted a few severed heads in that one, too. When I worked on some paintings of the New Orleans French Quarter, I was appalled that these paintings had to go over slot machines and compete with them for attention. So I put three figures in the balcony scene. One is pointing at the person who would be below at the slot machine; one has a martini and is looking very aristocratic and sneering at the slot-machine player. Then there's this other guy who is more of a caricature: he's got big buck teeth, a monocle, and an iron cross pinned to his lapel and has his head back, also laughing at the person playing the machine.

It's really hard to get away with anything more. I've been told to repaint fruit in still lifes because they were too suggestive. I didn't do it on purpose, but once they called my attention to it, I started to figure out ways that I could do it and get away with it.

GRAPHIC DESIGNER • ALEJANDRO

In 1981 I answered an ad in the newspaper for a graphic designer. Five months later the company gave me a call and asked me if I wanted to go to Saudi Arabia.

I ended up at a naval base in Jubail, Saudi Arabia. The company I worked for had just won the contract to train new recruits for the Royal Saudi Navy. Most Americans working there were rednecks, ex-military types, pirates and mercenaries — people who couldn't get a job anywhere else. I didn't like my job because I didn't really like the people that I was working with, and I didn't like the country — it was featureless and there was nothing to do there. I felt like I was doing time in prison but I just accepted the fact that I was there because I really needed the money. I was getting paid a lot better than I would have been in the States. A friend of mine said I was a "wetback with a vengeance" because I went all the way to Saudi Arabia to get a good-paying job.

I worked in the audio-visual department designing training aids for the school. I did things like make big wall-sized mock-ups of .45 caliber pistols, cross-section drawings of cannons and gun mounts, and charts that showed ten different ways to loop a rope. I put together lots of slide programs, from how to fight a fire to explaining basic electronics.

Forty percent of what we did was write the names of students on graduating certificates. For every class they took (and each person took about fifty to sixty classes) they got a little certificate. So, we would spend a lot of our time writing Arabic names in calligraphy on these certificates.

Every once in a while, the Saudis would get a hair up their ass and open up the training contract for bidding. After I'd worked there for three years, our company got outbidded and lost the contract. The people in my department needed money as bad as I did; so, to keep ourselves fully employed, we started to misspell the students' names on their certificates. We'd get some guys whose names we'd end up writing over and over again. We messed up as many as we could. Sometimes we didn't even need to fuck them up because when you write something in Arabic like Mohammed, is it Mohammed or Muhammad? There's no way of translating it literally. We were able to extend our contract for three months because we had to finish all of these certificates.

ART GALLERY ASSISTANT • BILL

There's no real concept of my job description because the manager and owner see me as a worker and themselves as the ones who sell the art so I have to do whatever they want. They don't care. They just pile shit on me. In that sense my work environment is tense. The boss has no idea what it's like to work and be bossed around. Not that that's atypical of any job.

I'm called the shipping manager. I don't manage anyone, I just manage the shipping. But shipping is just a small portion of my job. They really need two people to do the work but they only have one doing it, and that's me. My job involves everything from hanging art in the gallery to getting paper cups for the kitchen to shipping art all over the world.

The gallery is owned by a woman, and her husband manages it. He does all of the business stuff. He is an incredibly uptight asshole who does not trust anybody. He's always suspicious about the littlest things which is reason enough to hate the guy and not really give a shit about doing a good job.

We handle mainly fine prints by artists like Picasso, Miró, Frank Stella, Andy Warhol. All big names, we don't mess around. We have things ranging from $1,500 to $1,000,000. Sometimes people will come in and they have some money that they want to invest, so they get a piece for their house. Other times people don't give a shit and buy what they like. We have a couple of clients who buy thousands of dollars worth of art every year.

I don't have much respect for the art because I see it all the time. When you see the stuff in the gallery or a museum it might be interesting, but to me it's like handling cans of soup. It's just a commodity, an object. I have to haul it around the gallery at the boss' request. I end up carrying this stuff up and down stairs all the time so I treat it like a bag of bricks. When I'm overworked I don't

Employees show frustration with the work routine, coupled with the pressure of the work environment. ... Sabotage also can be caused by the Ivory Tower Syndrome. Workers feel that managers in the Ivory Tower send edicts down without cause or justification. Isolation of the managers in this form allows workers to feel that they do not matter, and as conflict builds, sabotage occurs.
— Supervision Magazine [3]

care that I'm handling a $20,000 Matisse because I have to unpack it, log it in the inventory and put it in a storage drawer.

I'm supposed to handle all of the art with cotton gloves so the oil from my hands doesn't ruin the art, but I never use them, I always "forget." I don't bother putting tissue paper between the prints to protect them, so some things get marks on them. I am really careful to dent the frames. I just throw the art in the drawers. I'm supposed to be careful with it, but I have too much stuff to do to worry about shit like that.

I once picked up a Matisse that was matted from a drawer. It was easily worth well over $50,000. Since the mat wasn't done very well the art slipped through it and ripped. I'm supposed to send any damaged art to the art restorer, but I never do that because it only adds to the backlog of work I have to do, and can get me in trouble with the bosses. So, I took the Matisse, rolled it up, and shipped it to the place it was going and didn't tell anyone.

Recently, I had to send a piece of art to a particular client and there was a small nick in the frame. I should have filled it in with plaster and painted over it, but all I did was color it in with a brown marker. If a print comes back from the framer with a dent or a scrape in it I just ship it anyway. I don't want to hassle the framer about a little nick because he's just a working guy like me. I don't want to screw anyone else. If the client does notice the nick then I just say that it was fine when I sent it out. That's the thing I do, I never take responsibility even if I'm responsible for it. I always remind the owners when they notice something wrong that I'm not the only person who handles the art and if I was, nothing would be wrong.

There's this common illusion that if someone gives you a job, they are doing you a favor. In reality they're going to take you for everything you're worth. So you stop caring. Sometimes you have to get certain things done and it's best just to get them done. Most people have a certain work ethic where they feel like they have to do everything their boss tells them to do. It gets to the point where people worry in advance about not doing a good job, much like ingrained intimidation. But after a while you stop giving a shit and stop getting excited about all of the work that needs to be done. You stop caring what your boss says, and you don't care about being yelled at anymore.

I used to have what I thought was guilt about not doing a good job or not doing things fast enough. Then I realized that what I felt wasn't guilt but rather a fear of being caught and fired. But once you create the illusion of being a good worker the chances of being fired are less. My bosses now say that I seem happier, which I am, but it's because I decided that I'm not going to get uptight if someone is breathing down my neck. I realized that I was being overworked. This is an objective fact. Second objective fact: my boss is a fuckin' asshole and does not have any conception of what my job is like day-to-day. The way I see it, people aren't assholes because they're bosses, they're bosses because they're assholes.

The men who work the hardest seem to do it by making other men do their work for them.
— *Reflections of a Bachelor*

All art expression can bring to people a new dimension of enjoyment, and a language of release from our highly mechanized world. From the artist can come a real contribution to our culture, but this is possible only when the individuals bravely bring forth their most personal concepts and visions.
— *It's Fun to Paint, Arnold Blanch and Doris Lee* [4]

5 EVERYTHING YOU WANTED TO KNOW

Knowledge and Information

TEACHER • KAT

When I finished college, I started doing secretarial jobs and I just hated it. One of my best friends was going through a teaching program and I thought it would be a good idea because I definitely didn't want to be a secretary for the rest of my life. So, I went back to school and got my teaching credential.

One thing about teaching in general is that there are too many kids. If you have more than thirteen people to a teacher, the learning curve goes down. We have between thirty and thirty-five kids. You have to compromise your ethics to teach at all. It really feels like the power structure doesn't want people to learn things. I don't think this is anything new, but to be teaching and knowing that, it's a big compromise. Sometimes I just feel like a martyr, that I'm getting fucked over just as much as the kids are. I think there's a lot of frustration among the teachers I know. There are a few who are exceptional, whose hearts are really into it and are able to do fantastic things with children and make being at school interesting. I think that most teachers just want to survive. A lot of them treat it just like any other job.

I substitute-taught for about two and a half years. The job was very tedious and I was treated poorly by the staff and the administration. As for the kids, the more I had to discipline them, the more we were pitted against one another. Most of the time there were no lesson plans or they just had boring stuff to do, so they just goofed around. I struck a balance with them: I let them get away with so much and let myself relax and not do as much work. I did this to survive because substituting is a very hard job. I often came away from it not feeling too good. More than once the administrator got mad at me because the class was too noisy. The best part of the job was that I didn't have a boss. I could walk away and work at another school if I didn't like the place or the principal. I liked the lack of responsibility. That's the only redeeming quality of that job.

I don't think the materials that we use present subjects in an appropriate way. I was teaching history and the kids were so freaked out when they read about Henry VIII. They asked how he could have killed so many people. How could he be a king if he was bad? How does somebody get to be a king and why were there kings? I explained to them that powerful people rule things and it's the same way here. They said that the President could never do something like that. I explained that he could, it's just not as obvious. I often go off on subjects like that.

I ended up teaching sixth grade science this year, and it was the first time I'd taught sex education. It's not really sex education; it's more like education about the reproductive system. I used the teaching materials I was given, but discovered that the way we teach sex education is to say that girls get periods and bleeding, and boys get erections and wet dreams. The material desexualized women by saying that they don't have erections or wet dreams. I told the class that girls have erections and wet dreams too, and periods are a whole other subject. I've never heard any other teacher say this. I don't know how the administration would have reacted if they heard me saying that to the class. Something that's not in the curriculum, especially something about sensitive issues, might be seen as harmful to the students. I guess one should discuss something new with the administration in order to get some feedback on it; but for me, it was something that wound its way into what I was teaching at the time.

HISTORICAL INTERPRETER PRIVATE CHARLES

I was a member of the Fort Ontario Guard at Fort Ontario, New York, on the shores of Lake Ontario. I had to dress up in Civil War garb and recreate the year 1869. Our daily schedule consisted of polishing our equipment for an hour, flag ceremonies and inspection. Once in a while we had drill, too.

Tourists came and the whole situation was very militaristic. It wasn't set up so that we were performing for tourists; rather, we were part of a drill squad and had to perform in straight military order. Some of the people on guard decided to make the military look as silly as possible. The inspections turned out to be pretty funny sometimes, because the commanding officer had to come up to each of us, inspect our equipment, and ask us all these questions about the different parts of the fort and the different parts of our uniforms. Of course, we always told the tourists that stuff so fast that no one could understand what we were saying. A lot of the tourists knew that we were goofing off and enjoyed it, but the more militaristic people didn't, and once in a while they'd complain.

Sometimes, a guard would mess up while we were marching and get punished. We thought that some of the practices were pretty unfair, considering the heat. We wore these huge, thick wool uniforms, and if we messed up a certain number of times, we had to run a lap around this parade ground. One day a guy was marching post and he just fainted. A few weeks later we thought, "Wow, that worked pretty well 'cause he fainted, and we didn't have to march post for the rest of the day." We decided to have him "faint" again when it was really hot so we could get out of marching post. Later we put in a complaint, and somehow the regional office found out about the punishment practices, and they were ended. It was much too much.

The biggest incident was when I was left in charge. I had been there a couple of years and was the second ranking person. Usually the guard was in charge of punishing people, but the assistant manager decided he was going to give out the punishments that day, which was totally out of line. He had a guy march the most brutal post for an entire hour. It consisted of standing stock still in the heat — you couldn't move a muscle. It was one of the hottest days of summer, and the hottest summer in thirty-three years. It was deadly, grueling punishment. I thought, "This is too much," and I took him off post. The assistant manager didn't like that. He also thought that a bunch of us were scheming together.

There were two outhouses that were considered the guards' domain — we used them as dressing rooms, and spent our off-duty time there. The assistant manager decided to punish one of the

The employee has to do the work as directed. Otherwise, he is subject to discipline. If his defense is that the work assignment was hazardous above the normal risks of the job, he is admitting a refusal to do the work. Then, the burden of proving a case may shift over to him.
— Supervisor's Factomatic, Jack Horn [3]

A little rebellion now and then is a good thing.
— Thomas Jefferson

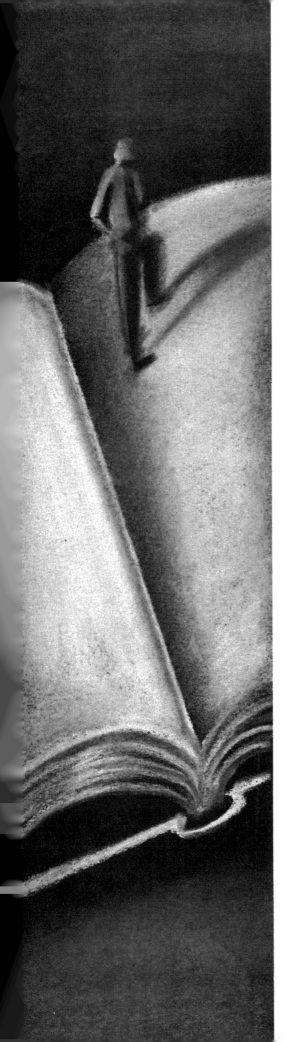

guards by making him switch outhouses. When he switched, I decided that we all had to switch. Management was stepping beyond its ounds: the assistant manager usually hung out with us, but he was pulling power trips and getting out of control. The whole circus atmosphere had boosted morale incredibly. It created a more tolerable place to work, because conditions were pretty tough. When they started cracking down on that, we ran into trouble. I got fired that day, and later the rest of the guards threatened to quit. The boss showed up at my apartment that night and begged me to come back. I didn't have any choice economically, so I did.

I think that they have been trying to move away from the drill squad concept anyway, because this one historian found out that it wasn't a drill squad there in 1869, but a bunch of old disabled veterans from the Civil War who were serving their last few months.

LIBRARIAN • ART

Long before I started working in the library, I had a vision of it as a universe, with all the possibilities for the literate mind that such a universe contains.

My first library job was working with periodicals. The fellow who sat across from me at the check-in counter resembled a morgue attendant; we became good friends. We had the same wry sense of humor. After several months, without ever discussing it, we simultaneously played the same prank on each other.

In the card file for the respective parts of the alphabet that we worked on, we created strange-sounding titles for serials or periodicals which the library was allegedly receiving. For example, I planted cards for *Public Equanimity: Its Construction and Maintenance* and *Stellar Inquest: the Review of Celebrities on the Slab.* He retaliated with *Roman Orgies: Then and Now.* They were generally of a macabre nature; that's where our humor was. Of course, the cards were supposed to indicate a bibliographer's interest in seeing the publication. We forged the initials of a deceased bibliographer and backdated the cards to cover our tails. Since it was a card system, the only way it could have been detected would have been through a file reading, when someone goes through the file card by card to see if they're in order. Since we read our own files, there wasn't much chance of anyone else catching us.

Having passed much of the last decade working in libraries, I know that our little amusement was nothing unique. In fact, many other library workers I've spoken with around the country play the same game of creating books or faking publications by cobbling together some kind of bibliographic shell. As an intellectual game, it is very appealing to people of a particular bent — or a bent imagination! With the proliferation of on-line computer systems, the possibilities become exponentially richer, because if you use a cataloging utility to create a record for a book that has no previous existence, it can take on a life of its own. I've talked to librarians in Texas and California who have amused themselves by inputting these fake records and following up by observing with great satisfaction the processing of inter-library loan requests for these fanciful titles. Admittedly, it does mean some poor schmuck has to trudge through the stacks in vain for a volume that will never be found, but I suppose there are more meaningless pursuits, like banking or law.

In the library world, the "authority file" is a file of names and versions of those names that people use when they write or publish. Keeping them all straight is a cataloguer's duty. You have to set it up so that people can search for it and pull the most number of records of titles by a given author. Because people have the proclivity for using many different names, "see" records are a part of this file, which refer you from one form of a name to another. I heard of one clerk who put a "see" reference for Reagan, Ronald Wilson, that said, "see 666." This made it into the microfiche catalog. It may have been a bit obvious. It was very quickly detected and "fixed."

Another one of my pranks has been to deface existing records with subtle alterations. Around the time Salman Rushdie was issued his death warrant, I went into the record for *Satanic Verses* and put in a special field which indicated that one of the library's copies was the special infidel edition, with an asbestos dust jacket. That particular description remained in the system for over a year, until somebody took it out. I wonder whether some pyro of the public came running to see the book, but I'll never know...

INFORMATION CLERK • CHRIS

My stint at the Downtown Community College lasted a mere three months, but for me it was a turning point for a couple of reasons. For one thing I learned word processing there, which catapulted me from $5 to $6 to $10 to $12/an hour jobs. It also made me aware that most people, especially in San Francisco, work in offices. I wanted to address this fact, since I, too, was suddenly an "information handler."

As an information clerk I sat right inside the front door and spent seven hours a day telling people where the bathroom was, when and where classes met and about English as a Second Language. The school provided two basic services, both primarily for the benefit of the downtown office world: basic training in office skills, and English classes for immigrants and refugees that prepared them for low-wage, rudimentary data entry jobs.

The job's nemesis was familiar — I wasn't allowed to read, even when there was nothing to do. I was supposed to "look professional," according to my corporate-climbing boss, Ms. Walton. She was appallingly dumb, and as far as I could tell, she hardly knew anything about goings-on in the school. I think she was an image-builder for the community colleges. Knowing little and being self-conscious about it, she was pressured to accomplish things she didn't understand, and she'd vent her fears by admonishing me for reading the paper at my desk during lulls.

I hadn't planned to stay long, and despite the two-year minimum I promised in the interview, I planned on a long summer vacation. About six weeks before I planned to quit, I composed a fake advertisement for the DCC and had it printed up. The ad summarized all my jaded views of the purpose of this training institute for the clerical working-class. About ten days before I had planned to quit, I began surreptitiously placing them inside the Fall schedules of City College, which I distributed at the front desk. A few days later the shit hit the fan. A co-worker came running up to me and asked if I had done the yellow leaflet that had the entire school in an uproar. I smiled and told her, "No, never heard of it." Nonetheless, it was obvious to my co-workers, who knew I had a bad attitude, that I was the culprit.

I was absent from my work station when the director, Dr. B., came in. She gave me a dark look as I scurried back to my position. Five minutes later the phone rang, and I was told to come to her office. She looked rather pale as I entered. She was boiling but tried to act calm. She pulled out a copy of the leaflet and thrust it at me, saying, "What can you tell me about this?"

I said, "Oh, is that the yellow leaflet I was told about? Can I see it?" I took it and sat down and slowly read it as if I had never seen it before. I chuckled at the funny parts, dragging out my feigned surprise until she finally exploded, "You are sick! You must be deranged to do something like this. It's damaging to our institute. You're fired!"

I had put her name and the school's actual logo on it, so I denied responsibility just in case some kind of lawsuit ensued. I protested that I wanted to complete my final week, but she told me to go. I felt quite satisfied with the extra days off before my vacation.

In 1983, Studs Terkel's 'Working' was deleted from the 8th grade curriculum in the Washington, Arizona School District. "When we require idealistic and sensitive youth to be burdened with despair, ugliness and hopelessness, we shall be held accountable by the almighty God."[6]

6 WITHOUT RESERVATIONS

Hotel

DESK CLERK • DUNCAN

The place was one-third old people who had lived there forever, one-third male and female prostitutes and the other third were transients who would stay for a night or two at a time. It took me a while to get used to the hours; plus, the wages were really low. The bosses were dicks, especially my supervisor, who was pretty weird. He was perfectly manicured, with permed hair and curled beard, hairy chest and gold chains.

One morning he came in at about seven and started bitching at me for some stupid little thing. I wasn't feeling too well but I said I was sorry anyway. But then he wouldn't let up. He went on for ten minutes. I felt too ill to work so I went home. I crashed out all day and got up just in time to go back to work. I grabbed some take-out food and was eating it at the beginning of the shift. The supervisor was there but not to work. He started hounding on me about the same shit that he had been going on about in the morning. I wasn't really in the mood for it and I told him so. He wouldn't stop. I was sitting in the booth and he was about ten feet away from me. He wouldn't shut up. Finally I yelled, "Shut the fuck up!" and threw my salad at him. It smacked him right in the face; the dressing got all over his beard, his clothes, and his hairy chest. It was wonderful. All the people around really loved it, and he shut up. After that he was so nice to me. Sometimes you have to set your limits with people.

I didn't get fired for that. I got fired later for being humane to the people who lived there. There wasn't a desk clerk there who wasn't an absolute turd. I was nice to people. I'd help them with their laundry and stuff like that. I'd go out of my way to make living there a little more pleasant for them.

CHAMBERMAID • KIM

It's a beautiful summer day, and as we approach the hotel it looks like a medieval castle on an artificial lake, with ducks flown in from some more hospitable land. Limos pull into the front entrance, but we head round back and park next to the dumpster already reeking from the sun. We walk down a concrete passageway with burnt-out bulbs and open a door where a blast of fluorescent light and humid heat hits us: it's the laundry room. We take the service elevator up one flight and there are a wealth of possibilities — effusive light, soft carpets, dark wood and polished brass. With the blue smock on we are invisible in this world — we are "the help."

There are several work crews in the housekeeping department and we're all partial to different kinds of sabotage. At 6:00 am one squad heads down to the bar. It's in a locked room with the inside modeled after an ancient hunting hall. There is little activity here early in the morning. All the lock needs is a plastic credit card and we're in. Workers jostle like newborn animals for position under the beer taps. They continue the day piss-drunk and vaguely happy.

There's a club that subscribes only to pranks. Membership is drawn mostly from the "houseboys," young men and women who

By its very nature, hospitality is a people industry — and thereby labor-intensive. To control labor costs, productivity must be achieved without sacrificing hospitality and personal service.
— Training for the Hospitality Industry, Lewis C. Forrest, Jr. [1]

Employee theft has a tendency to be contagious and cancerous.
— John Case, President of John D. Case and Associates [2]

People get their living by such depressing devices that boredom becomes a sort of natural state to them.
—H.L. Mencken

collect dirty linen and glasses from the chambermaids' carts. The sport of choice is throwing breakable items from high places. Some like to loosely wrap a bunch of glasses in a sheet and chuck it down the laundry chute. This creates a beautiful mess down at the other end and the screams of the laundry workers echo the length of the chute. Laundry workers hate the houseboys, but would never report them to management; in a twisted way everyone looks out for each other.

When these activities get boring, houseboys will go up to the roof and throw items directly off the building onto the back driveway. The coup de grace is when someone steals a fifty-pound container of milk from the kitchen. It's nice, quite nice. But all this throwing can get tiring. When houseboys are sleepy they let themselves into a linen closet, one on each floor. Towels and sheets are strategically placed on the front of the shelves and a cozy little sleeping nook is created in the back.

Chambermaids employ many types of sabotage but shirking is the most common. Housekeeping is the hotel shit-job that involves a bizarre intimacy with the customer. Front-desk folk may talk to these people but they don't have to clean up everything from used condoms and diapers to thousands of hairs in the tub. The key to survival is cutting corners.

Some chambermaids opt for the lazy approach. Instead of dragging out the heavy vacuum, just drag a broom across the carpet to make it look like it's been vacuumed. We're allotted eight hours to clean around fifteen rooms. If we can finish them in five hours, we then have three hours of leisure time. Chambermaids are skillful at disappearing. The trick is to park your cart somewhere you're not, and escape to one of the vacant cleaned rooms. Lie on the bed in the air-conditioned room and watch hours of soap operas and MTV.

Other chambermaids prefer to do a fastidious and painstakingly long job in each room. Clean a little and then perch on the edge of the bed and read a bit of the occupant's magazine. This is a little more dangerous because that occupant could walk into the room at any time. We have to be prepared to jump up and look busy at any moment. A chambermaid was once blown away while sitting on the bed reading in a dimly-lit room; a man sat up, who unbeknownst to her had been sleeping in the bed.

Members of all the housekeeping groups band together when it comes time for stealing. All bags are searched on the way out, but that's no deterrent. Bags are stuffed full of small items such as soap and shampoo, and the workers walk right out the main lobby door of the hotel. For more major thefts it's back to the rooftop. Workers with pick-up trucks drive to the back of the hotel. Others throw boxes of linen, shower curtains, towels, just anything, into the waiting trucks. A favorite item was the 1000-pack of chocolate mints put on guests' pillows. To this day, none of us can even look at a chocolate mint without gagging.

ROOM SERVICE WAITER • BORIS

For six years I've been employed at one of San Francisco's grandest hotels. It's prestigious, very expensive and prides itself on its fine

service and glitz. Being the type of hotel that it is, there's a big social division between the corporate types and the back house people.

Among the workers themselves there's a lot of respect. With the supervisors, it's kind of iffy. Some of them are well-liked because they don't give the employees a hard time and are amenable to feedback. The ones who do give the employees a hard time fit into a definite pattern: they tend to be people that go to hotel management training school. These people want to become the big cheese, and ways of doing that include handing out layoff slips, shitting on workers and pushing people around. Some tension is built around this.

There was this one asshole supervisor who was stealing really expensive bottles of wine, and everybody knew it. Someone blew the whistle on him. The security guards caught him, but of course he wasn't fired. If I had been caught doing that, I would have been out the door.

The most common form of sabotage we're really big on is eating food that we're not supposed to eat. They don't like people helping themselves. One time I saw these guys running out the kitchen during the graveyard shift and I couldn't figure out what was going on. It turned out that they had helped themselves to the shrimp scampi and didn't want the manager to see them because they would have all gotten in a lot of trouble.

We're constantly doing the sodas and the mineral waters, which are kept under lock and key. I know where the key is. It's a simple matter of waiting until my boss isn't looking and then getting the stuff out. Quite a lot of drinking takes place on the job, especially among the dishwashers. When there's a banquet going, there's lots of wine and champagne. Bartenders and waiters pop bottles open at every turn. When the party's over, all the open bottles go down to the kitchen on a huge cart and the late night dishwashing crew will drink what's leftover. If they're lucky they'll get a waiter to open them up a beer. It has some funny results. A few months ago they canned this dishwasher who got drunk and ended up pissing all over the delivery elevators. I've walked by guys who got so drunk during the late night shift that they'd be asleep in the hallway, oblivious to the world. We usually make them an espresso and make sure they're okay.

Most people who work there have a bad attitude. The longer people work there, the less gung ho they are. They'll do the minimum to keep their job but they'll show up late or hungover. They admit they don't care. Because of the union, it's very difficult to get fired. Once you get sick of it, you just fuck off. For places like that to be profitable, the workers have to give 120 percent. And here, they don't.

SECURITY GUARD • ROBIN

I found out about the job through an ad in the newspaper and I was hired on the spot. Only later did I find out that a security guard is seen as one of the lowest jobs in this country. It's easy to become one and most don't last that long.

Time is the measure of business, as money is of wares.
— Francis Bacon

A little thievery is a dangerous art
But thievery largely is a noble part
'Tis vile to rob a henroost of a hen,
But stealing largely makes us gentlemen.
—Representative Samuel S. Marshall

Propaganda, like indoctrination and advertising, conditions employees to act along lines which they like (or imagine that they like). Individuals may then want to do the things suggested for them. Managers may, for example, suggest to employees that "We can be the best in town!" Employees may strive to meet that challenge.
— *Training for the Hospitality Industry,*
Lewis C. Forrest, Jr. [3]

My first assignment was the graveyard shift at a 500-room hotel downtown. I was the only guard there. I had to secure the entire building, keep people from stealing and respond to emergency calls.

The first couple of months I was very professional and friendly. But after a while, I started to search through the entire hotel for places to sleep. I found two rooms where I made nests with mattresses and pillows. I used to put my two-way radio between my head and the pillow so when my supervisor called me, it would wake me up. I'm sure my voice always sounded like I had just woken up but it didn't really matter because whenever I got called to do something, I'd say I was busy.

I started to get bored, so I began stealing small things like food and beer from the kitchen. But when I start stealing from a job, it's like a snowball effect, an addiction, I can't stop it. I was supposed to make sure all the rooms were locked and secure, but all I did was check to see if a door was open, to see what I could steal. I stole TV sets, lamps, chairs and furniture. I would run from one end of the building to the other to take the stuff to the garage where I parked my car.

I made little plans for myself to steal all of the time because it's the only fun thing I could do at work. My main mission was to steal lots of things, and to see what was the biggest thing that I could take without being noticed. There was one room, which I didn't have access to, where they kept slide projectors and cameras. It was very tempting to me. I had a large set of keys to all of the rooms, but I couldn't get into that one. I figured out they must have an emergency key to open all the doors. I had the key to get into the maintenance room so I went in there, found the big drawer where they kept all the keys, and got the key for that room. I took about $700 worth of audio-visual equipment. I remember once when I took a slide projector; it took me about fifteen seconds to get the courage to take it and go down the secondary stairs and through the emergency exit to make a short run to my car. When I shut my trunk and knew the projector was in there it was like an orgasmic pleasure. I finally had it. After a while, the stealing got boring, so I quit.

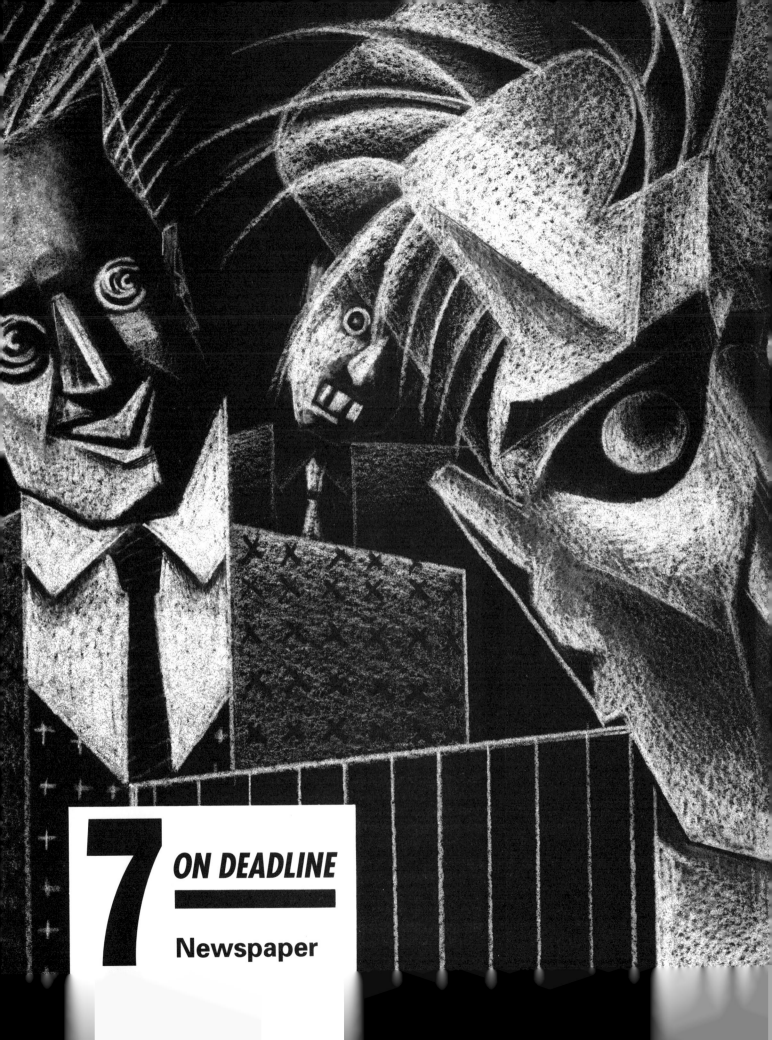

7 ON DEADLINE

Newspaper

PRESS OPERATOR • LEROY

I ran a web press for a small daily newspaper that is distributed all over the West Coast. I had worked there several months and had become friends with one of the assistants.

My boss was one of the worst tyrants I had ever worked for, and for some reason he hated the assistant, who was very shy and introverted. He took great pleasure in letting him know how small, stupid and worthless he was. The assistant was half Korean, half American, born in Korea but recently arrived in the U.S. with no family or friends. All he had was this horrible job. The boss fired him one afternoon in a frenzy of sadistic hatred. I argued with the boss and he asked me if I would like to be fired too. I said, "No," and went back to work.

It was 11:00 am and the paper needed to be printed by 4:00 pm so it could get delivered to air freight at the airport for delivery. I futzed around the press 'til the afternoon. Around 3:00 pm the boss came down and saw that the papers weren't printed yet. I said the plates weren't ready, there were technical problems, etc. Time wore on with the boss getting more and more agitated as the press sat by silently. Finally, the tension exploded as I started cursing him out for firing the assistant. I walked off the job, with no papers printed and no time for him to get a replacement printer. The "daily" would have to take the next day off.

DISTRIBUTOR • CHARLES

I knew the guy who had the distribution rights for a large daily newspaper. I was going to college and needed a job so I started working for him delivering newspapers. I was making very little money, but since it was a college town and jobs were had to find, I took what I could get.

To a certain extent, I managed the entire distribution thing because the guy I worked for didn't pay much attention to it. When I started working there the whole thing was a mess. There were six or seven routes and they were all screwed up. The route books weren't up to date. Nobody really knew what they were doing. I made sure that things were running more smoothly. I was doing a lot more work than I was supposed to be doing. I was doing it mostly because I couldn't stand the mess that was there, and also because I expected that my work would be appreciated.

I delivered about 300 and something papers to individual homes and probably 300 to 400 to paper racks. It took several hours, from 1:00 until 7:00 in the morning. I wasn't happy doing it at all, because I thought that I'd be getting more money from it. I asked for more money a number of times. It was always, "Later, later ... we'll see." I did not like the attitude this guy had at all because he wasn't really pulling his weight. If I hadn't done the stuff I did, the place would still be a mess.

My first idea of how to get a raise was to make myself indispensable, so that the place could not go on without me. That in itself didn't really prove possible because he simply didn't care. So then I thought I would make my route so impossible that nobody could

do anything about it. I didn't keep my route book up to date and any entries I made in it were completely confusing. They weren't lies, but they weren't easy for anybody but me to read.

It ended on a Sunday morning. The Sunday paper was a really big job because it was a lot larger and more people got it, so it took two people to do it. I would usually just hire someone for the day, but I told my boss that I couldn't get anybody, so he had to help me. I wanted to make sure he was there with me. Then I gave him an ultimatum: "You give me that raise that we've been talking about for such a long time, or I'll quit and then you're really going to be sorry." I told him that he would not be able to find anybody to do my route because it was so complicated. He didn't go for that. He would not flat out say, "No, I will not give you a raise." I did not really intend to leave that morning, but I decided it was a perfect opportunity because he would really be screwed.

I was so mad at him that that's what I did. He was left there with 500 Sunday papers and a route book he couldn't read. He leaned out the window and screamed at me to come back and not to leave him in the lurch but I said, "Too bad, you had your chance." As far as I know, he was probably doing that route well into the night.

PAPERBOY • BOB

I started delivering papers when I was eleven years old and I did it throughout high school because I've basically been on my own since age thirteen. I had to work, and how many other opportunities are there for a little kid?

I had about 100 customers on my *San Diego Union* route. The route paid fairly well, but since we were called "independent contractors" by the company, they would sell us the papers and we had to worry about collecting the money from the customers. It was kind of fucked because if a customer skipped town, the company wasn't out of the money, a eleven-year-old kid was.

The only way to get back at the company was to not put their shitty inserts in. The paper got dropped off at my house at 4:30 in the morning and sometimes there would be no inserts. I'd just fold the paper, put a rubber band around it, and start throwing it to people's houses. But a lot of days I'd have to put ad inserts in all of the papers, especially Thursday because of the food section. It really sucked when they gave us three ads on the same day. Usually it was one or two a day. If I was running late and had to put these inserts in, I would just say, "Fuck it," and not put them in. Sometimes I would get in trouble because so-and-so worked at May Company and didn't get their ad in the paper that day. Basically, if they treated me like shit, I wouldn't put their inserts in.

They had various ways of treating the paperboys like shit — being ultra-harsh on us if we were a few minutes late delivering papers, or trying to get us to deliver them earlier. I never got them out on time. It wasn't always done on purpose, but if someone got their paper at 7:00 instead of 6:30, I didn't lose any sleep over it. It was all based on an honesty policy and whenever I put out my trash, I'd hide the inserts, so when the delivery guy drove by in the morning, he wouldn't see them.

ASSEMBLER • DENVER

Mailers are responsible for the handling and assembly of newspapers. We operate inserting machines, tying and stacking machines, and other equipment related to the production of finished bundles of papers. We do all the work between the pressroom and circulation.

In August 1988, the Denver Mailers' Union, having failed to sign a contract with the new owners of the *Denver Post*, was attacked with forty-two percent to fifty-five percent pay cuts. At the time, all other unions had contracts. We were isolated and vulnerable. For fourteen months we conducted a campaign against the paper.

We came up with several ideas which we did not act on, because they could have led to prison. Perhaps we should have taken more action — hostile, militant and illegal — but $8.60 an hour, even if it's far from $15.03 an hour, is better than prison. We had informational and boycott picket lines. We used a bullhorn to tell drivers stopped at lights to boycott. We leafletted any promotional event sponsored by the *Post*. We had Jobs with Justice rallies. We had radio ads and we were on TV several times. We had a phone bank to get cancellations. We would drive through different neighborhoods writing down addresses of subscribers, look up their phone numbers in reverse directories, and then call them and ask for cancellations. It's just as easy to get someone to cancel as it is to get them to subscribe. And, we worked to rule.

Working to rule means doing just what you're told to do — nothing else. Don't draw conclusions, act like you're expected to act and don't in any way think for the boss. If they ask you to go do something, go do it. Did they ask you to come back? How do you know you're supposed to? Maybe they will come to where they sent you and ask something else. If asked to train new hires, train them to fight. Part of learning how to do the work right is learning to do the work wrong. Show them how to be sloppy, not to worry about production. After all, if they cared about production, they wouldn't make us work understaffed and underpaid, so why should we care? Take your time. Take as much time as you can to do anything. You can even do some jobs so carefully, so meticulously, that it amounts to a slowdown. Just be prepared with answers if questioned or hassled. Be polite, unless you're in a situation when the company has made an error according to its own dictates. Then, you can probably get away with causing increased stress for the boss.

Some things which come to mind like a thunderstorm: some machines have sharp corners or burrs. Try to wear them smooth by dragging inserts over them. Also, a thumbtack inside a glove can do a lot of clandestine tearing. Ride power equipment while applying the brakes. This saps the charge. Stick paper in conveyor belts — enough paper will jam it. Load compactors on one side — also good for a jam. It's easy to drop palmed "surprises" into the buckets — any unpleasant item will do. Drop inserts on the floor, kick them around, tear out pages they need like the TV guide. Develop speech impediments for the bosses and stare at their bellies if they're fat. Everyone start whistling different songs if

---

Direct action means you gain all of your objectives on the job rather than the ballot box.
— *Jack Miller, Industrial Workers of the World*

Sabotage means primarily the withdrawal of efficiency. Sabotage means either to slacken up or interfere with the quantity, or to botch in your skills and interfere with the quality of capitalist production, or to give bad service. Sabotage is not physical violence; sabotage is an internal industrial process.
— *Sabotage , Elizabeth Gurley Flynn, 1916 [2]*

If a job's worth doing, it's worth doing well.
— *proverb*

It might be said that the ideal of the employer is to have production without employees and the ideal of the employee is to have income without work.
— *E.F. Schumacher*

there is downtime. Also, laughing together at downtime is good. Screw around with adjustments on equipment. Call office numbers at crucial times, tying up the lines. Remove a stack of papers from a vending machine on Sunday. Return them a week later into the same machine and take out the new ones. Save the new ones for the next week. Be creative, and don't be afraid to take some chances. But don't take chances with your workmates' safety or property. Don't threaten those who refuse to sabotage. Don't damage company property that you need, like sinks, toilets, etc. Do have fun with the sons-of-bitches; it's all they're good for.

REPORTER • LEE

After I graduated from journalism school I got a job with the *Burlington County Herald,* a daily paper in south Jersey. I was making a whopping $150 a week and wasn't a happy camper. The editor and I did not get along. He kept berating me for failing to write my lead paragraphs in two sentences with one-syllable words. He was upset that he had to edit everything I wrote.

One day he got really mad and assigned me to the police beat. My job was to call up every police department in the south Jersey area and write a recap of the evening's events for the morning paper. I wrote the headlines, the leads and the story, which was very unusual in those days. The editor was again hassling me for my extended lead paragraphs for these minimal stories. It got to the point where he threatened to fire me so I said, "Fine. You want short paragraphs, you got 'em."

The very next day two articles appeared in the paper. One headline read "Dead." This was followed by "Dateline: Medford New Jersey. That's what Harry Serbronski was after his car hit a telephone pole at eighty-six miles an hour." The other headline was "300 pounds burnt." At the time, the police were raiding a lot of pot growers and everybody assumed, after reading the headline, that another pot grower had been caught. But the next line was "Dateline: Marlton, New Jersey. Flash fire went through a farm building killing one obese woman weighing 304 pounds."

The family of the woman sued the paper on grounds of malice. The paper was taken to court over the story and lost. I got fired the next day. I had no regrets. I didn't care.

8 INSIDE THE OUTSIDE

Growing and Cutting

X.

COMBINE DRIVER • TAD

I got a job with a custom cutter, the people who follow the wheat harvest from Texas on up to North Dakota every summer. The combines we were using were a new model series on loan from International Harvester. A fleet of eight or ten of us went along in a big row through the fields and checked out the new models to see how they were performing.

We were all pretty young, between fourteen and twenty-two, and would rather fuck off than sit on these things for twelve hours a day. Once or twice a week we would slug the combine, which means we'd cause the combine to feed up so much material that it would bind up the cylinder inside the machine. We would shut down two or three machines. Then they would set them aside and take us off the field. International Harvester representatives would come out, tear apart the machines, and try and figure out what the fuck was going on.

We did this intentionally so we could slack off. We got a kick out of these guys with ties and clipboards going over the machine. We thought this was tremendously funny because they seemed very concerned since they had millions of dollars at stake. It was beyond them to think that we would do something like that because, like most employers, they thought their employees were a lot dumber than they really were. I think this is true for most non-unionized, off-the-street labor. They generally assume that you will never pull any stunts. Everybody on the job was in cahoots together. We got to sit around in hotel rooms while they looked over the machines.

GARDENER • WILLIAM

When I got a job at a country club golf course, I thought it was going to be great, because I was hired to do the type of gardening I specialized in: pruning and planting. But the first day I was there, I was mowing lawns and blowing leaves. I had never done either in my life.

After several months, I started to get frustrated because I wasn't doing what I was hired to do. I decided to write some letters to the club's beautification committee. I wanted to show them that I wasn't a mow-and-blow type of gardener. I explained what gardening needed to be done, what plants were planted wrong and why nothing was growing or looking good. The place needed big changes and I made it clear that I wanted to get the work done.

When I finally met with the committee, my plans for the club met with a positive response and we set down certain priorities to get the place looking good. We decided to start on more pruning and to cover the hillsides around the golf course with wildflowers. After that, however, absolutely nothing was done because the person in the middle was my supervisor.

My supervisor thought he was the greatest golf course superintendent in the world. He had a good looking golf course but only because he had an exceptional crew. I don't think he realized this because he thought he did all of the important work. He liked to flex his muscles and show his power over his employees. He

thought if he treated us like shit we'd work harder, and for him to fit in with the club's exclusive membership, he had to show off by making us look like scum.

I started getting the mowing and blowing done as quickly as possible and going off to something creative, like working with the plants. I made the time to do what I wanted to do, but that's when I started to hear shit from my supervisor. He'd ask me what I was doing, yell at me, then make me go blow some more leaves.

I then submitted a detailed report regarding each hole of the golf course to the beautification committee. Again, they liked what I suggested and wanted me to start working on planting beds that would be in full bloom by May twenty-first, when the club was going to host an important golf tournament. I started to feel even more heat from my supervisor because now he felt threatened. The place needed someone like me, who could recognize certain problems and solve them. The committee loved what I was doing but my supervisor hated it because I went over his head. I made suggestions that he should have made, which made him look bad.

Suddenly my supervisor started making me do more pointless tasks. There were at least 8,000 plants that needed planting but I was still forced to mow the lawns and blow the parking lots. I asked him for help but he said everybody was busy and that I'd have to do it all by myself. He knew that I wanted to get the plants done on time but he wanted to put me under as much pressure as possible.

I didn't start planting until May. Because I knew it was his fault, and I knew it would be obvious, I decided to go at my own gardener's pace. I knew I could plant those bedding plants quickly, but I decided to plant them with the utmost care. I planted each one as perfectly as possible. I looked at each plant, unfolded their roots, gently laid them in the ground, then carefully applied the mulch and soil around them. I was definitely being overly efficient. I had been planting for years and could have gone much faster with just as much efficiency. But I decided that I was going to take my time for the entire month. Nothing was in bloom by the time the tournament happened and the club became very aware of how inefficient my supervisor was.

MILLWORKER • CRAWDAD

The Fort Bragg redwood sawmill is owned by Georgia-Pacific, a large company with interests in building materials and chemicals. Workers used to call bomb threats into the company. They waited until 1:00 pm on Fridays, in spring, when it was balmy and glorious. They would call the dispatcher, the same person they called in sick to, and say "I put four charges of plastique in the powerhouse. It goes off at 4:00. Nobody works today!" and hang up. Then they'd get a cold-pack and a gram of hash and drive out to the river. The tactic quit working around July, when it wore out from overuse. The dispatcher was instructed not to tell anybody, and no one looked for the bombs anymore.

The bomb-threat callers only wanted the occasional afternoon off, and took advantage of the political struggle then taking place between ownership, woodsworkers and the first wave of reform-minded hippies and political radicals, who made it a point not to

The more that S.O.B. pushes me, the longer I'm going to take, even if it kills me.
— Anonymous millworker

On an orchard farm in the state of Washington a disagreement arose over conditions on the job. A strike took place. The I.W.W. members among the strikers immediately telephoned to the union in the nearest city. When the employer arrived in town looking for a new crew he was rather surprised at his speedy success. Full fare was paid for the men and the railway train was boarded. At the first stop, about two miles from the city, the whole crew deserted the train. They were all members of the union. Returning to the city, the farmer picked up a second crew. He arranged to have them pay their own fare, same to be refunded upon arrival on the farm. This crew went through all right and worked for a while under the farmer's direction. Thinking the strike was successfully broken the employer finally busied himself with other matters for the rest of the day. Next morning upon visiting the work the farmer was surprised to find that 1000 young trees had been planted upside down, their roots waving in the breeze as a mute evidence of solidarity and sabotage. No further argument was needed to convince the farmer of the justice of the demands of the original crew.
— Sabotage, Walker C. Smith, 1913 [3]

We were instructed that there were three kinds of tomatoes in the field: the red ripe, the pinks, and the sunscaled. We were to pick the red ripes and the sunscaled but were to leave the pinks. Everyone takes baskets and puts them out at intervals along their row. As you fill one basket you move on to the next one. The tomatoes in the field were very poor. We were only supposed to pick red ripe ones. Everyone, however, was picking pink ones and rotten ones; more or less anything to fill up the basket.
— Work In Market and Industrial Societies, Herbert Applesbaum [4]

A good nursery manager is cognizant of the fact the most important factor of production relates to the employees. The proper and timely granting of employee rewards can have a major impact upon the success or failure of the business.
— Nursery Management [5]

get jobs in mills or timber.

Another favorite (but rarely successful) tactic is to drop metal and glass into the Hog, a machine which chops wood trimmings and waste into Hog fuel, or chips and dust to be burned for power generation. A metal detector and a full-time worker guard the Hog against such foreign objects, although the odd aluminum soda can will get by, and everyone then enjoys a half-day or so of relaxation while millwrights attend to the damaged blades. The mill loses between $100 and $200 per minute while the Hog is broken. Anyone caught intentionally dropping foreign material onto the Hog-feed chain is subject to stern discipline including termination, so it is not done lightly. Equipment breakdowns are fairly common events, and I always enjoyed them to the fullest while bosses got all red-faced and stood around wishing they could fix it with a hammer.

I suppose sabotage also might include hiding between the loads of lumber with three or four buddies and copping a buzz. At least half the workers I know are regular marijuana users, and their motive is to reclaim their minds, or at least to render them useless to the company. It's also a way to relieve the crushing monotony. They've instituted pre-employment urinalysis since my day, and they work harder at propagandizing the smoker against seeking peace through drugs, but let's be honest about this: getting a mill job is the quickest way to get on drugs. Speed is not quite as common as pot, but the effects are more profound and users are truly dedicated. And then there's alcohol.

Acts of sabotage are likely to be appreciated by some workers. Many seem to have no opinion. Others are so much in debt that they find ways to work even when their co-workers are sent home, and they are against sabotage.

PLANT NURSERY WORKER • RYAN

I was the lowest one on the ladder, so naturally I was treated like dung. My main duties were carryout assistance and plant care — watering and stocking. I was also in charge of spraying very potent weed killer on the wild grass around the outside of the nursery. After having been accused of stealing items from the yard, I became very displeased with my job and my boss.

I knew where the weed killer was kept. Having access to the yard thanks to a section of iron fence that was wide enough to squeeze my ass through, I strolled in one evening and gave the plants a little drink. Starting with the expensive trees, I worked my way down to baskets of seeds, drenching them with that deadly cocktail that would soon take its toll. I used approximately seventy-five gallons of the poison in all. I got fired the next day because the boss said I was "too slow" and "unmotivated."

About a week later I cruised by the nursery to pick up my last check. I noticed that all the plants in the nursery were brown and dead. I also found out that a friend who also worked there had told the boss to fuck off the same day I was fired. Since I left on a good note (no argument or harassment), he was blamed for my deadly deed. Taking one last glance at the yard which was now a foliage cemetery, my heart swelled with hellish triumph.

★

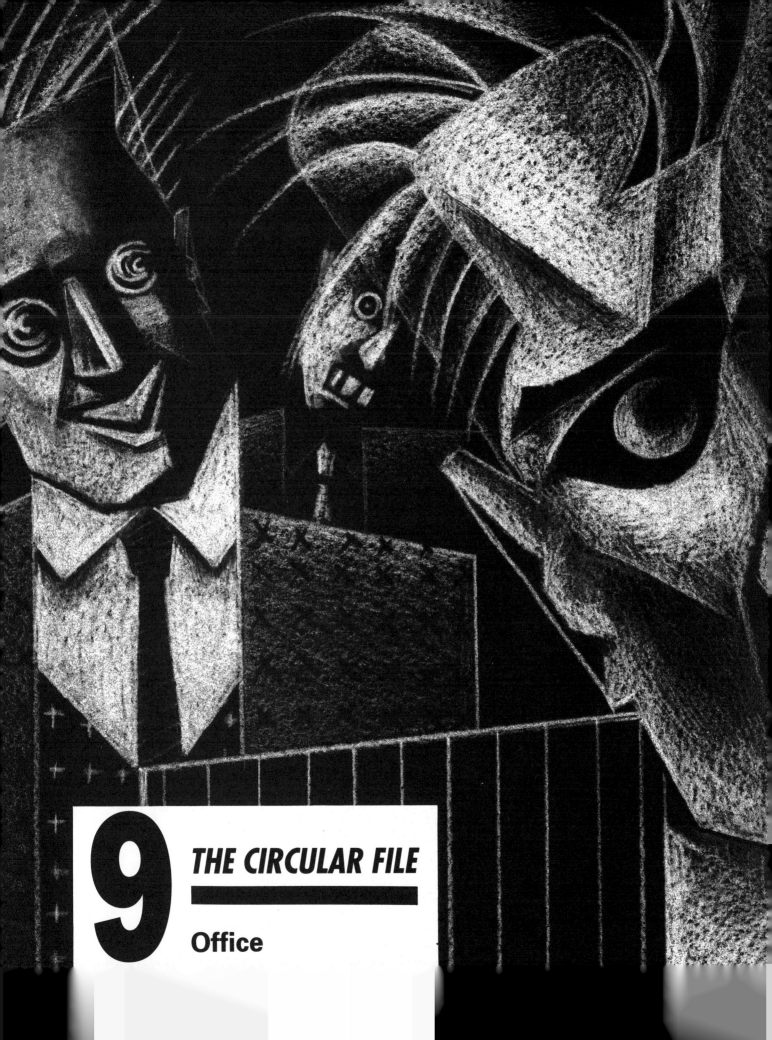

9 THE CIRCULAR FILE

Office

PARALEGAL • GEORGE

I worked for a personal injury law firm. It was one of those firms that you see advertised on television so there was never a shortage of clients. At any one time, we were handling about 1,100 cases in that office. Compared to the large amount of work, the staff was fairly small: there was the boss, three attorneys and usually ten paralegals.

My particular job was to handle cases from intake all the way through litigation. This means that if someone were in a car accident and hurt their neck, we'd get a hold of the police report and witnesses for them and write to the insurance company on their behalf, demanding money for pain, suffering and inconvenience.

There was a lot of autonomy in the job. When you started out you basically got your own office or a huge desk space. No one seemed to get in your way, which was nice. However, the workload was incredible and the clients were awful. The boss led these clients to believe that they could dictate when their settlements would come and how much they would be. Anything he could get away with he did, and we had to deal with all of the repercussions.

Starting salary was $7 an hour with a review in six months, but we never got a decent raise. Instead, we got $7.50 an hour plus twenty hours a week overtime which really makes no sense when you think about it. There's no way anyone could have worked overtime at this job without going nuts.

There was a very high turnover rate. A lot of people would only be there for a week. I worked there for two and a half years and the only way I lasted was by scamming.

We handled our own clients and essentially nobody really saw the cases. We were reviewed occasionally but never consistently. Often, out of the 150 cases we would have, five or so we called M.I.A. These were clients who were missing in action and hadn't been around for three or four years and their case was waiting to be settled. The insurance companies were calling us up wanting us to settle, but we couldn't without the authorization of the clients.

Well, some of us would find the authorization — that is, forge the client's signature, settle the cases, and distribute the money to the doctors and the attorneys who needed to be paid. The remainder went to the paralegals. It was good money. We felt that we had a right to the money. This guy was underpaying us and I really felt that he owed me. Even the born-again Christian woman I shared an office with did this, as did the top paralegals. It was a secret we all shared.

I don't know of anyone being caught. But as long as the doctors and attorneys got paid, why would the boss question anyone? If the client were to resurface, I suspect the boss would know what the paralegal did. He'd know that his business name would be in jeopardy if word got out, so he'd just pay off the client. I don't think that it could ever get out.

Like I said before, it was good money. Too bad I quit. It got to be very stressful. Even though I was only working about five hours

---

Who first invented work — and tied the free — to this dry drudgery of the desk's dead wood?
— Charles Lamb

There are as many ways to steal from an employer as there are kinds of business.
— Nation's Business [1]

Employees are doing the right thing when they report their suspicions because internal theft cannot flourish without the sanction of co-workers. It's extremely rare for large scale theft to occur without others knowing about it or becoming suspicious. Employees who immediately report their suspicions are preventing a small problem from becoming a major one, and this will benefit all employees who work in the company.
— The Peter Berlin Report on Shrinkage Control [2]

All of us on the insurance company "floor" were continuously aware of the constant surveillance — so aware that we had developed ways of appearing busy when we were actually socializing with our fellow workers. Those of us who had telephones found this easy: we simply used the old call-your-neighbor-on-the-phone trick. Thus both of us looked busy.
— Work in Market and Industrial Society, Herbert Applesbaum [3]

a day and getting paid $2,300 a month, the lying was very unhealthy. I always had to look over my shoulder to protect myself.

INSURANCE FILE CLERK • RANDALL

One company was in the process of taking over another and needed to convert the old company's files to their system. I was working for a temp agency at the time and was called in with several other people to do the job.

About one-third of the files were people who weren't able to make their insurance payments. In the files I read a lot of letters from people explaining why they weren't able to keep up their payments. Some were pregnant, others couldn't find jobs and they had been sending in letter after letter telling the company that they wanted to keep in touch, and that they didn't want their credit fucked up. Most people *wanted* to pay back the loans, they just needed more time. Yet the company went ahead and put the loans on default. It wasn't like the company was going to fold if some people delayed payments.

Even though I had a boss looking over my shoulder the entire time, it was still pretty easy to let an defaulted insurance policy go on through without being checked. The boss only checked the file numbers, which were the laminated tabs that we were putting on the files, so if those numbers were right he didn't check much further. I started deliberately fucking things up by putting a paper in the wrong file or writing down one wrong number. I targeted the people who were in the most trouble. Once I put the wrong number on a file and it resulted in delaying an entire stack of defaults that were going to be mailed out the next day. What I did might not have helped them in the long run, but at least it gave them some time, and the company some trouble.

A nice fire would have done that place some good, but they had a good sprinkler system.

SECRETARY • ALICE

I worked part-time for a senior sales director at a cosmetic company. I was a secretary, handled the mail, made the bank deposits, ran errands and spent half my day at the copy shop. Some days it was hectic, some days it was slow; it just depended on what time of the month it was.

I worked there five years and the job was okay but towards the end I couldn't wait to get out. I wasn't making any money. The woman I worked for was one of the main directors and she made big bucks. She started me out at $5 an hour and the first year I got a quarter raise every three months, so I ended up at $6 an hour after the first year but I never got a raise after that. I was forty-four when I started and I needed a job at the time, so I took it thinking I would gradually get raises. I asked her for them and she always told me that she couldn't afford it. I knew she could afford it because I knew what she was making, I was handling her finances. She would go out and buy beautiful clothes. She just didn't want to pay *me* any more.

Into the third year of working there, I realized that it was lame and that I wanted to quit, but I needed the money and I didn't have much confidence. I started leaving early, maybe padding an hour here and there. She was out recruiting most of the time because the more people she had working for her, the more money she made. So I was there by myself most of the time. To me it was just a perk; I thought I deserved something, a little bit more than what I was getting. If there was nothing to do I would leave, which was OK, but I had to keep track of my hours. I would leave at 3:00 pm but say that I worked until 4:00 pm. She never knew the difference.

She offered me a ten percent discount on all cosmetics when I started, but shortly after the first year she took that away, saying she couldn't afford it. I never took anything without paying for it, but I would pay a little bit less for it. She never looked at the sales record. I didn't buy a lot of the stuff she sold because it was expensive and I didn't use that many cosmetics, but for the few things that I did use, I gave myself a discount.

I never really felt resentful towards her. Well, actually there was a period where I *did*, but in the end I figured that was just the type of person she was. She was cheap towards others but very good to herself, and I wasn't worth anything. She was so beautiful and elegant and I felt like a little dud.

I worked hard and these perks made me feel like I was getting something for my work. I did everything I was supposed to, and then some. She definitely took advantage of me and I knew it at the time. I now know that I shouldn't have stayed on as long as I did. I've never done anything like that before. I'm a very honest person but I feel like what I did wasn't wrong.

EXECUTIVE ASSISTANT • CHRISTIAN

For ten years I was the executive assistant to the merchandising manager of a Fortune 500 retail corporation in the Midwest. My region included 120 retail stores where I bought and distributed inventory.

I worked really hard. Three months after I started, I was handling the largest volume of stores for the company. I maintained a very high profile and was very vocal. I moved up in the company for the first three years but was never promoted beyond that because there weren't any women in top management positions. That really pissed me off.

About six years ago I decided I wanted to do a publication, and I was trying to think of different ways to do it. Contributors sent me information, which I photocopied with no charge to them, because I had access to this incredibly beautiful photocopier at work. I usually got to the office at 6:00 in the morning — about an hour and a half before my co-workers arrived. I would be standing at the copier, filled with anxiety and thinking that someone was going to catch me. Occasionally the security guards would make their rounds and scare the hell out of me, but they probably thought I was an incredibly hard worker, doing work early. I had a box under my desk where I'd stash all of these papers. I always carried a knapsack to smuggle the stuff out little by little — a total of 8,000

A female secretary employed by the True Value chain in Kansas was stealing at a rate of $1600 in four days. She said she stole a total of $10,000, but the total was probably more. Her boss says, "If we were a single-store operation, we would have been out of business."
— Hardware Age [4]

Women do two-thirds of the world's work ... yet they earn only one-tenth of the world's income and own less than one percent of the world's property. They are among the poorest of the world's poor.
— Barber B. Conable, Jr., President, World Bank

One third of the people in the U.S. promote, while the other two-thirds provide.
— Will Rogers, The Illiterate Digest

sheets. It took about three weeks to get them all out. I published the magazine for three years. When I stopped, the company couldn't figure out why they all of a sudden had this huge backlog of paper.

I stole anything I could get my hands on and sold it at yard sales — a lot of supplies, an electronic stapler machine. It didn't even have to be anything I needed or wanted. With my extensive background in juvenile delinquency and petty theft, this kind of thing came naturally to me. I've always found it oddly justifiable, something like a company benefit. At times, it was highly profitable.

I didn't feel any guilt about anything I took. I figured out the value of the inventory I was buying and shipping, how much the stores were profiting from one day of my work, and how much I was getting paid. They could have paid me thirty times more for my work and it still wouldn't have come close to how much they profited from me. I never felt any remorse. I think good mischief is well worth the personal effort, especially when people are so incredibly underpaid for their effort.

PUBLIC RECORDS RESEARCHER • ALEC

My job doesn't occupy my mind very much but I still find it interesting. I'm asked to extract anything as mundane as a birth or death certificate, or as important as a foreclosure on a house. It always amazes me that people pay me extraordinary sums of money to retrieve this type of information, when they can easily get it themselves.

I don't work in an office, so the company I work for doesn't have any real control over my workday. They beep me and give me job assignments. At the end of the week, I send them all the work that I've done. Since the company has offices all over the world, I get calls from different branches to do the work, so no one really knows what I'm doing unless I tell them. I'm supposed to be cost-effective, productive and efficient. I'm not supposed to have any down time; I'm supposed to account for every fifteen minutes of my time. They don't want anything in writing; they want numbers and categories.

I simply overreport my time. It's based on my mood at the end of the week, when I report. I regularly report thirty-five to forty hours a week of work but I actually only work about twenty. My company is aware that this could happen, and once they sent my supervisor to follow me through a typical day of work. But because I do the job every day and she doesn't, I drew out the search and I took longer than I normally would.

I said that the only real inefficiency was the time I had to spend on the phone talking to the branch office. "If this other office would just behave, I'd be the most productive corporate citizen you have!" As a result, my supervisor directed the office to give me my work in a completely different way. She thought this would save me two hours a day but it actually made my job even easier. My supervisor was content and said I was working hard and doing my job.

UTILITY FILE CLERK • HARRY

In certain sections of Pacific Gas & Electric people violently hate the company, and it doesn't take much to get people to talk about how much they hate it. In the elevator, people make jokes about going back to the salt mines. Many people have mentioned to me that they know that most of what we do is pointless and wish they could somehow arrange for the company to send them their paychecks at home and never come in. Management are all happy little monkeys committed to the corporate cause, but a lot of the regular workers aren't.

One particular section I worked in was involved in litigation with some of the employees who were either being hassled by the company or trying to get back at them for injury claims. I forget all of the legal jargon but there was a particular notice informing the company lawyers that the court date was on such-and-such day at such-and-such time. If the company didn't get the notice, their lawyer wouldn't show up, they'd forfeit the case and the employee would automatically win. One of my fellow clerks would fill brown bags with these notices. The bags would go out with him when he went on his break and they wouldn't be with him when he came back. They were gone. The guy knew it was all shit.

TELEPHONE SURVEYOR • IRIS

Sometimes the surveys were short and lasted five minutes, and other times they lasted forty-five minutes. We did surveys for political parties, lobby organizations and sometimes even for private businesses who needed to find out people's favorite deter-gent or hairspray. The surveys went from very menial to very opinionated.

The owner was a total asshole. He seemed to think he was high and mighty. It's almost like he hired younger people just so he could push them around and so he wouldn't have any confronta-tions on his own level. The job was so trivial and meaningless, but this was his life and livelihood. He felt he was doing something great for society.

It really wasn't very difficult work. Being able to talk and dial a phone were the only job requirements. We would sit at a desk and call people for six hours and fill out the surveys. The company would tell us how many surveys we were supposed to do every hour. Not only did we have to do the interviews, but we had to record if the person hung up and at what time.

Most people didn't do the interviews at all. We would make up names and answers for people we supposedly talked to. If we actually did call someone, we only put in some of their own answers. Sometimes if it was a survey about something that we felt strongly about, we wouldn't ask them certain questions, but just fill in our own answers.

The ironic thing was that with so much fucking around and every survey was so ridiculously wrong, the owner still had this big bulletin board with newspaper clippings of statistics based on

surveys that we had done. We would die laughing, because we knew all of the answers were wrong. They weren't even close to being accurate.

I don't think most people consciously fucked around; most did it because of the environment and the way the business was set up. The job was so tedious and the wages were pathetic. The way I see it, when you're in a situation that's unreasonable from the start, you have to compensate for it. That's just the nature of work. If people were getting what they deserved for working, there would be no need to screw around.

COPY EDITOR • BILLY

My job was to keep track of the word processors' errors and to monitor how much work was going through the system.

The word processors would be given all this work and they'd be under a lot of pressure to get it done quickly. They had to work really fast to keep their jobs, but when they worked faster, their error counts went higher. If their error counts were too high, the supervisors would chastise them for it. The supervisors would constantly threaten the word processors with this standard of productivity.

The management was trying to work both ends at the same time. They wanted them to work really fast, but they wanted their errors to be low, too. It's a completely unnatural expectation and these were just normal human beings. Besides, word processing anywhere is one of the worst jobs. It's the equivalent of piecework in a factory. So the word processors' morale would be low and the supervisors would be pushing them extremely hard, and then they'd ask for that little bit of extra effort.

My colleagues and I managed to sabotage that system by giving the word processors really low error quotients. We'd do it even if they made lots of errors. Everybody on my shift had an unspoken agreement about it. The word processors knew that we were on their side, which helped us when we had to deal with management later. It was always a tight rope situation because we didn't want to lose our own jobs. We had to make sure a reasonable amount of errors got recorded so the supervisors wouldn't realize what we were doing.

We ended up telling the supervisors about what was going on. If we hadn't, they never would have caught on. We explained to them that the system was completely illogical — they were undermining their own attempts to get the work done and forcing the word processors to make more errors than they ordinarily would. They eventually got rid of this system because it was so unmanageable. Because of our efforts, the word processors' jobs became more tolerable.

PARALEGAL • FRANCES

One Friday afternoon a memo was circulated through the law firm where I work. It informed employees that due to escalating health

Work avoidance includes employees hanging out at the water cooler or trying to look busy while not really doing anything

— Fortune Magazine [7]

When a man tells you he got rich through hard work, ask him whose.

— Don Marquis

"People who purposely abuse their paid working time are stealing from their employers, just as they would be if they stole money or products," says Robert Half, the employment expert who first identified — and named — time theft. "And time is a commodity that can never be replaced, replenished or restored."

He also announced the results of a nationwide survey of leading corporations. According to the personnel directors and top management executives who were interviewed, the major types of time theft are, in order:

1. Constant socializing with other employees and excessive personal phone calls. The largest form of time theft, by far.

2. Faking illness and claiming unwarranted "sick" days.

3. Inordinately long lunch hours and coffee breaks.

4. Habitual late arrival and/or early departure.

5. Using the company's time and premises to operate another business.

6. Creating the need for overtime by slowing down during normal hours. [8]

insurance prices, the firm would no longer allow employees to waive their insurance costs and have the $190 a month premium included in their paychecks. There are 155 employees in the firm and about thirty-five have waived their health insurance. The firm was going to continue paying the insurance costs for those employees who didn't waive it, and those who did would have to enroll in the plan. The company thought that with 100 percent enrollment their premium costs would be lower.

We were all pretty shocked at this idea because many of us had waived the insurance when we began working here. When I was interviewed for the job, I made it clear that I wanted to maintain my private insurance. The company agreed and said they would apply the premium to my paycheck. I felt they had broken my employment contract.

We immediately understood that our salaries would be cut. We were upset, and I don't think any of us worked for the rest of the day. The whole week after the memo was released there was a lot of talk about what we could do to protect ourselves. We wrote up a petition and got about twenty people to sign it. I didn't care that I was spending time on this petition instead of work. I don't care about work, I care about protecting my income. I wasn't doing the work that I was being paid to do, but I said to myself that they were screwing me over and it was tit for tat.

If the company doesn't want to take care of their faithful employees who make their profits, then forget it. I'm not going to feel guilty about what I do. They are only looking to cut costs on the business end; they're not looking out for their employees.

TYPESETTER • LINA

I've been a typesetter for twelve years and I've never met a typesetter who didn't steal his or her own services from an employer. I've seen it happen when I was working for magazines, advertising firms and commercial print shops. We make anywhere from $10 to $15 an hour. Typesetting services are billed to the client at $75 to $150 an hour. Every typesetter knows that his or her labor is not being compensated at the rate at which it is being sold.

Over the years, I've produced thousands and thousands of dollars of free work. When I typeset outside jobs, I use the company's equipment to make money for myself. When I typeset my name and address for my mailbox at home, I'm stealing for my own use. I also trade my typesetting for services; I haven't paid for a haircut in over ten years.

Oddly enough, when I had a very high-paying typesetting job, I felt no need to do outside work. In jobs where I've worked at the low end of the scale, I've always wanted to rip off the company. If I feel like somebody's treating me fairly, I don't want to steal from them. "Fairly" means a decent wage for my work and the feeling that I can do my own outside work once I've finished my work for them without having to hide it. If I have to hide it, I just feel more compelled to do it, as a way of saying "Fuck you!" It's human nature. If someone feels like they're not being ripped off, they won't feel compelled to rip off the person they work for.

PHYSICIAN RELATIONS MANAGER BARBARA

I worked for a large inner-city hospital. My job was to increase physician loyalty to the hospital by helping them be more successful and happy with the hospital. Then, they would be encouraged to use it more. I helped solve problems and identify concerns that physicians had with their practices. I was paid a base salary of $50,000 and a bonus on top of that.

Because I represented the hospital, I had to know everybody in the hospital and how the hospital worked. I not only had to get to know the physicians, but I had to get to know every department head and manager.

I had excellent relations with everyone at the hospital. The only block I had was my boss. She came into the hospital as a high-powered consultant, but had no experience and very poor interpersonal skills. She had never worked at a hospital in a managerial capacity. Instead of developing relationships with other vice presidents, she came in with her master plan and tried to implement it. The other V.P.s resented that.

She had conflicts with me because I had developed strong relationships with the department managers. They were all telling her that they liked me, but *she* wasn't getting along with any of them. She knew that people would come to me and talk, but they wouldn't come to her and that bothered her.

Her managerial style was very controlling; I couldn't meet with anybody in the hospital without her approval. But to do my sales job, I needed to have a long leash. Here I was, a very well paid manager, but I was not allowed to talk with any physician or members of the office staff without her prior approval. I wasn't allowed to talk to anyone on the hospital's marketing staff because she didn't like them. I was not even allowed to go to the second floor of my building because that was where their department was located.

After a couple of months of harassment, my boss ended my relationships with the physicians associated with the hospital. She put together a ridiculous sales call list of physicians not on the hospital's staff. She gave me the list to deal with as a way to farm me out. The physicians on the list would take years to get on staff, if I were to get them at all.

I decided that I wasn't going to waste my time doing these bogus sales calls. I drafted up fake sales reports and sat in the office and read all day. I looked up the physicians in the medical society's directory, got all the information I needed, then wrote up various reasons why they weren't good prospects for the hospital. I figured that if she was going to make up a bogus sales call list, I was going to make up bogus sales call reports. I know some people would respond to a situation like this by getting more into their work and blocking it all out, but my response was to do nothing.

She wouldn't let me do the job I was hired to do. At the salary I was being paid, I should have at least been able to make small decisions such as whether or not I wanted to talk to an office manager. Because I wasn't allowed to think or do anything on my own, it was obvious that she wanted me to be her glorified secretary. I refuse to feel guilty about not working for someone who doesn't acknowledge me as a fellow human being and a professional.

Stumble out of bed
and stumble into the kitchen
pour myself a cup of ambition
and yawn, and stretch
and try to come to life
jump in shower and
the blood starts pumping
out on the street and
the traffic starts jumping
with folks like me on the job from 9 till 5

Working 9 to 5
what a way to make a living
barely getting by
it's all taking and no giving
they just use your mind
and they never give you credit
it's enough to drive you crazy if you let it

9 to 5
for service and devotion
you would think that I would deserve
a fair promotion
want to move ahead
but the boss won't seem to let me
I swear sometimes that man
is out to get me

They let you dream
just to watch them shatter
You're just a step
on the bossman's ladder
But you've got dreams
he'll never take away
You're in the same boat
with a lot of your friends
waiting for the day,
your ship will come in
and the tide is gonna turn
and it's all gonna roll your way

9 to 5
they've got you where they want you
there's a better life
and you think about it, don't you
It's a rich man's game,
no matter what they call it
and you spend your life
putting money in his wallet
         — "9 to 5," by Dolly Parton[9]

    Yesterday I was a dog. Today I'm a dog. Tomorrow I'll probably still be a dog. Sigh. There's so little hope for advancement.
         — Snoopy

10 WHITEWASH

Maintenance

CONVALESCENT HOME JANITOR • HERB

I had to clean the rooms, scrub toilets, mop floors and empty garbage cans. The place had two wings: one in the front and another in the back. I was always assigned to the front wing, so if I wasn't there, the other two janitors on the shift wouldn't notice unless someone specifically needed me for something. I was virtually unsupervisable.

I actually had to work hard and fast cleaning the wing. It takes a lot longer than you would imagine. The nurses would be yelling at me and all of the patients would be saying, "Get my bed pan!" I just felt like, "Fuck you. I'm sick of this." But the people who lived there were more important to me than the boss. They were all old people who didn't mean any harm, and they paid a lot of money so they wouldn't have to look at shit. They were the ones I felt I had to answer to.

Unfortunately, I couldn't sneak out of the building using the front door because I'd pass the nurses' station and the supervisor's office. This problem was quickly remedied with a bit of cleverness. When the employees' lounge was empty, I would sneak in, take the screen out of the window, jump outside, then put the screen back in the window. Now, the possibilities were endless. Usually I would walk down the street to a nearby dental complex, hang out in the shade for a half-hour or so, then climb back in through the window, punch out, and go home. Usually when I came back from a little stint, people would ask me, "Where were you? We were trying to find you." I would just say, "Oh, I had to go to the bathroom," or some bullshit like that. As far as I know, no one ever missed me.

UNIVERSITY MAINTENANCE WORKER ADAM

We get in and out of the buildings very easily without being questioned. We always look like we belong wherever we may be because we wear work gloves and have a truck with the university insignia on it. The university spans across an entire city in New Jersey, so we can go wherever we want without our supervisors thinking anything of it. This gives us a lot of freedom to do whatever we want. We regularly drive the truck to one co-worker's house and go to sleep for a couple of hours, then we go back and punch out.

The university was renovating an academic building and they put a lot of the furniture, carpet, space heaters and track lights in a warehouse that our department shares with whatever department was being renovated. It was all just piled up and none of it was labeled. I figured no one would miss anything. One day I told my boss we had to work overtime because there was a lot to do. Then three of us loaded up the university truck with two dressers, two desks, three chairs, three beds and some lights. Later I went back and got two carpets. A guy I worked with got two mattresses and track lights.

I took most of the stuff because I was moving into a new

In April 1971, President Nixon told the Republican Governors' Conference at Williamsburg about his thoughts on the rewards of honest toil. "Scrubbing floors and emptying bedpans," he claimed, has "just as much dignity as there is in any work to be done in this country — including my own." In September of the same year, before a joint session of Congress (and three days after a Labor Day statement containing the same theme), he again declared that, "No work is demeaning or beneath a person's dignity if it provides food for his table and clothes and shelter for his children."
— *Where Have All the Robots Gone?*
Harold L. Sheppard and
Neal Q. Herrick [1]

Boredom, after all, is a form of criticism.
— *William Phillips*

One security professional says: ten percent of the people you hire will never steal; ten percent will steal regardless of what you do; and eighty percent will stay honest if you create an environment that discourages and detects theft. Our job is to keep the first ten percent, to identify and get rid of the second ten percent, and to protect the other eighty percent against themselves.
— *Nation's Business [2]*

apartment. I didn't own any furniture and I needed it. It was free and very easy to take; no one questioned us and I don't think anyone even noticed. They were so incredibly disorganized. If they *did* miss the stuff, they probably just chalked it up to the move.

If I had to rationalize doing it, I'd say that there wasn't a revenge motive, just fair give and take.

CEMETERY GROUNDSKEEPER • JERRY

For two years I worked at Sunnyside Cemetery in Long Beach. I did everything from general maintenance to funerals — you know — burying people.

When I first got the job I didn't fuck off much, but then we got a new supervisor. He had been a navy captain for forty years and wanted everything in order just like in the military. Sometimes he would just follow me around, checking up on everything that I did. He made us work when there was no work to be done. We had to cut the grass even if it didn't need it, just to keep busy. He was so gung ho and jumpy that it pissed me off, so I didn't even try to work.

I got tired of breathing the gas fumes from the lawn mower, and found that I could go out to the yard and just pretend that I was mowing the lawn. The yard was a thirteen acre circle so once I got a couple of acres away the supervisor couldn't hear if the mower's engine was running. Usually there were other machines going which helped increase my cover. I never turned the motor on. I just faked it; pulled the line and just walked around. I'd be out there for hours just pushing a switched-off mower around. Sometimes, when it was too hot and I was completely out of the supervisor's sight, I would stash the mower behind a grave marker and climb up into a tree and hide. I'd just sit up there and relax.

I would never fuck with any of the funerals or bodies because that was disrespectful to the families. It would be like doing something to somebody that you didn't know.

GOFER • SPENCER

The place was an old ice house which had been converted to a wholesale furniture and design mart with hundreds of designer showrooms. I was one of the people who worked for the building manager. We had to do things like water the plants and replace lightbulbs; if the tenants of the building needed something, we were there to help them. We were basically gofers. When I first started working there, the manager liked me, but then he realized he had married a monster.

The slimeball manager had this cutesy idea to promote the building. He bought this block of ice every day and stuck it out on this old scale in front of the building, in reference to what the building was originally built for.

I was friends with one of the owners of a small company in the building who had her cocktail every afternoon at 4:00 pm. The ice-making machine that made the party ice was broken and had been for several days. She would call up the office everyday and com-

plain, but the boss never did anything about it. This woman got very upset because they didn't keep the ice machine in good repair. As you can imagine, not having ice can seriously hamper the beginning of cocktail hour. So she had me paged and sent up to her showroom. She said, "You gotta do something about this ice." I said, "No problem, be back in a moment." I figured we weren't meeting our commitment to the building's tenants; the cocktail hour isn't happening; cocktail hour must happen. I grabbed a sledgehammer and, with one of my other goofball gofers, went down to the block of ice and smashed it into two million pieces. We picked up as much party-sized ice as we could, delivered it to the showroom, and proceeded to have cocktails with the owner.

11 IT'S NOT JUST A JOB, IT'S AN ADVENTURE

Military

INFANTRYMAN • JACK

I didn't really have any special outlook on life. I hadn't gone to college, I didn't have any skills or job interests, and I'd been arrested. When I finally got the draft notice that had been hanging over my head, it sort of came as a relief. I wouldn't have to worry about a job or car payments.

Because of my blue collar background, I didn't resist the draft. I realized that everybody was going and it didn't occur to me to not go. I figured my only options would be to go to jail or to Canada. I didn't know anybody who went to Canada, and I had been to jail myself and knew what that option was like. Getting drafted just seemed kind of exciting because at that point I had a really dull life. I didn't really think they would send me to Vietnam and I didn't think they would put me in the Infantry because I thought that I was a pretty smart guy. I thought they would give me some special job to do in Germany.

By my first or second day in the Army I wasn't too pleased with my situation. I didn't do well for the same reason that I didn't do well in school: I don't like being told what to do. I didn't like the people I had to deal with and my frustration just built up more and more. Before long I was in Vietnam.

My job description was to walk to the top of a hill and dig a hole. Through the night I would sit in that hole or sleep by it. I would get up at dawn and walk to another hill and dig another hole. If I ever saw anybody who didn't dress like me I was supposed to kill him.

As with most of my peers, sabotage was part of the daily routine. Some of this sabotage was malicious, much of it to relieve the tedium of life on the battlefield or to ameliorate the effects of drudgery, exposure and exhaustion. Some of it was done for profit. Some of it was homicidal.

When I first got there, I threw away a lot of food, ammo and explosive devices because I was so overburdened with equipment I couldn't carry it all. I would dismantle incendiary devices to use the plastic C4 explosive as a source of heat to stay warm or as a way to cook food. When I was on guard duty, out of boredom I dismantled fifty caliber tracer shells to make fireworks. We just destroyed stuff out of boredom.

I put a huge rock in a friend's pack when he wasn't looking so he would strain himself to delirium on the march, just so we could laugh. When we were sent out at night to pull an ambush, we found a place to hide instead so we could sleep. I fell asleep on guard duty because I was too tired to stay awake, but I got caught for that. I refused to take anti-malaria pills in the hopes I would get malaria and be evacuated out of the bush. I jogged in place with a full pack in noonday sun in a brush fire in an attempt to get heat prostration. I disobeyed direct orders from an officer on the battlefield. I challenged my platoon sergeant to a fight. I was caught smoking pot. I allowed my weapon to become rusty and caked with mud, gambled when I was supposed to clean my weapon and slept when I was supposed to be packing up my gear. When I walked point I went really fast so the company would get hot and tired and pissed off. Sometimes I would lead the squad to a place were there was no

Labor is discovered to be grand conqueror, enriching and building up nations more surely than the proudest battles.
— War, William Everly Channing

1.8 million gallons of airplane fuel at the huge American supply base at Cam Panh Bay, Vietnam, blew up in the night on May 24th. Military authorities were quick to attribute the mysterious incident to a declining level of carefulness and the rise in drug use among US soldiers, even though no contact was made with the enemy commandos and no US losses were reported. Officers were unable to give an account of the enemy's methods in attacking the fuel storage area, but simply stated that "they obviously got past someone who should have spotted them." They are either not aware of what's going on around them or they have chosen to cover up what is most obvious to us: that this action was carried out by resisters inside the army.
— RITA (Resisters Inside the Armed Forces) Newsletter [1]

In August 1977, Lieutenant Colonel Lindsay L. Baird, Jr. (USA ret.) told a Senate subcommittee that while he was provost-marshal of the United States Second Division, Korean criminals, military people, politicians and police conspired with United States Army enlisted men to manipulate the Army's inventory of supplies in Taegu. The thefts occurred in the early 1970s; they involved Schneider-like deception, and cost the United States government $28 million a year.
— Controlling White Collar Crime, John M. Carroll [2]

likelihood at all of running into the enemy. Why look for trouble? Once while on a march I fell to the back of the company, planning to blow my brains out; another soldier changed my mind.

In the end, I vowed to never forget what those bastards made me do. I still haven't.

CORPSMAN • RAMIRO

Talk about a bureaucratic nightmare — the military wastes millions of dollars just in paperwork and the manpower to manage it. It is so bogged down with numbers and rules that nobody really knows what is going on. It is so easy to screw up the process — just add numbers here and there. I entertained myself by causing as much confusion as possible.

I was a quiet sort of guy who kept to himself. The thing I enjoyed most was destroying important documents. Whenever I found one, I would crumple it up and flush it down the toilet. Because I was senior corpsman, I was trusted and had access to military records. I found the executive officer's health record and threw the whole thing away. He had to be re-immunized because he had no medical record. He was really pissed.

I was also in charge of ordering supplies. Once I ordered some bandages and added some extra numbers on the form to see what would happen. A generator for a ship had the same exact number I used and this stirred up a lot of problems. I made sure that everything was wrong. There was no way to check on my work. There was so much to check, who would take the time to do it?

SONAR TECHNICIAN • MICHAEL

In 1978 the USS Cook pulled into Hunter's Point Navel Shipyard in San Francisco. A few crew members and one officer frequented the Mabuhay Gardens during that period, catching Negative Trend, Crime, the Nuns, Dead Kennedys and many other bands. The core of this crew became colorful proponents of punk on board the Cook. The officer quickly found the subculture at odds with his Naval career. He resigned his commission, but not after bringing some members of Magister Ludi onboard for supper in the wardroom, the inner sanctuary of "gentlemen officers" on board ships.

At that time Jim Williams began recording his own music in LAPS, the space that contained the generator that powered the Cook's sonar system. Coincidentally, most of the ship's punks were sonar men. LAPS became their focus. The space's unique closed air system allowed them to get high without fear of getting caught. A powerful vent sucked any offending smoke into the system. Roaches were disposed of in the same way, never to be seen except during monthly filter cleaning in which the sonar men recycled their reefer during "dry times" at sea.

For me the Navy was a job, an unpleasant one. I tried to escape, but got arrested on the highways for hitchhiking. I arrived onboard the Cook as a deserter, having gone AWOL three months before. I was brought to the ship in handcuffs with another Cook runaway,

John S., who introduced me to the other Cook punks. Being a sonar man myself, I eagerly became a member of this group of outcasts.

A few months later, when John S. claimed to be bisexual, he became the first Cook outcast to be cast out. He was discharged under less than honorable conditions. Disgust and hatred towards us from the rest of the crew grew precipitously after John's discharge. Alienated and increasingly out of touch with punk subculture in general, we hunkered down in LAPS getting stoned, listening to whatever music we could get and recording our own bare-bones music.

During a long overseas cruise, bigotry against us reached its zenith. One guy was constantly harassed and attacked, especially after he carved FTN (fuck the Navy) in his forearm. I found myself in trouble constantly, going before the captain three times in as many months.

After spending two months off the coast of Iran during the hostage crisis, the Cook got its order to head home. Somewhere along the way Jim W. and I decided we were going to put out a fanzine for punk gobs (slang word for sailors). Late at night, with keys borrowed from friends, we snuck into the personnel office and used their typewriters and xerox machines to produce the first issue of *PDL* (Punk Dialogue).

Soon after PDL came out, Jim was discharged. We tried to get another issue out, but the command discovered our use of government property and stopped us from putting out another "anti-Navy magazine of a subversive nature." It would have included a guest editorial from Mike H. about his recent bust and harassment for having one marijuana seed in his pocket, among other things. Then Mike was discharged. Dispirited, all of my co-conspirators gone and Darby Crash dead, I became depressed and dove headfirst into my own nightmares.

I spent the rest of my naval career being just about the only person into punk onboard. The Navy began cracking down on drugs and issued random and frequent piss tests. I straightened up, didn't get into too much trouble, and became the division's supply petty officer. In that position for nearly two years, I was able to order notebooks, pens, staplers, stationery and other tools to be used after my eventual discharge.

MECHANIC • A.J.

The military claims to have a big concern for safety. They were always telling us, "Be safe. It saves lives." The side effect is that when an accident occurs, there's usually a lot more damage to the machine than to people. People are cheap, machines are expensive. The military is concerned with keeping things intact machinery-wise because that's what costs money.

When I was sent to a base in Germany, it was my job to help keep the equipment in running order. Most of the equipment was manufactured in the 1940s and was really poor quality or jerry-rigged to work. The stuff had seen years and years of neglect because of a military tradition: inefficiency. If we could get away without fixing something, we would. If we could get away with

Two former Air Force base security policeman who pleaded guilty to stealing three fighter jet engines worth nearly $10 million were sentenced in Salt Lake City to federal prison terms. The case grew from a two year Pentagon investigation of thefts from bases in the West and Southwest that resulted in charges against nearly three dozen military personnel and civilians.
— LA Times [3]

When you have no control over a job, then besides the various withdrawals from work such as absenteeism and sickness we are likely also to find sabotage — "the conscious act of mutilation or destruction" that reduces tension and frustration.
— Cheats at Work, Gerald Mars [4]

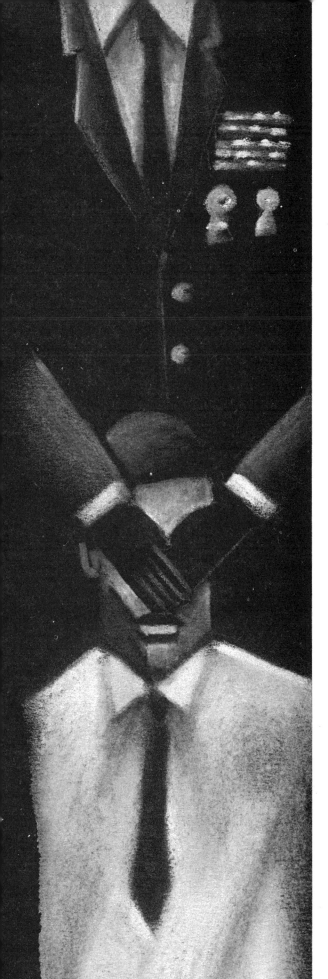

destroying something, we would. The army was like any other job: you did what you had to do and got away with as much as you could.

The sabotage I did was intentional. I covered my ass by pretending I fucked up. Every chance I got, I fucked something up. I found out that if I put grease in the bearings of a truck, it destroyed the whole axle system. I was supposed to check the oil in the trucks, but why should I? I would purposely run it 'til it died. I would sit under the truck, smoke cigarettes, and enjoy the day. If someone came by, I would pick up a wrench and pretend I was working.

You can find out what deadlines a truck. There's criteria, like if the brakes are out, you can't use the vehicle. If you don't drain it, it fills up with water. So, of course, I would never drain the tanks and they would fill up with water so the brakes wouldn't work. It would be deadlined and I wouldn't have to drive it.

I figured I didn't want to deadline where it'll be fixed in three days. I wanted months and months of delay. We had this generator that ran on gas and we put diesel in it. It took them three weeks to run the exhaust system clean and then it never really worked right again. They have these panel switches: if you don't turn them off, current runs through it and it drains the battery. It's really cold in Germany during winter and power drains real fast. So you leave it on, and the battery's dead. When I left the Army, it was still dead. They said they didn't have any batteries, because they're items that they couldn't just replace, they had to trade them in. So first we had to get the battery, send it, wait for it to come back and then they put it in and we would break it again.

CORPSMAN • HARALD

I joined the military in 1967 to get away from high school and my parents. I ended up at Great Lakes Naval Training Camp and became hospital corpsman so I wouldn't have to fight in any war. The ironic part was that I didn't even know there was a war going on at the time. When I got to the hospital corps school I met this man and he told me that he was getting the hell out of the place. I asked why and he said, "There's a war going on in Vietnam and if you're a hospital corpsman that's where you're going to go." I hadn't even heard of Vietnam so I stuck it out and stayed there. I didn't really do anything but finish at the bottom of my class. I don't think it was because I was stupid, but more just that I wasn't interested in doing a lot of homework.

Later on I ended up at Little Creek Amphibious Base where I worked in a dispensary. By this time I was frustrated with the military because they controlled my time and work habits. I got orders for Field Medical School at Camp Lejune in North Carolina. I spent a month there learning jungle training and how to take care of patients who had been blown apart. Then I spent five months on a ship in the Caribbean, three weeks of that in Panama. It was 1968 and there were a lot of demonstrations going on and a lot of alternative scenes started growing. Even though I was in North Carolina, I could see, through the media, what was happening. When I was in Panama I realized that I might die, so at that point I decided I was going to resist.

I became involved with radical politics. I admired people like Ho Chi Minh, Malcolm X, Huey Newton, and Karl Marx, and put pictures of them in my locker on the base. We had an inspection and everyone had all of their clothing laid out on their beds. I had given my uniform away so I had none. When the inspecting officers came to me, I opened my locker and they saw all of these photographs. Everyone went totally bananas. They stopped the inspection with me. They didn't look at any more people, beds, lockers or anything. That afternoon I had liberty, and when I came back, I found out that everyone who had associated with me was being interrogated to find out if I was trying to convert them to Communism.

I used a lot of drugs, never dressed properly and always tried to get away with not getting a haircut. These actions may seem insufficient to a lot of people, but in the military, not having a haircut is the ultimate form of rebellion. You can make a major or general's face turn red just because your hair is an eighth of an inch too long.

I guess it finally came down to the fact that after spending two years getting ready to go to Vietnam, I knew my number was going to happen and I knew I had to take a more direct stance against the war. I ended up deserting a number of times, the longest time being a month. When I came back I demanded a court martial. Reluctantly, they gave me one. I spent a month in the brig. It was a horrifying experience. I witnessed a person getting beat to death by the guards. After I came out, I went AWOL a few more times. I spent another two months in the brig and when I came out, that was it, my military career was over. They finally gave me a psychological discharge.

The soldier's body becomes a stock of accessories that are not his property.
— Antoine de Saint-Exupery,
Flight to Arras

Most of us are on the verge of revolt a good deal of the time, but we don't do anything because we're too tightly harnessed.
— William Feather, The Business Life

12

IT'S BUSINESS DOING PLEASURE WITH YOU

Sex

PROSTITUTE • JANE

I slept with men for money. I worked in a brothel that was advertised as a massage parlor with five other women on an eight-hour shift. The majority of customers were just married, middle class men. Some guys were disabled and had a hard time finding someone to be with, so it was easier for them to pay for it. The owner was this 700-pound deadhead man who was really friendly and had a deadhead wife. He never messed with any of the women who worked there, and didn't treat us differently than if we were working at any other job.

The owner got tired of the business so he took on this new partner. This new guy couldn't handle things and stopped coming into the parlor except to pick up the money at the end of each night. So, we got to manage ourselves. We were in charge of all the money, but our rent, bills and the cops were all still paid by the owner, which was the best part.

The men would come in and pick the girl they wanted. When we got them in the room alone, we would find out what they wanted. The guys would pay $25 for a half-hour, and everything else went to us except for our room fee, $10 per customer. We got paid average to what women in other brothels were getting paid.

We were making pretty good money — but then we decided to up our rates. It was supposed to be $60 for a hand job, $70 for a blow job and $80 for a full service, which is what we called sex. We started charging $80, $90 and $100. The customers couldn't really argue with us because we could do practically whatever we wanted. Sometimes we kept the place open later or opened up earlier than we were supposed to. Everybody was supposed to do three customers a day; that was the average. The owners didn't know how many customers came in on a night or how much each one was charged.

Each night we picked a woman to run the books. She would keep track of the money that came in, the room fees, and if a customer used a credit card. The woman doing the books would document most of the customers but leave out three a night, which would total about $60 that she got to keep. Each night we took our turn doing the books. We all agreed to it and it worked out great. We worked really well with each other and all became friends.

This gave us the feeling of being more than just prostitutes, because we had control over our bodies and what we were doing. I think we all deserved the extra money. For sleeping with someone, you should get all the money you can.

STRIPPER • DAISY

I've been working in the sex industry for the past nine years. I started out working as a street prostitute. When I turned eighteen, I started dancing as a stripper. For the next few years I worked sometimes as a dancer or stripper, and sometimes as a call girl. For the past four years I've pretty much been dancing steadily, working as a stripper at clubs or at bachelor parties where an agency sets me up.

In San Francisco, most of the strip clubs are run and owned by

men. At the one where I work, the men always want the women to do more for less money. The word will come down and quite often the women will simply disregard it. There's not a lot the owners can do. If they want us to do a particular show we don't want to do, it just doesn't get done. If they don't want to pay for something we charge for, we simply won't do it unless we figure out ways to do it and get paid for it. We get away with it because they're not there during every interaction with a paying customer.

Where I work, the customers pay the club to get in the door. If they want to see private shows, like table dances or an individual girl dancing in a peep show situation, they have to tip the girl extra. We basically call the shots when we're in private. There's nothing they can do about it. They want us to give certain kinds of shows away for free. They try to orchestrate it so that we do it and it simply fails because we just don't do it. The women charge anyway.

Most of the women I know fake it all the time. Even if you're just a dancer, men will ask you if you get off onstage. I say, "I'm a dancer. I dance all day." That's part of the job, faking it. We're actresses, acting like we're sexually turned on all the time. We're in an entertainment industry. They come there to be sexually turned on and entertained that way, so that's how we act.

A lot of the time, call girl or bachelor party agencies that send strippers out on calls will try and get them to go places that they don't want to go. They'll try and get you to go somewhere where the guy isn't going to pay you all the money that you want to get paid, or that's too far away. They'll threaten you with not giving you any more calls or parties. Sometimes you'll talk to the customers on the phone and it won't feel right; it doesn't feel safe. If you don't have a good feeling about something, you don't want to put yourself into a situation that could be dangerous. Out calls and even bachelor parties, which I do now, can be dangerous, even with a male escort. Sometimes you really have to argue with the agency you're working for, and you have to be willing to simply tell them no. Even if they try to blackmail you into going somewhere you don't feel comfortable, you know that you can get work elsewhere. All kinds of agencies will try to get you to take parties and go on calls that you don't feel comfortable doing, because they're going to get their fee. The sabotage there is just refusing, or going along with your instincts, setting your boundaries and your price, and sticking to that.

EROTIC DANCER • RICO

The place was a small, dark, gay adult theater. It catered mostly to tourists and businessmen. They had four or five shows a day; I never did more than two shows daily. The money was good. I got $35 for the show and then tips, so sometimes I would walk out with $50 for fifteen minutes of work.

My "official" job description was erotic performer, but they called us jack-off artists. We'd get on stage and do a little erotic dance, take our clothes off, get hard, then jack off and hopefully have an orgasm on stage. The owner had this rule that we had to go down into the audience and let these men feel us up and stuff dollars in our socks. They weren't allowed to touch our genitals or ass, but everything else went. It wasn't very pleasant and I never felt too good about that.

I didn't like the owner to begin with, and I didn't like how he operated the place. He fired people all the time, often without paying them for their last show.

One night I went on, did my show, collected my tips, went backstage and as I was getting dressed, the owner came back. He said, "You didn't open the curtain." (There was a curtain that blocked off the movie screen when we were dancing, and we were supposed to open it up when we were through.) But I *had* opened it. He said, "Go out and open the curtain," so I went out on the stage. He came out and said, "That's not far enough," but it was all the way open and wasn't blocking the screen at all. He kept saying to open it up more. He was being very demeaning. I went backstage and he came back and said he didn't appreciate my attitude and that he didn't need me around anymore. I knew he was pulling the same shit that he had pulled on the other people but I thought I'd make it harder for him by making a scene. For show, I begged him to work just another week. He turned around and said, "I don't know why I hired you in the first place and no, I'm not going to need you anymore."

I got right up in his face and said, "You're the biggest piece of shit that I've ever laid eyes on. You can't get away with degrading people and tossing them aside the way you do. I don't know what kind of power trip you're on, but it's not going to work with me!"

He slapped my face. I had my motorcycle helmet in my hand and after he did that, I started pounding him with it. He turned around to leave and I grabbed him by the back of the collar and punched him in the face a couple of times. I threw him down on the floor and kicked him really hard in the side, then I went out to the audience and yelled, "I want everybody in this room to know that this man just struck me backstage."

He came out holding his side, and tried to make me shut up. He said, "You'd better get out of here or I'm going to call the cops."

When he mentioned the cops, a few people in the audience got up and left. I said I wouldn't leave until I got paid. I went to the front of the theater, where the cash register was, to get my money. The owner told the guy at the cash register not to pay me. He said he had called the police and they were coming and I said, "Fine, let them come." I told him I was going to go to the Health Department to tell them that he makes me go down into the audience where guys who have come all over their hands stick their fingers up my ass. I knew the Health Department wouldn't be too happy about that, and would close him down in two seconds.

After a few more threats, he finally gave me the money and told me to leave before the police came. I thought, "Fuck that; I'm going to wait to tell my side of the story." When the cops came, I told them what I had threatened to tell the Health Department; they believed my story and the owner never pressed charges.

To succeed in business you must learn how to get people to do what you want them to do.

— B.C. Forbes

Violence suits those who have nothing to lose.

— Jean-Paul Sartre

13

FROM THE GROUND UP

Construction

DEMOLITION WORKER • ANTHONY

The wicked New England winter had set in. There was no more work haying fields or picking apples. There was food from our livestock and from what we could put away from our garden, but no money for anything else. My friends and I drove our beat-up station wagon to the nearby "city," population 5,000. We went to apply for food stamps and possibly general assistance. The caseworker wouldn't hear of it: "There's plenty of work in this town. I know for a fact that they're hiring workers across town at the old grain mill."

We bundled ourselves against the bitter cold and went over to the hulking remains of an enormous grain mill that was now in a state of disrepair. We found the boss in his little warming shack relaxing next to his diesel space heater. "Sure I need more men, can't pay the going rate, but it's work. It's payin' buck-fifty an hour." This guy was in cahoots with the state and he wasn't even paying minimum wage. We took the job.

Our job was to tear apart the huge grain mill and strip the parts into piles, so he could sell the bits and pieces. The planks from the hardwood floors, the electrical equipment, the I-beams and metal work, the plumbing fixtures — all this would be resold, plus he would get paid for the demolition itself. He sent us out with crowbars, hammers and little else.

We were working on subflooring on the top of a three-story building. The roof had already been removed so we were totally exposed to the snow and howling wind. The floorboards were frozen and difficult to budge with crowbars. We attacked them with hammers and catspaws. We were in danger of freezing to death or slipping on the icy walkways and falling to our deaths. We worked all day while the boss huddled inside with his jet powered space heater. We went home bitter with cold. We returned day after day in search of that elusive paycheck. Some days it wouldn't climb above zero degrees, and we'd be out sawing flooring apart, disassembling metal conduit or cutting I-beams with cutter torches, watching them fall perilously below. At lunch time, we would munch on our cheese sandwiches in the comfort of the warming shack, while the boss would stand by watching the clock. We were perhaps twenty, all young men, most with wives and new babies. The wives would come around at lunchtime to bring sack lunches and show the baby to their freezing husbands. There was a sick, desperate feeling most of the time, as this miserable work was the only way to escape the bitter impoverishment winter brings to small towns.

At the end of the day, on payday, we waited for our checks. The boss looked sheepish. "Look boys, see that pile of hardwood there? I expect to have your checks as soon as I sell that pile. Then there'll be plenty of money. Tomorrow, no doubt." We stood around and stared in disbelief. The next day came and still no money. A week passed with all of us sawing boards, tearing down walls, chainsawing through subflooring, sparks flying as we hit nails below. The anger was building.

Finally, one morning, we threw our tools down. Gathering all

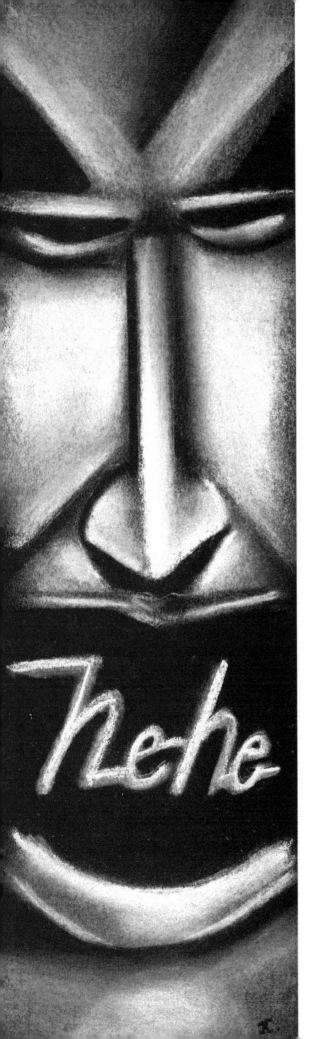

around, stomping our heavy boots trying to warm our feet, we plotted our retaliation for working several weeks with only promises of a paycheck. We knew he had in fact sold much of the material, and had even bought a new pick-up truck a few days ago. We picked up our crowbars, stomped down the remains of the stairs and barged into his office, the twenty of us prominently displaying our crowbars. We demanded our money. He swore he didn't have any. We said we'd have to pay ourselves then.

We left the warming shack and fanned out over the plant, grabbing anything of value. We brought our vehicles up close to the gate and started filling them with anything we could possibly resell — the tools, chain saws, materials, electrical equipment, anything and everything. The boss just stood by nervously, not even bothering to call the police as the five or so cops in town wouldn't mess with the twenty of us with crowbars. When we were satisfied with our booty, we waved our bars at him, called him the scumbag he was and drove away. Never heard from him again.

ROOFER • FRANK

I worked for Artcraft Strauss, a big sign company in New York City. They own all the large lighted signs and rent them out to companies like Coca Cola, Panasonic and Fuji. They're in Times Square and all over New York. It's run by a family who have pretty much tied up all of the leases for forty to fifty years.

First I re-roofed their whole headquarters. I worked with three other guys who didn't know how to do roofing, and they put me under a supervisor who also didn't know how to do roofing. He did a roof like it was a piece of cement, because that was his trade. So we did it wrong and it was fucked up, and I'm sure right now it's leaking.

When we finished the roof, the company had me sweeping the floors of the workshop because they were too incompetent to get me started on the next roofing job. The company had a supervisor give a new excuse every week. After a while, I just got fed up the situation because I was hired to do roofing, not sweeping.

One day when I was sweeping in the workshop, I banged the broom into a new sign that was being built for Times Square. I busted a couple of the sign's neon lightbulbs. I did it completely by accident but it gave me an interesting idea.

When I came in the next day the lightbulbs had been replaced and the sign was ready to be trucked out to Times Square the next morning. Most workers had already gone home, and I was just hanging out in the shop with my broom. When I was sure that no one was around, I grabbed a screwdriver and opened up the sign. I fiddled around with the wires inside and pulled out some electrical stuff and threw it in the garbage. I closed it up and left it looking exactly how it was minutes earlier.

The next day they put the sign on the truck and took it away. After installing it up on the building, they went to turn it on and one entire section of the sign didn't light up. They had to take down that section and bring it back to the shop for repair. That sign was dark for at least a month, which meant the company couldn't collect rent on it.

It was the big Canon sign; you see it in movies sometimes. Every time I see it I laugh to myself.

PLUMBER • PEDRO

Like my father, I've been doing plumbing pretty much my whole life. Our family was kind of poor, so I worked through high school. I was a cook for two years, but I knew that the money that I was making cooking was a lot less than what I could make plumbing.

I was mostly self-taught. If you're mechanical, you can pick up plumbing really quickly. There are smart people who aren't mechanical. My neighbor's a lawyer, and he calls me over to help him change a lightbulb because he can't figure out which way to screw it.

A friend and I had a job where we were doing the plumbing for a house under construction. It was a side job, working directly for the owner. We had done all of the copper pipes that go underneath the concrete floor of the house. The concrete had been poured over the pipes, which had been looped up through the floor to hook up to the fixtures. It was at this stage when the owner started going back on his word. He said, after the job had been done, that the quote that we agreed on was too much. He said, "I can't pay you for this and I'll only pay you for that." Then he said something like, "You're not even licensed, so I might not pay you at all." The guy thought he could save money and finish it himself.

We immediately got bad attitudes. We packed the water pipes full of nails. We didn't do all of the pipes, but we put enough nails in there so he would have a problem. We could have used a high pressure hose to blow the nails out if we knew we were going to finish the job, but it never happened, so we left them in there.

He came back to us later because every time he turned on the faucets in his brand new house he heard all of this rattling. What he didn't know was that not only was he going to have the noises, but in time the nails would rust up, wrecking the washers in the faucets.

We definitely got more satisfaction than guilt from what we did. We didn't have anything to lose. I still think we got fucked because we didn't get paid, but he got fucked too. You gotta cover your ass any way that you can. If they fuck you, you gotta fuck them back.

WATERPROOFER • DON

I'm a sub-contractor. The contractors that hire me are my bosses because they have financial control over me. It's a typical boss-worker relationship without the benefits; sub-contractors don't have a lot of recourse if they don't get paid by a contractor.

There's an extreme amount of pressure in my job. I can get sued if someone before me does the job wrong or someone behind me fucks up what I did, even though I may not be guilty of anything. You only need to make one mistake to screw yourself out of the business. Luckily, I haven't made any mistakes in 4,000 jobs.

We had one contractor that wouldn't pay us. It was a hundred and some odd bucks, not a very large amount. He tried to shield himself from us with a lawyer. He didn't want to talk to us, but I made it clear to him that the money he owed was such a small amount that I could easily make it cost him a lot more not to pay us. He ignored everything I said and wouldn't return my calls. One day, I went over to his office and filled the locks to all three of his doors with Loc-tite. We got paid very soon after that.

One contractor owed me $500 for two years. I did some work for him and he didn't pay me. I went and locked the gate to his house with a really strong bicycle lock, so come Monday morning he wouldn't be able to get out of his house. Sure enough, he had to call a locksmith because guys like him generally don't have tools. I'm still working on collecting from him. Before the Christmas holidays I go out in front of his house and spraypaint on the street that he's a thief. I make the message really big and bright so his neighbors and relatives see it when they drive up to his house.

The pressures and difficulties of my job make me even more determined to get money from the people who owe it to me, no matter how small an amount. It always seems that the most fucked jobs, the worst ones, are where the guys will screw you. It just burns my ass when somebody screws me.

MODEL MAKER • DENNIS

I was working for Bechtel, which is a major engineering contractor. Their main job is to design and act as general contractor for very large engineering projects. When I was there they were working on several nuclear power plants, coal fire power plants, oil refineries, and on military technology for separation of plutonium from fuel rods taken from power plants. They were working on the international airport in Riyadh, Saudi Arabia. They also worked on mass transportation systems, like the one from San Diego to the Mexican border. They're a private corporation — there's no public stock in it — owned by the Bechtel family.

When I was there it wasn't a bad place to work at all. We only reported to our own foreman in the model shop. We were allowed to dress down and we could be in two or three different places at once, so people had a hard time keeping track of us. The general rule in the model shop was that if you could wrap it up in paper, you could take it home. There were thousands of dollars worth of Plexiglas that went out of that office. Everyone did it — the bosses, the workers. It was great.

To avoid mistakes with large engineering projects, all designs are built to scale and checked off before they're actually put on a final drawing and sent to the field for construction. A model maker's job is partly to create a model and partly inspection and checking. You have to be aware of the American Mechanical Engineering standards for piping, electrical conduits, steel and the like. If you see a mistake, you call it to the attention of a designer or engineer, and at that point have the drawing changed.

I worked primarily on Coal Strip Unit Three, which was a coal-fired power plant in Coal Strip, Montana. The model for Coal Strip was done on a scale of three-quarter inches to the foot, so it was thirty-five feet long by five feet wide and probably five feet tall. The model took over five years to build and cost over five million dollars in time and materials. It was a large model. We worked on this model in an office in a skyscraper downtown. We also had a model shop a few blocks away which had all the power tools and machine tools. We worked back and forth between the shop and the design floor, where the actual designers, engineers and support services were.

Things started to tighten up on the design floor while I was there. The foreman, a guy named Bob, started getting pushy and arrogant. He was trying to make it into management and they were sending him to management training school. Once a week he'd go to these seminars and come back with paperwork he would lock in his desk. We would stick a big screwdriver in the top drawer and strike upward on the handle and open the file drawer. We'd get out his notebook from last week and read all the company policies. We were especially interested in policies about absenteeism, discipline, and giving information to potential employers if you were changing jobs. We learned what management could and couldn't do to us, and what we could get away with. We ran it off on the Xerox machine and passed copies around to everyone so they knew what was going on. As time went on and people got mad at Bob, things would happen to him. He would find his safety glasses glued to the base of the model. We glued his toolbox shut and generally tormented the guy as much as possible.

We were a bit of an uncontrollable crowd, which made it fun. We built really ridiculous fake equipment and installed it in the model to see how long it would take for some engineer or designer to notice. We had to glue different pieces of plastic on the model base to indicate spaces that had to be kept open for specific reasons. For example, a piece of orange plastic indicated a pull space, where equipment has to be pulled out. I would use a completely ridiculous color that wasn't being used for anything, like purple Plexiglas, and label it "Space reserved for future nonexistent equipment" — and see how long it took for someone to see it.

One of my buddies was working on the Hope Creek Nuclear Reactor project, on the reactor core. As a joke he started modifying some of the drawings, and then initialing them, which meant they were signed off on an intermediate design check. Over a period of a few weeks he put a run of piping going from one place to another on a complicated course all the way around the reactor core and attached the end of the pipe to the beginning of the pipe. So the pipe began and ended nowhere, and just ran around the core. I don't know how many weeks it took for someone to finally notice, scream and have someone take it out of the model. There's a chance something like that could get onto the final model and even get out in the field and be partially built before somebody notices it.

TRUSS AND TIE ROD WORKER • JOHN

I had to climb up into the roof of a newly framed house and put ninety degree clips into the 2x4's that made up the roof's trusses.

Academic authorities have at times pointed out that work sometimes offers less opportunity for self-expression than might be considered desirable. However, workers sometimes find their own ways to express their thoughts and feelings on the job, to exercise their own creativity.
— Common Sense for Hard Times, Jeremy Brecher and Tim Costello [6]

There is no doubt that crime exists in every society. Criminal behavior is so pervasive that some social theorists have asserted for various reasons that crime is actually "normal."
— Security Management Magazine [7]

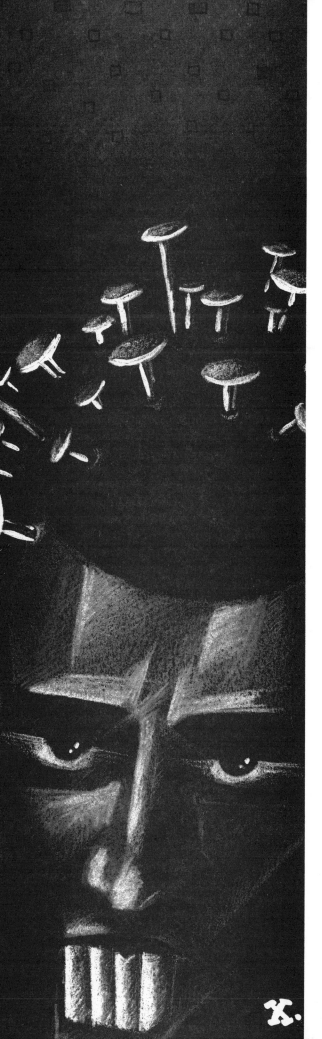

They were called hurricane clips and they reinforced the roof under extreme weather.

I did the job really well because I was small. I scurried in and out of the trusses and bashed the clips in with my hammer. I had never done construction work before but I think I got the job because the other guys got tired of bumping their heads.

The guy I worked for was a fly-by-night contractor. He was always behind in his bills and never had enough equipment to do the job right. At the time, new construction was booming in Florida, so it was easy for even a disorganized guy like him to have fifteen houses going up at once.

As far as I was concerned, he was an idiot. All of the guys who worked for him would bitch and moan constantly because he owed all of them back pay. He didn't treat me very good either. One day he docked me for half of a day's pay because I was sitting down on the job. It was a perfect way to make someone a disgruntled employee.

The long 2x4's used to make trusses are very expensive. I met this guy whose dad did construction. I asked him if I could get my hands on some brand new 2x4's, would he buy them from me? He said, "Sure."

From then on, when I put the clips into the trusses, I wouldn't nail them in correctly. I only put in only two nails instead of a bunch so the clips would be very easy to take out. As early as an hour after I left work, the guy who wanted the 2x4's and I would come back and just fuckin' steal 'em. I'd climb up to the trusses, take them apart and put the wood in the guy's truck.

We did this about twenty times. Sometimes we stole 2x4's three times from the same roof. I'd come in the next morning and the first thing I would do is put in new 2x4's to replace what I had stolen the day before. There were always a lot of people working on a house so no one knew what the fuck was going on. Even the boss never caught on.

ROOFER • JEFF

I became unemployed when the shipyard where I worked shut down. I was married and I had a little boy so I needed to get a job. My brother-in-law asked me to come work for his roofing company. I was the third employee hired so I got in on the ground floor and learned everything that I needed to know within a year.

I became the company's first foreman. My initial crew consisted of about seven guys who became the nucleus of the boss' company. I trained them in every aspect of roofing they know today and eventually *they* all became foremen.

The boss promised that once the company started growing, I would become the vice president. But when that time came he hired someone else, someone completely new to the company. I had been with the company for four years, listening to the boss' promises, and then I was treated like shit.

At first I took it in stride but then it started coming home with me. Like I said, my boss was my brother-in-law, so my wife was caught in the middle. I was bringing home the money that fed and clothed her and bought her all of the nice things she wanted, yet her brother was employing me. I wasn't getting any support at home so I knew I had to do something at work to relieve the tension and keep from going nuts.

The first thing I did was slow down my work pace. When I was expected to take off thirty squares a day, I'd back it up to twenty. I'd encourage the people I was working with to go slower and my bad attitude carried over to them. When they saw how I was getting shit on they didn't want to work either. There was no room for advancement if a guy like me wasn't getting it.

I purposely laid a roof that would leak. It was a ballasted roof, which is made up of a layer of insulation and a big sheet of rubber on top, and all weighted down with stones. The only thing protecting the building from Mother Nature is the one thin ply of rubber. All I did was make a little hole where the water would pond the most, and covered it back up with stones. It's almost impossible to find a leak on a roof like that. The roof started leaking after about eight months, ceilings were caving in, all kinds of good stuff. Including the internal damage to the building, it cost the company $50,000 to fix.

My stepfather told me about how he once put Prestone Radiator Flush in somebody's gas tank; it takes a long time before it starts affecting the car. That's exactly what I was looking for. I did this to three brand new trucks that were going for $17,000 when the company got them. It was a slow breakdown but it messed up every system in the trucks. They started stalling out at lights. Soon you couldn't pass on highways and I swear to God, we'd be riding down the road, and the radio would come on by itself. The first time one of the trucks completely broke down, we went into the office and tried to explain what happened. I said, "Well, the radio came on, we couldn't turn it off, the heater came on and we couldn't turn it off so I got on the cigarette lighter and called you." I was the only one that got any chuckles out of that one. Eventually all three trucks had to have new motors installed, all their lines had to be flushed out and the electrical work had to be redone. The company ended up spending $9,000 to repair each vehicle.

To this day, my boss hasn't found out a damn thing. I eventually got fired for having a bad attitude. But the thing is, I didn't have one going in, I got it by being shit on by my boss.

People ... may engage in destructiveness so as to feel a sense of mastery and control over their environment which they cannot achieve through conventional, nonviolent means. Sabotage, therefore, may be a symbolic way of telling oneself that one is not at the mercy of management.
— *Journal of Business Ethics* [8]

Revenge is sounding especially sweet these days, and managers must prepare for it.
— *New York Times* [9]

14 RETURN TO SENDER

Mail

MAIL HANDLER • JUDI

The Washington Bulk Mail Center is one of twenty-one centers in the United States. I worked there from 1976 to 1980. They spent lots of money and put together factories that just plain didn't work. These computer nerds design factories and they've never seen one in their whole lives. They didn't want to admit that it didn't work. They set an efficiency rate for the factory but since the machinery didn't work, they couldn't achieve that rate. Instead of hiring more employees and admitting it was a failure, they forced us to work overtime. We worked at least sixty hours a week, and in December they would work us eighty-four. A major problem was that we worked all the time, and started to go crazy.

Overtime was the main issue, but accidents and industrial injuries were two other ones. General harassment was a problem too — they give a ten point preference to veterans, so everyone thinks they're still in the army. The real army ass-kissers rise to supervisor. Since you don't have to make a profit in the post office, it lacks the semblance of reason you get in capitalism. In the post office it didn't matter how much money was wasted.

I unloaded and sometimes loaded trucks. It was supposedly all mechanized. We had these great big things called extended conveyor belts that went into the trucks. We froze our butts off in the winter and roasted in the summer.

Parcels and sacks were unloaded and sorted separately, but the machine was always jamming up. The best way to break up the jam was to throw some sacks on the parcel system because they were heavier and would push the jam through. This of course meant that they'd be landing on the parcels and squashing them to bits. That was a kind of sabotage that was actually endorsed by management because they wanted us to work faster.

There's no back-up system in the plant. If there's a tangle somewhere, the whole line shuts down. When the non-zip chute backed up, everything we wanted to know the zip code of would shoot back up, and everything going to that place stopped. For every piece, you had to have a non-zip option, so if the non-zip chute closed down, the whole line closed down. We'd key everything in as non-zip, and the system would overload. All the red lights came on and everything went down. When New York was in a wildcat strike, we keyed everything to New York.

As we began to feel our collective power, people got more obvious and flippant. We started doing little things like sending things to the wrong place and deliberately shutting things down. But as we got to be more organized, one of the games we played when we were bored was to deliberately break the machinery and make a bet on how long it would take the mechanic to figure out what was wrong. We'd try to break it in a bizarre manner. One of our favorite things to do was to turn off emergency stops to see how long the mechanic would take to figure out which one it was. We would take turns banging on the sides of the trucks while we were unloading them. The supervisors would get very upset and run back and forth trying to figure out who was doing it.

Eventually we began to do really organized things. When they ordered us to work overtime on Thanksgiving, everybody left. We

There is dignity in work only when it is work freely accepted.
— *Albert Camus*

Most people would feel insulted if it were proposed to employ them in throwing stones over a wall, and then in throwing them back merely that they might earn their wages. But many are no more worthily employed now.
— *Life Without Principle, Thoreau*

were real proud of that one. Another time, we did a sick-out, where a lot of people went home sick at the same time.

We weren't allowed to strike. We met between the two shifts — there was an hour break in between — and I stood up on a table and gave a speech in the cafeteria. We drew up a committee of twelve and a list of demands, and eighty of us did a walk-in (since we couldn't do a walk-out) to our supervisor's office and gave her our list. Her reaction was to put locks on the door between the plant and the administration office so you couldn't get in. You had to have a computer card and a combination and all of that. Short of going on strike, the culmination of our action was the trash-in. They were famous for losing our paychecks on the night shift. The forklift drivers would drive around and tell everyone that they lost our checks again. We'd cause machines to wreck (which was pretty easy), the forklift drivers would drop pallets everywhere, and everyone keyed everything non-zip. One night we brought the place to a standstill. We trashed everything that came in.

The unions were very corrupt and the overtime didn't decrease in most of the country. But we won. They stopped giving us overtime. As we did such a horrible job on the parcels, people started using UPS more and the post office less. The volume started to go down, so the trashings and overtime and accidents went down. The safety conditions improved. After a year, when we did the wildcat strike, the union crumbled and fell into our hands. We ended up taking over the union and I became the Chief Shop Steward (the highest position in that plant) and began to expedite grievances. They got rid of the worst of the supervisors and brought in new ones specifically to appease us.

Everyone makes jokes about postal workers smashing up mail because they think they don't care. But postal workers don't like the fact that we can't do a good job no matter how hard we try.

LETTER CARRIER • OTIS

I've been a letter carrier for eleven years, which isn't really that long. Contrary to popular belief, the work is not that strenuous. You get to be by yourself and work outdoors. It's one of those kind of jobs that once you get it, you keep it for life.

I've got around 230 deliveries on my current route, which is considered small, but it befits a man of my seniority. When you've been around a long time, you get to choose the route you want, and only fools pick long routes if they've been around a long time. The way I see it, the less work, the better for me.

I take a lot of liberties when I deliver mail. A lot of the time I play god as far as deciding what mail is important and what's not. I'll go out of my way to deliver any letter or postcard. I'll handle checks with kid gloves. I don't consider bills important, and junk mail is definitely not a priority. Magazines are a low priority because I usually want to read them first.

On my route there are a lot of houses on hills that aren't that easy to get to. If there's just a bill and nothing else for one of those houses, I'll usually decide they don't want it that day. I'll deliver it the next day when they get more mail. I think most carriers will skip houses if it doesn't seem worth their time or effort.

Triviality and drudgery may not have the same family name, but they are twins at birth.
— Work, Workers and Work Measurement, Adam Abruzzi [1]

Not snow nor rain nor heat nor gloom of night stays these couriers from the swift completion of their appointed rounds.
— Motto of the U.S. Postal Service

I'm supposed to work eight hours a day but my job usually doesn't take that long. I go in at 6:30 in the morning, sort the mail for my route, which takes about three hours, and then I deliver, which is supposed to take about five hours. If we get done with our routes early, we're supposed to sort whatever mail came in that afternoon, which is usually just junk mail.

Most carriers finish their routes in three hours and don't go back early, because if they do, the supervisors will add deliveries to their routes. Some carriers pace themselves so their route takes five hours, but I'm not very good at pacing myself. I usually finish mine in three hours so I just do whatever I want to do. I like my route because it has a park on it, so I can sit there for a couple of hours and read, sleep or listen to music.

When I first started the job, this old guy gave me a portion of his route to do. He told me, "Don't come back early." I wanted to show him up and prove that I was a good worker. I finished the route early and when I came back, I could tell right away that the old guy was real pissed because I made him look bad. Another time, I did a whole route in three hours. When I came back the supervisor said, "Yeah, that's the way it's supposed to be done," then gave me more work to do. It got back to the carrier whose route it was and I'm sure he was pissed off, too. After about a month, I got my own route and quickly learned that it's in my best interest to set my own pace. You err on your own side if you want to last as a carrier for thirty years.

MAILROOM CLERK • REGGIE

I worked at the Heritage Foundation, a conservative think-tank on Capitol Hill. It's a group of attorneys, columnists, whatever, who crank out — daily or weekly or whatever — information. It's printed downstairs, in the xerox room, and distributed to senators, congressmen, and other influential people. In a couple of cases I delivered packages addressed to Ed Meese. That gives you an idea of what kind of people work there. My basic duties were to collect mail in the mornings from the post office, sort it, distribute it, and so on. I pretty much did everything myself and I had a lot of responsibility.

I got the job right after high school. I had never heard of the organization, and just found the job through the newspaper. When I was working there, I would occasionally glance at what they were putting out; the more I read, the more I thought about it and realized they were doing fucked-up things, like defending business practices in South Africa and U.S. investments there.

They have a big fundraising deal, and when they sent out fundraising requests, people would mail in checks. Sometimes they'd be huge amounts, and sometimes they were piddling. Checks came in from individuals as well as companies. So I'd randomly take an envelope, open it, see how much it was for, and throw it in the shredder. I started doing it more and more. I could tell if it was a check by holding it to the light. If so, I'd toss it, dump it or shred it.

MAIL CLERK • DOLORES

Huge mail sorting facilities were built by the Postal Service during the seventies to house obsolete junk machinery which our great nation paid billions to acquire in kickback boondoggles with mega-corporations like Burroughs and Pitney-Bowes. The Burroughs Corporation manufactured the Edsel-like white elephant junker known as the LSM (Letter Sorting Machine). It takes twenty clerks and a mechanic to run one, and a building the length of a football field to house one. There are thirteen of them in the biggest sorting facility in Los Angeles, which is a building bigger than ten football fields.

A big sorting factory runs around the clock, but most clerks are on the swing or graveyard shifts, when the mail collected from mailboxes comes in. There might be 500 to 2000 employees in these big, windowless warehouses. With gigantic sack-sorting machines, LSM's, flat sorters, canceling machines and conveyor belts all running at once, the continuous noise level is 83 decibels. OSHA, the Occupational Safety and Health Administration, allows 90 decibels and Cal-OSHA allows 85. Hearing loss occurs at 55 or less. In short, you cannot communicate with another human being on the workroom floor without yelling. Most clerks wear Walkman-type headphone sets. The union fought a hard battle for those. Clerks get two ten-minute breaks and a half-hour for lunch. You must clock in within 120 seconds of your scheduled reporting time or face disciplinary action for "tardiness."

Mail is transported in large steel containers, called OTR's ("over-the-road" containers). They are stupidly designed, ill-maintained, invariably in bad repair and extremely dangerous. But someone in the American Can Corporation made plenty of money selling them to the Postal Service, so there they are and there they will stay. Scores of OTR's were easily incapacitated by cutting a very simple cable-spring mechanism, making it impossible to release the doors to get mail in and out of them.

A powerful magnet was used to suck the computerized "brains" out of some giant LSM's, sending thousands of letters to the "zero bin" and shutting down the machines for days while baffled management scratched their heads figuring out what had gone terribly wrong and calculating the major expense required to repair it.

"Big Joe" was management's name for a large, hydraulic lift used to load and unload containers and other items off of trucks. Mail handlers and dock clerks became intimately familiar with Big Joe. One early morning, when no one was working, someone reached underneath it and cut the thick electrical cable that powered Big Joe from its deepest, darkest underside. No one in the area got much mail the next day, and it was probably pretty hard for the special mechanics they called in to repair it. They had to use another lift to raise Big Joe to a level where they could see, reach and fix the problem, because there was no way Big Joe could lift itself anymore.

Wadded up balls of soft paper products will plug up a toilet, and

Sabotage will also be used in places where the union organization controls negotiations and official demands, but not the forms of actions used on the shop floor to win immediate concessions.
— Sabotage in Industry, Pierre Dubois [2]

In order to gain certain demands, without losing their jobs, the Austrian postal workers strictly observed the rule that all mail matter must be weighed to see if the proper postage was affixed. Formerly they had passed without weighing all those letters and parcels which were clearly under weight, thus living up to the spirit of regulation but not to its exact wording. By taking each separate piece of mail matter to the scales, carefully weighing same and then returning it to its proper place, the postal workers had the office congested with unweighed mail on the second day. This method is more effective than striking, especially when used on a large scale.
— Sabotage, Walker C. Smith, 1913 [3]

> *I don't know of anything that can be applied that will bring as much satisfaction to you and as much anguish to the boss as a little sabotage in the right place at the right time.*
> — *Bill Haywood, Industrial Workers of the World*

management's seemed to get plugged quite a bit, necessitating their use of the employees' restrooms. There, besides the distastefulness of having to eliminate their bodily wastes alongside the lower classes, they might encounter themselves personified in obscene graffiti. They had separate restrooms for the different echelons of management: supervisors and middle management had theirs, right on up to the postmaster who had his own very private restroom. When his shitter overflowed one day, the supervisors started locking all the bathrooms — except ours, of course!

In the big facilities the front offices are usually glassed-in, plushly carpeted affairs where top management passes the time with one another, happily oblivious to the conditions in the windowless, deafening hell of the workroom floor. They "work" between 9:00 and 5:00 — no time clocks for them! That made nights a particularly good time to do things like drive by with a high-powered rifle and shoot out the glass walls of a particularly odious top level manager or spray graffiti on exterior walls.

By far the most effective and powerful sabotage of respect for management resulted from our crude but uncompromising Local newsletters, distributed to employees and mailed to other Locals which would reprint cartoons or other stuff ridiculing management. A network of these union "zines" was in constant circulation among the 250,000 members of the Postal Workers Union across the country. Ours was the best and most radical. I think it was the real reason I got fired, effectively busting our Local.

15 PLAYING THE RINGMASTER

Entertainment

CARNY • DINO

I ran the games, the "joints," for an independent concessionaire with Ray Kamick Carnivals. We were with the unit which travels through Missouri out to California and up to Canada. I was an agent, a concessionaire.

My boss, Ed, didn't like me much. He'd shave off the money that I made and tell me that I made less than I did, so I wasn't even making enough money to stay in a hotel. (We were paid a twenty-five percent commission.) After a while I got tired of it because I wasn't making enough money to keep myself clean. Usually we'd chip in and one guy would get a hotel room and everyone else would clean up there. But it wasn't working out because we were hitting dead spots like the border towns in Texas and New Mexico. We weren't even making enough money to go over to Mexico and get a hotel.

The boss was dogging me all the time. It turned out that his bosses were ragging on him because I was the only one there with long hair and a beard. I was only fourteen years old when I first went into this place. I had my dad sign a piece of paper saying that I could travel with the carnival, so Ed took responsibility for me and acted as my guardian. He couldn't fire me, so he just didn't pay me. I worked for thirteen or fourteen hours a day, so I started pocketing some of the money that came in so I could eat. He never caught on to that.

To get more customers I'd hire a "stick," a kid to walk around the carnival with a big stuffed animal to tell people he'd won it at my place. That way, I was making more money than anyone else on the whole midway. I took this one Indian guy for his whole check on the bushel-basket game. He was real mad and came back with his wife and kid and said he was going to get kicked out of his place. I felt real bad about it and I didn't want to see him out on the street. But when he came back, my boss was there, so I couldn't give him back his money. If he had come earlier, I would have given it back.

Another guy came in and I started working him out of money by doing this con called "double up and catch up." I got about $400 out of him and he got real mad and complained to the carnival owner that I was ripping him off. We had to call a "patch," who takes fifty percent of everything you make and patches things up with customers who have been beaten really bad. The patch didn't work and the guy came back real irate. So I told him that to straighten things out, I'd sell him the rollercoaster. He really liked that idea because he said he owned some closed-down movie theater and could run the rollercoaster right there. It was the last night we were in town. I made up a bill of sale and for an extra $200 plus the $400 I took him for, I gave him the deed to the rollercoaster. From this money I was able to pay the Indian guy his money. The guy who bought the rollercoaster came back later that night and everyone was gone, including the rollercoaster. The whole carnival had split and gone to another town. He followed us to the next town, which was out of the state. When I found out that the guy was in town, I left.

The guy who bought the rollercoaster got back to my boss and got him in a lot of trouble. It ultimately came out of my boss' pocket, because the guy started really ragging on the owner of the rollercoaster, and showed him a bill of sale with serial numbers and this name on it that nobody recognized. My boss had to pay the guy who had the bill of sale $250 out of his own pocket.

MOVIE THEATER WORKER • BEN

After I got out of drug treatment, my first job was selling candy at a movie theater. After I had been there awhile, I occasionally worked in the ticket booth, or as a doorman. I was working for the GCC Corporation, which has gotta be the greediest, shittiest company on the face of the earth.

Luckily, most of the people I worked with were pretty cool and I quickly found out that $3.50 an hour wasn't the only thing I could get out of the company. At GCC theaters, they figure out how much popcorn and soda has been sold by counting how many cups and popcorn buckets have been used. If fifty popcorn buckets are gone since the last count, fifty must have been sold. That is, unless you grab the buckets and cups that people have thrown in the trash, wash them out and resell them. This provided a nice little profit for peons like me. It's debatable whether or not this was a clean, hygienic practice — I doubt it — but nobody really cared since most of the customers who came in were complete assholes anyway.

For some reason, people who come into movie theaters seem to think they have the right to vent all their frustrations on the employees. I can't tell you how many times I've listened to some fat, slobbering, white bread cunt whine to me about the price of a fucking box of Goobers. Whenever I resold something, I always tried to make sure it was to a whiny asshole who obviously deserved whatever germs the previous owner of the bucket of popcorn had left behind.

Of course, you always had to be careful that the manager didn't come down and bust you for pulling a scam, but my manager spent most of his time in his upstairs office, probably trying to figure out why he was slaving his ass off for $12,000 a year.

Eventually, a friend clued me in to a great scam. Movie theater tickets are attached to each other in huge rolls, which are fed through a machine that pops them out through a slot to the customer. All the tickets are numbered, in order, and at the beginning and end of each shift, we figured out how many tickets we sold by subtracting the ending from the beginning number. On a busy night, a hell of a lot of people will hand the doorman their ticket and keep on walking without waiting for the stub. Thus, if I went about my work at a slower than usual pace, it was extremely easy to end up with a fistful of unripped tickets which I gave back to the ticket seller who resold them. At $5.50 to $6.00 a pop, we turned a sizable profit on a weekend night.

DRUG DEALER GUARD • PETER

I was employed as a guard and doorman at a drugstore of an illicit nature. It sold primarily low-grade hallucinogens such as mari-

juana, hashish and mushrooms. My duties entailed greeting people who came to the door and answering the telephone. I screened people to see if they were customers of long standing and a respectful nature, or if they were intruders who had to be forcibly removed from the premises. I also rolled marijuana cigarettes for customers so they could make a choice as to what to buy. I was to prepare the various samples, as well as engage in pleasant conversation and make the customers feel wanted. I passed the time most amiably while the dealer sat there and raked in the money, which really began to irk me.

I noticed that many consumers, unlike the previous generation of pot smokers, were really reactionary. Their drug consumption was no longer a political statement, but rather commodity fetishism. I began to engage in a method of subliminal sabotage against the customer and my employer. I began to make very unpleasant conversation with the customers. I no longer felt I could give them the social interaction necessary to make them feel validated.

A social worker came in on a Friday afternoon and was complaining that his clientele, welfare recipients, were self-defeating, that they reinforced their own misery and would never get off welfare and that it was their own fault. This guy was disgusted with the situation and wanted to buy some high-power sinsemilla to forget the misery of dealing with this fucking trash day in and day out. I got in an argument with him about class and made him aware of the contradictions in his attitudes.

In the days and weeks ahead I engaged in more conversations where I questioned the consumer's very presence at the drugstore. As time went on, my employer began to receive complaints about my behavior and I noticed his supply of customers was dwindling by a good twenty to thirty percent. My employer couldn't keep me on in this capacity because I was destroying the clientele that he had assiduously built up over the years. At the time this was the best job that I'd ever had: I was making $13.50 an hour, yet my growing disgust and revulsion ended with my termination.

VIDEO DATING SALES MANAGER NANCY

I've been working for a large video dating service for about four years. I started as a member, but they were short-handed so I got a job. The work isn't really that hard. I mean, it's a great idea, and if people who are ready to do it come in, they just do it. I don't have to push too hard to sell a membership.

I work for a nut. If he can't have his way, he throws temper tantrums. He makes up rules for work as he goes along. It's just ridiculous. He's always out of his mind and takes his temper out on all of his employees. You just don't know what he's going to be like one day to the next. It's really hard to work with somebody who's nuts. Everybody always feels tense and stressed out. I just go in and close my door and pretend he's not even there. The only reason I've lasted as long as I have is that I work part time.

To ease the tension we do petty things that make us feel better. We use the stamp machine whenever we want. People have mailed all their Christmas cards with the stamp machine. We use the copy machine, the fax machine and, of course, the telephone for long distance calls.

None of us are supposed to date the clients because the company doesn't want the people using the service to think that they have the salespeople to compete with as well as the other people using the service, but we all do anyway. Several of our consultants have gotten married to clients. We have first pick. If our boss caught us, he would fire us, but we all see it as a perk.

We don't feel any remorse because we feel that he's technically wrong for treating us the way he does. If he were ethical, he would do nice things for us, but he does stuff like give us a Christmas party and then say, "Oh, by the way, you're not getting any bonuses because I had to use them to pay for the party." That's really typical.

CASINO POKER DEALER • PEGGY

I saw an ad in the paper that said "Deal blackjack on weekends. No experience necessary. $10 an hour." I answered the ad and was put into dealer school. They set up an audition when they thought I was ready to work.

I got a job at a casino that had over a hundred tables. After dealing a couple months of pan, I started dealing poker: draw, seven card stud, lowball and a few others. You could work your way up to different levels of tables and make more money as you went. Every dealer got minimum wage but the tips increased as you moved up to the higher-betting tables.

When I was in dealer school it was explained to me that a dealer had to be tough, you couldn't let customers upset you. They were going to take it out on you if they weren't making money. It didn't help if someone won; they sorta blamed that on you, too, by saying "You're my lucky dealer. Here, have an extra tip." Then the other eight people at the table resented you more. When you get started in a casino, the bosses make it clear that you can't talk back to a customer, no matter what the situation may be. You have to smile, take it all and of course keep the game going no matter what the customers say to you. I had customers tell me that I was the reason the machine gun was invented. People told me they were going to beat me up outside after I got off work. Some threatened to break my hands so I couldn't deal anymore. If someone physically assaults you or is about to, the casino security steps in. It's not for *your* protection, it's because if a dealer gets knocked to the ground, they can't keep dealing hands every minute, and therefore the casino loses.

Sometimes the pressure from dealing with the customers built up inside of me until I had to start kicking myself so I wouldn't yell, "Fuck you!" It got so bad in one game that I couldn't deal another hand. I laid out the deck in front of me and said, "I'm not dealing another hand to you people until my half-hour shift at this table is over." That made all of the customers really mad. It also made the floor manager mad. He took me aside and told me to never, ever do that again.

You're expected to keep the action going and deal an average of thirty hands every half hour. It's to the dealer's advantage to work fast because you get more tips, but if a customer was giving me a hard time, it felt good to deal the cards like I was underwater. I used to slow down the pace of the game a lot by dealing the initial hands out slower than usual.

I used to fuck up people's winning hands by touching them with the muck pile. Once any card touches the muck pile, it no longer counts. When all of the players show their hands at the end of the game, I could quickly put everything in the muck pile and no matter what the player said, it wouldn't matter. One time I did this and the player called the floor manager over. The manager found the man's winning hand in the muck pile, but explained that it had touched the muck pile and that he couldn't do anything about it because of the rules of the game.

I used to deliberately misdeal by giving out too many cards to a person or messing up the order of the cards, in which case you have to deal a whole new hand. The customers hate this because they just want to get their cards and play poker. They don't want any interruptions.

Giving a tip back to a customer was another big no-no. No matter how big or small the tip was, you were supposed to smile and say, "Thank you sir." You're even taught this in dealer school. Sometimes the size of the tip can be an insult but you still have to take it with a smile, no matter what. One time I threw a quarter tip back at the customer. The only reason why I got away with it was because I did it on the night that I quit.

I eventually left, because more and more the customers got to me. I actually liked dealing cards, but it got to the point where I was crying every time I went to work, on my breaks, and on my way to a new table. I couldn't bring myself to work there anymore. I wish I could have done more to the place and the customers.

16 THE CUSTOMER IS ALWAYS RIGHT

Retail

DISCOUNT CHAIN STORE STOCK CLERK KARL

Working at Kmart was your typical teenage shit job. The job was boring. Everyone who worked there hated being there; it was drudgery. The aspect that was really depressing was seeing people who had families work there, making the same amount as a teenager. It was sad to see people support their kids on shit wages. I don't think any employee, except for upper management, made more than $15,000 a year.

The day after Christmas, 1979, the store laid off a lot of people, even people who had been working there longer than I had. To get even with the company, I started stealing.

The first things I took were two music cassettes that were in the stock room. I stuck them in my sock and walked out. When I got into the appliance department I gave my friends discounts on batteries and cassette tapes. Everything was minor until I was moved into the camera and jewelry department where I was under a lot of pressure. I couldn't take it anymore. I knew that other people were taking stuff but everyone was really quiet about it. I had a friend come in and I gave him a shopping bag filled with six Minolta and Pentax cameras — about $400 each — and a couple cases of film. I charged him $1.99, which was the price of some batteries. I made sure that I stapled a long receipt onto his bag. Then two security guards walked up and we engaged them in a twenty minute discussion about shoplifting. Later, my friend walked out the front door. After that, it was easy.

I was transferred to building materials, where I had access to a large garage door. My friend had a big car and we loaded it up with garage door openers and ceiling fans. At Kmart they only went by department sales — they didn't have I.D. numbers like other big stores — so they didn't know what item was being sold. We could sell a load of plywood and the company would think we had sold a load of garage door openers. My friend would go out and sell the stuff and we would split the profit. We did this three or four times a week. I think we stole close to $100,000 worth of merchandise. We wouldn't give a second thought to leaving the shelf empty, and when we ran out we would order more. I told some of the people who worked there what I was doing and most would say, "I couldn't do that." Then one day I saw my friend going outside with a huge box filled with about $20,000 worth of stuff, everything from gold chains to stereos.

In 1981, Kmart 3399 had the worst yearly inventory of any Kmart in the country. The store had $500,000 in invisible waste. That year we fudged the inventory: instead of marking one ceiling fan we would mark five. The same people who were stealing were doing the inventory, so we were able to cover our asses real good, but it made us wonder who was taking the rest of the stuff. In reality, the store probably had lost between $750,000 and $1,000,000 to invisible waste.

An ironic story is that one Christmas I took four cases of Atari games and gave them out as presents at the store's Christmas party. I later found out that security was taking stuff too. The person in charge of the warehouse was taking stuff by the forklift load and putting it in the back of his pickup. Nobody ever thought to check that guy.

I don't think I did that much damage to the company. In 1982 the company blamed the store's problems on management, most of whom were transferred to other stores. The store never fired or caught anyone stealing, but the store's reputation did bring management morale way down. Just think, they were in charge of the worst store in the entire country.

TOY STORE FLOOR MANAGER • RON

I worked at Toys R Us in Tampa, Florida. The job was boring, but I found a number of ways to entertain myself, other employees and even the customers.

One Christmas the store had a Barbie Doll house on display and every night I would create a different scene by dressing the dolls up in strange outfits and setting them up in unusual situations. One time I dressed the Ken Doll in a clown outfit, tied Barbie against a balcony, and set Ken up so he was whipping her. One day during the summer I found a Barbie Doll on the floor with half a leg chewed off so I attached a peg to her leg, resealed her in a box, and sold her as Peg-Legged Barbie. I found a ripped-up Cabbage Patch Doll, and a friend and I took the doll home and resewed part of it, took it back to the store, and sold it as an Anatomically Correct Cabbage Patch Doll.

Once, I cross-dressed a Ken Doll and repackaged it. A lady and her daughter saw the cross-dressed Ken Doll. They bought it then took it to the newspapers because they thought it was the result of some mix-up at the factory. About a month later, after I got fired, my girlfriend called the papers and told them that I was responsible for the doll. The next thing I knew, radio stations and newspapers from all over the country were calling me. Until I went public with the story, Mattel was going through all of their security systems trying to figure out how something like this could have happened. I know Toys R Us didn't want to tell Mattel what happened. Toys R Us does not like any publicity whatsoever, good or bad. Eventually I was fired, not by my boss, but by a big representative from the company. My boss liked me and tried to defend me, but the representative had the last word.

I had some fun with what I did. I'm not trying to sound like a jerk or anything, but I was the best worker at the store. If they gave me three things to do I would do five. I kept the other employees amused. I saw it as a necessity for surviving the type of job I had, but I would have to say that I probably went a little farther than other people.

DEPARTMENT STORE CLERK • PAUL

Some twenty years ago I was working at Uncle Bill's department store. I was just a floor clerk in the miscellaneous department which was paints, hardware and stuff like that. There was a manager named Virgil James. It was a long time ago but I still

I don't want to grow up, I'm a Toys R Us kid.

— Toys R Us slogan

When you are saying something that doesn't mean much, you must say it with a great deal of authority.

— Virgil Thompson

From our examination of various measures of an individual employee's perceived economic difficulties, we found very little evidence to support the hypothesis that employees become involved in theft because of greater economic pressure.

— Theft by Employees, Richard C. Hollinger and John P. Clark [3]

remember him, a real tight ass, prim and proper. Mr. Business.

Keep in mind that twenty years ago it was real easy to get a job. We knew that if we fucked up and got fired, we could find another job. Back then, a job wasn't really a matter of pride to me, it was a matter of funds to get things I wanted. I never had big plans for that job. It wasn't a career move, it was just a place to go. I didn't take a lot of sick time off. I needed the money so I wanted to work. I was a really good employee. I was courteous to the customers and I did the job well. I didn't really even think about it, it was just the way that I carried on.

Everyone that worked there were friends, longtime friends. We all knew the company was fucking us over because they'd never give us raises or anything. They might give us a nickel or something and then make a big deal out of it like they made some big sacrifice. They paid us shit, so we compensated for it. I'll give you some examples. Our friends who were cashiers would give us super discounts. A friend of mine worked in the hunting department. I wanted a twelve gauge shotgun and he sold it to me for $12; it was an $80 gun. There was a twenty-five percent mark-down table with damaged items and stuff they were trying to get rid of. So we would take the new merchandise, make up tickets for it, put it on the mark-down table, and buy it at the reduced price. If I wanted a big tool box I'd just drive my car to the back loading dock. A couple friends and I carried this tool box that took me two weeks to fill up with tools. We're carrying the tool box back to the warehouse and this Virgil James started to walk back to the warehouse. So we just threw the tool box off the back of the dock and right through the plastic window of my '59 Dodge convertible top. Never caught us, never caught us at all.

GROCERY CO-OP CASHIER • DIANE

The first thing that interested me in working for the co-op was that they paid well, had paid holidays and health benefits. When I started there, I didn't think of it as a company because everyone supposedly had the same interest in providing food to the public at a cheaper price. Later I saw that the structure wasn't really arranged that way and that all support workers, myself included, were being used to make the co-op "fat" for the people who ran it. Nothing I said made any difference because everyone made more money and got more benefits than I did.

You were hired as either a collective worker that did a bit more of the office backroom type of work (and got about $2.50 more an hour), or as a support worker who did more of the grittier work like stocking the shelves and doing the cash register. It was mainly a difference of duties and pay. It was kind of sketchy who got to be a collective worker and who got to be a support worker. There were collective workers who were really inept and support workers that were completely capable of doing any part of the job. The company decided which position you would be in. A lot of it had to do with if you had a college education or not. It was frustrating to be a support worker and know that you weren't getting paid as well as collective workers, who seemed to have an easier job than you, when the place called itself a collective.

As managers, our fundamental purpose is to build a department and organization that we are proud of. Our unit in many ways becomes a living monument to our deepest beliefs in what is possible at work. We strive to create both a high-performing unit and one that treats its own members and its customers well. Each time we act as a living example of how we want the whole organization to operate, it is a positive political act.
— The Empowered Manager, Peter Block [4]

How many employees steal from their employers? Experienced private investigators believe that one-half of the work force engages in petty theft from employers; taken are paper, pens, and other small items. Of those fifty percent, however, half also steal important items, and from five to eight percent of all employees steal in volume. A study by the U.S. Chamber of Commerce found that up to seventy-five percent of all employees steal at least once and up to forty percent at least twice.
— "Employee Theft: A $40 Billion Industry," American Journal of Political and Social Science [5]

Although larcenous customers are more numerous, employee thieves seem to be greedier. A survey of eleven major retailers by Jack L. Hayes, a Stanfordville, N.Y., loss prevention consultant, found that shoplifters who were caught stealing outnumbered their employee counterparts, 92,212 to 8,197. But the average shoplifter's take was only $57.31 of merchandise, compared with the employee's $890.
— New York Times Magazine [6]

The longer any support worker worked there, the less able they were to be collective workers. See, support workers got disgusted with collective workers because we got a better view of the whole structure by not having the power that other people had. The people in the collective couldn't understand why we, of all people, should get our insurance paid for, even though we made less money and couldn't afford doctor bills. Because they paid us less, they felt we should get less benefits. These are the same people who sign petitions for Justice for Janitors and other noble causes, but wouldn't look at what was right under their noses.

Over time, I got more confident about what I could get away with. Sometimes I'd let things completely slide through and not ring them up. I wouldn't let the customer know I was doing that. I would give the twenty percent employee discount to the elderly and people that used food stamps and just write down that they were workers. I would purposely mark down new shipments of inventory that came in. I would make a basic guess about the price, then lower it. With produce, a lot of the time they would mark it up then add five cents because they figured a percentage was going to go bad or get bruised. When I priced the produce, I usually didn't include the extra markup, just for the hell of it.

I got frustrated that the company wasn't really living up to what they claimed to be and that they had a reluctance to deal with support workers' questions about the company structure and why things were the way they were.

I think what I did was some type of self-empowerment. I never thought of it as revenge. It seemed like the only outlet to vent my frustrations. The little things I was doing were so nit-picky, that if I wanted to do something to drastically undermine the company, I would have looked at it from a completely different angle. I was just splitting hairs but it made it easier for me to work there.

RECORD STORE CASHIER • OWEN

I worked for Wherehouse Records and Tapes for three years in three different stores. At that time they had 105 stores in two states. Now they have five or ten mega-stores.

The rumor was that the owners knew zero about the record business and had no respect for any artist who wasn't white and a million seller. I was hired as a clerk because I had classical record experience: I listened to two Mahler records and I qualified.

I started at a store in the suburbs that only stocked Peter Frampton and Barbra Streisand records, which was fine. Then I was transferred to a store in a black neighborhood. At Christmastime, the store had 300 copies of Peter Frampton's latest album and not a single Randy Crawford record. We would have to beg them to send us one copy. We were pretty disgusted with management by this time. I transferred to a store closer to where I lived and we ran into the same problem: only white mainstream artists were stocked. Again we had to beg for current hits and could never meet the demand for the records that were being requested.

One day, me and a couple of women who worked there were griping about the situation when one of the clerks who had been in the store forever said, "You know, there's a way of handling this

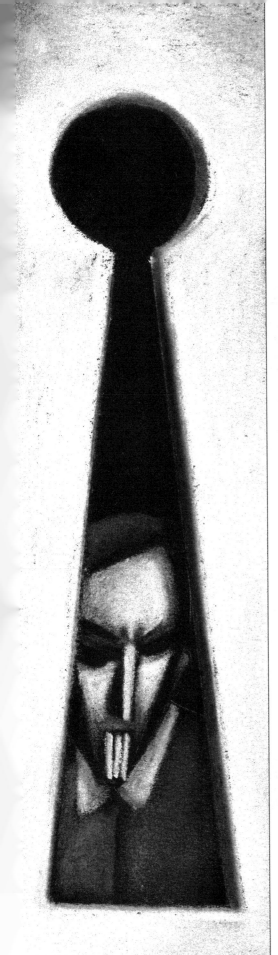

problem." He showed us a grade-B technique of tapping the till, which was basically ringing up a sale and not giving the customer the receipt. The next sale that goes through you open the drawer, make the change, and give them that receipt. Anybody could do it.

Soon, all four of us were doing it. It started with $20 a day for lunch. Pretty soon the store was making six or seven sales a day on the books while we walked out of there every night with armloads of records that we sold to secondhand record stores. We made some pretty good money. The company was so blind to what was going on that they sent us a new manager to see if she could save the store, but of course she couldn't. She ordered thousands of dollars of these off-the-wall records that we told her to order. We took them home and told her the next day that they had sold. Everyone from the regional managers on down had no idea what was going on.

We also let shoplifters come in and steal from the place. If we thought they were getting greedy, or if we didn't like their attitude, we'd stop them, but we had a nice class of regular shoplifters who would pick and get what they wanted. If we saw that someone had refined taste we would encourage them and recommend other albums.

DEPARTMENT STORE STOCK CLERK VICTOR

I didn't care that some schmuck on third shift started doing graffiti on the bathroom walls. They put locks on the doors to keep him out, but left me in the cold. They had no right. I had to make those fuckers pay.

I was in aisle thirteen pocketing a screwdriver as an elderly gent headed for the bathroom. I shadowed him and waited outside the door, paper towels in hand. As he exited I caught the door and entered under the pretext of filling the towel dispenser. He was out of sight and I figured it would take him about three minutes to stroll up to the office and deposit the key into the hands of the next eager poo-goer. I worked fast. Inside of a minute I had disassembled the lock and removed it from the door. I lifted a ceiling panel and shoved the whole apparatus up there, along with the screwdriver. I began to wash my hands as a revelation struck me: I wanted them to find it! They should know the underlings were disgruntled. Quickly I pulled the lock assembly from the ceiling and entered my choice stall. I lifted the cracked porcelain seat and splashed the lock into the toilet.

COPY SHOP CLERK • ALAN

I've never dealt with so many fucked-up managers as when I started working at a busy, downtown Minneapolis copy shop. We had to do a lot of work, took a lot of shit from customers and got paid beans. Actually, it was one of the best jobs I've had because everybody that I worked with was really fun.

Maybe they call it take-home pay be-cause there is no other place you can afford to go with it.
— Franklin P. Jones

The good work strike-workers pro-vide consumers with better service or products than the employer intended — for example, they undercharge shoppers or give free bus rides.
One good side effect of the good work strike is that it places the onus of stopping a service on the employer.
— "Strategy For Industrial Struggle," Solidarity pamphlet [7]

U.S. News and World Report found that 34% of 18-29 year old employed individuals felt it justifiable to steal from their employer.
— James D. Walls, Jr., Senior Vice-President of Stanton Corporation [8]

Employee theft is a $40-billion-per year disease eating away at the health of American companies.
— "Employee Theft: A $40 Billion Industry," American Journal of Political and Social Science [9]

There is really no category of harm-less theft. A company that does not stand firm on all issues of theft will find the rules bent and broken in every way.
— Security Management Magazine [10]

One day, a friend from work and I decided to go to a movie, until we realized how absolutely poor we were. The only one we could afford had a $1 admission. We decided we weren't being paid enough, so we started to pay ourselves — from the cash register. We got to the point where we couldn't work a day unless we got $40 each, on top of our daily wages. If a manager got on our case to work faster, we laughed and took $20 out of the cash register for harassment. We found out later that we weren't the only employees taking money. It seemed to be a common practice. Eventually, we got so fed up that we decided we weren't going to charge anyone for anything all day. This became known as the "Free Day." The three of us gave away hundreds of dollars' worth of services and products. We didn't charge anyone for time on the computers, laser printers or copiers. If anyone came to pick up a big job, we just gave it to them. A lot of customers were very shocked. Some people almost got to the point of demanding we take their money, which, when you think about it, is silly. We told customers it was part of a promotional campaign or that the cash register was broken and we couldn't take their money at the time.

The owners started to notice money was missing, and that at least one employee was stealing, but there was nothing they could do because the store was open twenty-four hours and they didn't keep good track of things. I think they still don't know just how much money we took.

Our bonus checks were paid according to the number of good customer evaluations we got. We would go through them (even though we weren't supposed touch them, much less look at them), and if any bad ones came in we'd throw them out. If we didn't meet our end-of-the-month quota for good ones, we just made some up with fake names and addresses, and wrote how great the employ-ees were at that particular store. The results would be published in the company newsletter each month. We were rated the best employees and the best store. The management never thought employees could make money by faking these evaluations. We faked hundreds of them. To this day, when I get together with other people who worked there, we always have a good laugh.

CONVENIENCE STORE CLERK • MARC

For two summers I worked part-time at a large discount conve-nience store which was part of a large national chain. The work was tedious and boring. The attitudes and practices of local managers and the corporate owners didn't make the job any better.

While working at this store I learned from one manager that about $15,000 is lost to shoplifting each year. I also learned that they counter their losses by marking up most of the merchandise twenty-five percent over the retail price. For example, products that are bought for about $.99 to be sold for $1.99 were often priced at $2.59. Even fixed prices on products that the corporation manufactures themselves — the store brands — were often in-flated.

What also bothered me was that, had the store avoided stocking up on many products that could never sell in the first place, they'd

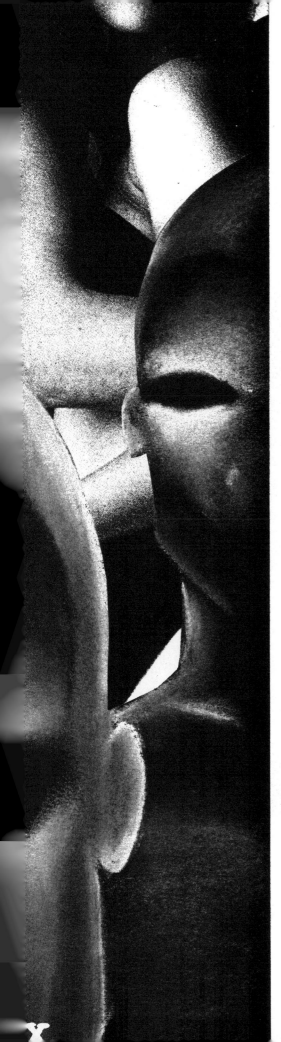

have been able to market everything else at a fair price. Anyone who has ever spent much time with typical American children could predict that Mr. T. Shrinkydinks and toys from the TV show *Ghostbusters* weren't going to be a hot item. But this store loaded up on these products, and now they're stuck with cases of useless merchandise. Rather than assuming responsibility and seeking a reasonable solution, such as hiring someone with a stronger eye for market trends, the store chose to recover their losses by marking up all the other merchandise. Simple math shows that the store probably turns a pretty hefty profit, more than making up for what they lose to shoplifters.

Seeing customers being ripped off every day, over and over again, showed me that people were accepting those prices as retail. The store had frequent sales which made shoppers think they were getting bargains. In actuality, they were finally getting products at retail value or a little bit less. Also, many of the store's customers are elderly men and women who don't have much money to spend for the household products they really need. Many of them no longer drive, so rather than walking at least a mile to a store like Kmart, which has a larger selection, they bought from the chain I worked for.

My job mainly consisted of working the cash register, pricing merchandise, and walking around as a sales clerk. As a cashier, I was able to see which products were especially popular. I also learned that memorizing the prices of popular items is relatively easy for cashiers, since they see the same merchandise purchased over and over again. I got all the information I needed to aid me in my scheme. All the other assistance I could want was provided by the nonexistent security system. Employees used to monitor and secure the store and, unlucky for my managers and co-workers, they trusted me.

I put new merchandise on the shelves at the inflated prices my managers demanded. While I priced these items at their intended prices, I priced other items at twenty-five percent to fifty percent less than retail. Instant sale, but I was the only one who knew about it. You cannot peel off a sticker without destroying the sticker under it as well. This conveniently prevented anyone from lifting a sticker and seeing the old price. To prevent suspicion, I left extremely popular items alone. Any other items I marked down. No one is going to take the time to check the merchandise receipts or catalogs to check the retail price, especially if the store is understaffed. To the best of my knowledge, no one ever suspected a thing. By the time I stopped working at this store, I cost them at least several thousand dollars while giving consumers merchandise at reasonable if not heavily discounted prices.

The ironic thing was, the name tag I had to wear at work read "Customers First!"

VISUAL MERCHANDISING MANAGER JIM

I was hired by the largest department store in Hawaii as a visual merchandising manager, which really means a display manager. I had a crew of assistants, called trimmers, who helped on the displays. We did all of the windows and interior displays, and dressed all of the mannequins in the store.

I'm a little more relaxed at work than most people. I figure if the work gets done and it's professional work, what's the difference? I can't stand being uptight at work all the time. To me it's a job, and I can't believe that I get paid to dress mannequins. It's pretty silly when you stop and think about it, but there are a lot of people who take it very seriously.

There was a newly hired woman trimmer who was very talented and beautiful. At first, we were nothing more than co-workers. About a month after she started working, we went to lunch together and discovered we were attracted to each other. With time, we got a little more involved and eventually started going out. We found more than enough time to get away and have sex at work. We could have done it at her or my place but we decided, "We're here and the moment grabs us."

In most department stores there are these little passageways behind the display windows. Only the display people had the keys so we would go down there once in a while. We did it in sitting rooms before the store opened, or up in the production room where we dressed the mannequins. Because we were doing display work all over the store, our choices were unlimited. We were never gone longer than a half hour and there was a pager system that we could hear from anywhere in the store, so if anyone wanted us, it wasn't a problem.

The manager of the store was very tight-lipped and straight-laced. She thought this woman and me were spending too much time together and would give us dirty looks every time she saw the two of us going to lunch together. I think she thought that something was going on but she never caught us in the act. It was always kind of a kick to do it and think of what would happen if this woman had ever seen us. It was like taking a chance because I would have been fired instantly if we had been caught.

DEPARTMENT STORE MATERIAL HANDLER SANTA

I snuck out the back door of the store during lunch hour, pushing five shopping carts into the woods behind the store, every day, for close to a month. Then I would pull out some rope, which I stole from the hardware department every morning at seven, and tie these five carts onto the rope and hoist them up various trees.

Finally, twenty-seven working days and 135 shopping carts later, a store manager walked into this "forest of sabotage" and discovered where all the missing shopping carts were. After a lengthy investigation, the store never found out who committed this act. It took three hours to pull these carts out of the trees.

I committed these acts partly out of boredom and partly out of revenge. What better way to spend a lunch hour than to string up shopping carts, pretending they're my bosses? Naturally, I did not feel any sort of guilt and laughed many times thinking about it.

It very seldom happens to a man that his business is his pleasure.
— Samuel Johnson

No office anywhere on Earth is so puritanical, impeccable, elegant, sterile or incorruptible as not to contain the yeast for at least one affair, probably more. You can say it couldn't happen here, but just let yeast into the place and first thing you know — bread!
— Helen Gurley Brown

The kind of actions that one can undertake at the workplace are only limited by the imagination of the workers themselves.
— "Giving Them The Gears," Open Road 11

It is very clever to know how to hide one's cleverness.
— Francois, Duc De La Rochefoucauld

POS/EM (Point Of Sale Exception Monitoring) catches dishonest sales associates in the act, at the point of sale. POS/EM is effective against cash register losses such as: cash theft from the drawer, under-ringing sales, even credit card fraud. This new loss prevention system from Sensormatic records the attempt and the transaction data on videotape, providing positive documentation of what actually occurred.

During the surveillance mode, if POS/EM "sees" an exception it has been instructed to monitor, it selects the appropriate camera, automatically aims the camera at the register, and superimposes the transaction data over the video picture of the cashier and register. This information is then stored on videotape. In addition, POS/EM can supply you with hard copy of the transaction via a standard 80 column printer.
— Sensormatic Electronics Corporation brochure [12]

Workers are amazingly candid about their own stealing when questioned anonymously. The University of Minnesota sociology department discovered that while carrying out a three-year study with a $250,000 grant from the Justice Department's National Institute of Justice. About one-third of all employees in three industries — retail, hospitals and manufacturing — reported they had been involved in stealing company property during the preceding year.
— Nation's Business [13]

EXOTIC FISH STORE CLERK • MAC

Before the store went out of business, it was the largest one specializing in both fresh and saltwater fish in the Northwest. I pretty much did whatever the management didn't want to do. The one boss that I always dealt with liked me. He let me spend most of the time maintaining the aquariums and dealing with the fish. This was great, because it was something that I was interested in. Back then, fish were my thing.

The place was extremely profitable, but it was mismanaged. One day we were told that the State Comptroller was closing us down because the store hadn't paid sales tax for the last nine months. They wanted us to stay on for a week to clean up the tanks and get the fish ready to go back to the wholesalers.

I was working with two guys that I never really got along with. There was deep-rooted jealousy on their part because they had accomplished far less than I had, and I was a lot younger. They were put in charge of the clean up procedures.

I came in the day that we were supposed to start and these two guys were blaring a tape. I asked them if I could put on a tape. They said, "Yeah, whatever. Hurry up." Within a couple minutes of listening to my tape they pulled it out of the tape deck and threw it across the room — the tape casing shattered. Just because they didn't like the music. It kind of pissed me off.

I had mentioned I wanted to take home a certain fish. The first thing they did was to pull the fish that I wanted out of the tank — a really expensive one — and one of them puts a cigarette out on it. So it fucks it all up. A little later they tried to put a cigarette out on me. Then they started picking fish out of the tanks and throwing them at me. It was just getting stupid. I was getting really angry. I said I was going home and one of them went, "Fuck, yeah, you're going home. You're fucking fired!"

I went in the back to wash my hands. There's a big holding facility there for all of the saltwater fish which are very expensive, ranging from $50 to $500 a piece. Those two guys were planning to steal a bunch of these fish for their tanks at home and, little did I know, they also had a couple of their own fish in there too. I grabbed a gallon bottle of bleach and poured about four cups of it into the tank's filter system. I calmed down almost instantly like it was no big deal. I was just about to leave when one of the guys went back there and started freaking out. He was throwing shit around, yelling, "What did you do this for? Oh my god!" My only alibi was that the back door had been open. I said, "Oh man, somebody must have come in through the back." I started to freak out to make it look real. The bleach killed about $2,000 worth of fish.

Luckily, I got away with it. I think the boss that I was friends with knew I'd done it but ended up paying me anyway. I didn't admit anything. That was the one and only time I've ever really done something that drastic. Looking back on it, I couldn't say that I wouldn't do it again. I mean, they deserved it, fuck.

17 QUALITY: BUILT THE AMERICAN WAY

Manufacturing

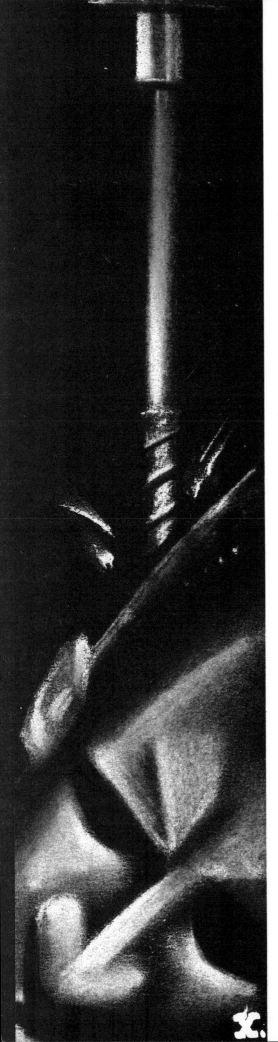

MACHINIST • BURT

I worked for a small company called Gray's Manufacturing Company in Inglewood, California. They made specialized airplane parts for companies like Boeing and Lockheed. I was the low man on the totem pole, working for two rich brothers who were trying to outdo each other all the time. One brother had done really smart things with his money and had made good investments. But the other brother, who owned the company, was always losing his ass on small business ventures. He always put it off on his little brother who took his frustrations out on me. It was like passing the buck.

What it boiled down to was a really shitty job: deburring, which means cleaning the parts when they came off the machine. I had to run this big piece of sandpaper across each part five or six times, bore it with air and water, and check it with calipers. I had to wash my hands every time because if I got just one little piece of grit on my calipers, it didn't measure correctly. It's a really screwy job. They were charging the company a lot of money for these parts — about $25,000.

I was frustrated doing the work and having the boss come and check stuff that I knew was accurate. He would be frustrated because of the bad deals he was making, so he'd knock the parts around and make them so they weren't any good, then blame me. If one part hits a certain place on another, it's not going to be any good. After he screwed up half of the parts I had done, I had to go through and figure out which ones were screwed up and fix them up just right. I got really tired of this and knew it was going to come out of my paycheck. So I thought, fuck it! I'm going to ruin every one of them.

I made it *look* as if the parts were okay. I took ten-thousandths of an inch off more than I should have, or I bored a hole wider than I was supposed to. Then I wrapped them up, packed them and got them ready for delivery. The boss didn't catch anything because I'd always make sure the top three in the batch were okay, and he'd only check those when they were packed. All the ones after the top three were screwed up. The company only got $4,000 worth of good parts out of a $25,000 job. It really ended up costing them a lot — probably $21,000, not including shipping — and what it cost to recall the parts.

The pay was low, they treated me badly, they were running a shitty company, and their ethics were rotten. I still think they owe me for all the shit they put me through. I did really good work. They kept promising me a raise, but it never came. They ended up going out of business.

COIL WINDER • JAY

While working as a coil winder in a big transformer factory, we workers faced the dehumanizing "science" known as Minutes Times Motion, which is where a computer estimates how long it should take to complete a task such as building a transformer. Every day, we would check the number and type of transformers built, and at the end of the week we would get a computer-generated analysis of our efficiency rate. If we "beat the clock," we would get a happy face on our evaluation report. A frown face would mean that we were just not up to par, as far as our computer was concerned.

To get a grip on this bad situation, especially in a non-union plant, we required a total conspiracy amongst workers. Starting with the guy I knew the best, we each agreed to slow down production on one of the transformer types. We each handed in approximately the same number of units as our co-workers. After a few frowning faces on our monthly reports and a talking-to by the supervisor, the management had to readjust their computer time accordingly. It makes management look bad to have a product constantly come in under production goals. Adjusting to our new time made them come out around 100 percent again. This victory encouraged other assemblers to do the same, with equally good results.

As we became faster at winding, we would overproduce and thus we would have to store some units in our lockers. We soon saw the wisdom of having a bank of units, in case we didn't want to work as hard one day, or a friend needed one because they messed one up. We earned more free time at work, and were still working at 100 percent, as far as management was concerned.

CARBURETOR ASSEMBLER • EUGENE

It's common to hear people complain about American cars breaking down and having problems; there's always some goddamn thing wrong with them. It's almost always internal, and they have to take the car back to the shop and figure out what's wrong with it. It's not an accident or a fluke. These machines are designed by engineers who know what they're doing. They're precise. It's the people putting them together who aren't quite as precise as the engineers would like them to be.

I worked manufacturing carburetors in Detroit. There was one particular carburetor that you could place a BB in and it was there for life. The only way you could see it was if you x-rayed it. The only way to fix it was to replace the carburetor. It would be an intermittent problem with your carburetor — you'd never know when it was going to strike. Usually it would hit you when you were going downhill.

Anytime we got a chance to do internal parts, like a carburetor, we would screw them up purposely. We would put in bolts that were the wrong size. We would do anything we could to make the carburetors dysfunctional. We did this to as many carburetors as possible.

I inspired and taught many others. They were bored out of their minds. It was such a relief for them to take that screwdriver and damage that part internally, knowing that no one would know they did it.

The goal was to wreak the most blatant destruction without getting caught. The most insidious thing, of course, was dealing with internal parts of engines and inside door panels. Workers might take a pair of pliers and pop off just one cog on the end of

---

What is property, that it is so sacred, that it must not be destroyed if it stands in the way of human life and justice?
    — New York Call, 29 June 1913 [1]

The Boeing Co. today is trying to find out who cut hundreds of electrical wires in a new 737 being assembled at Boeing's Renton plant.
    Officials say it looks like sabotage. Mark Hooper, spokesman for the Boeing Commercial Airplane Group, said Boeing believes the cuts were deliberate, although an investigation still is underway.
    "The cuts were found in dozens of places at different times during several systems checks and performance tests," he said.
    A motive is unknown, although some workers might be upset by recent layoffs of production workers. About 650 people, mostly in Everett, lost their jobs last month.
    The case is believed to be the first sabotage in a Boeing commercial airplane plant. Boeing produces fourteen of the 737s a month at the Renton plant.
    — Seattle Times [2]

"These are sensible and mature sorts of people — in their own outside environment these sorts of acts of vandalism and sabotage would never be tolerated. But in the workplace it was a different kettle of fish. ... Ford's probably killed, mentally, more people in their time than any fucking company. So consequently whatever action was ever taken against them, I can feel very humane in favor of the people who performed that action." (autoworker interview)
    For the managers of car factories, sabotage is no doubt a 'social problem'; for the 'saboteurs' the work itself is the problem. Sabotage is one of the solutions.
    — Sabotage: A Study in Industrial Conflict, Geoff Brown [3]

"When I was working on the line back in the sixties, if there was something I wanted from the supervisor and didn't get, I would let trucks go by without doing my job. I was no angel. Like everyone else, I would get away with whatever I could. They couldn't do anything to me, and that was the best way to retaliate against the supervisor: get his ass chewed

the plastic crank. There's a gear inside that's plastic and when you roll the window up and the cog is popped off; eventually that window won't work. With wiring and electronic parts, you could do countless things so that initially it works, but later on you'll have problems. You can't find out the source of the problem, who did it, or how it happened. That's the beauty of it.

Sabotage is different than revenge because it's a means by which you can express yourself and free yourself from oppression and dehumanization. You aren't attacking a person, you're dealing with an issue. It's satisfying to know that you're causing long-term problems for the industry. For the first time in my life, I saw other people like me who were drudging through life, making pretty good money and benefits, but whose lives were shit. Being human is so wonderful. If we're pushed apart from that, we tend to struggle because you can't be human in America and work in industry.

When you work for the auto industry, profit is number one. Although they say they're not doing it anymore, they've cut back on quality. They're trying to compete with Japan, but the only way to do that is to treat the most important person in the industry — the worker — as a human being.

They don't treat you like a human being, they treat you like a robot, and your function is to produce the profit. You're dehumanized. The carburetors were our way of equalizing the situation.

I caused a lot of damage. Not only did I teach and encourage others to do it, I caused many Americans strife and heartache and taught them the lesson not to buy from that particular company. The auto industry got a bad rap because of it. The fear and dissatisfaction from driving a car that breaks down all the time are going to stick.

WELDER • TAIT

For close to three years I worked at a family-owned company doing welding and general fabrication work. There were six employees, three of which were the owner and his two daughters. The place was really tense. I didn't let it bother me at the beginning, because I'm very tolerant. Things tend to roll off of me real well. I'll take it and take it, then all of sudden I'll say, "No, this is enough."

This guy was my supervisor when the owner wasn't there. No matter what I did or how I went about it, if it wasn't his way, it wasn't right. I've been doing what I do since 1980 and I've gotten used to working in my own methodical way. My supervisor didn't do shoddy work, but he was always in a hurry. He wouldn't stop and think where I would stop and think a job through. The owner never cared how I did a job as long as I got it done and did it right. This supervisor was the exact opposite: he would get me mad, then leave me alone for the rest of the day, and then the next day nothing would happen. After I quit this job I found out his theory was, "if you're pissed off, you work better."

I started getting really stressed at work. I was getting headaches by ten in the morning. It started spilling over into my private life, because I would be totally on edge. I spoke to a doctor and he said

I had stress headaches. He asked me what I was exposed to at work and I just laughed and said "an asshole." He said that maybe I should quit my job.

I started to purposely get mad. With that and the tension headaches, I decided I didn't want to be there anymore. I called in sick more, I would go in for a while and then say, "I'm sick, I gotta go." I wasn't really sick, I was just sick of working there. As I said, I'm a tolerant person until I'm not. I would just get into a mood and not want to go to work. I never purposely did shoddy work because of the situation, but I'm sure that it took a toll on my thinking and my general quality of work.

ASSEMBLYLINE WORKER • NICK

I worked for a year in a typical World War II-style plant with a sawtooth tin roof and smoke stacks billowing oily gray smoke. There were 1,000 of us poor bastards working there, doing mindless arm and wrist repetitions thousands of times per day, producing a basic industrial product.

The accident rate was enormous. Our sign out front read IT'S BEEN _____ DAYS SINCE OUR LAST ACCIDENT. It had no number on it as it would be too embarrassing. Almost every day there was a work-time lost accident. There were three shifts a day, and most of the accidents happened in the wee hours of the morning, say just after your 4:00 am lunchtime of chili con carne served warm in the can from a vending machine. The nurse was only on duty during day hours, when no one got hurt.

One time a co-worker got his leg jammed in a machine. The foreman pulled me off the line and ordered me to take him to the hospital; an ambulance cost too much. I ran to get my car and drove around town looking for the damn hospital, which I had never been to before, while my buddy moaned in deep pain. Once there, I helped him out to the emergency room and they took him away. I had to stay up front to fill out the papers. When I told the admitting nurse where we were from, I didn't even have to sign anything. She said, "We have an open account with your company."

This was a union shop and contract negotiations were on. The contract expired and the big union bosses told us to work without a contract. We walked instead. To prepare for the walkout, it was essential to plan ahead. Production went way down so as not to have a big stock of finished goods. The last shift to work before the walk-out had a myriad of mechanical problems. It was uncanny. The laser quality assurance probes started breaking, their bloody red eyes getting skewed every which way. The box machines started getting jammed and glue was dripping all over the conveyor belts. Forklifts were falling apart, parts from them disappearing mysteriously. Finally, with the factory so disabled, we walked off the job. The next shift was massed by the main gate, cheering, taunting the bosses and pleased at not having to cross the gate and enter the monstrous plant. The international union boss and the company boss ordered us back, but no one balked. Out of 1,000 people perhaps seven went back, and we took their pictures for future shame.

During the strike, the management desperately needed to truck the warehoused goods to market. Often, however, dump trucks of broken concrete would get dumped in front of the plant gates, preventing the big tractor trailers from entering. Despite not having strike benefits (the union had declared our strike illegal) and no unemployment benefits (the company lawyers got it cut off), we stayed out for a month until we won the strike.

STEEL WORKER • RICH

At the large steel manufacturer where I worked, we made everything from carburetor parts to grid irons for buildings. I started out on the ground floor of the shop. My job was to cut tubing.

I learned how to work most of the machines from going to a trade school. I loved working with the machines and building things. I was ambitious and learned every machine in the shop. The machine I used was expensive but inefficient. So I went to the lathe and made a particular part to make my saw work better and make my job easier. Soon I started working on other machines to make them more efficient and make life easier for a lot of the workers. The foreman didn't like what I was doing; not only was I doing things that the engineering department should have done, but also, I was making him look bad. The foreman made me stop — so I quit — but before I did, I caused the company thousands of dollars in damage.

I shortened every single tube I cut by at least one-thirtysecond of an inch, which made an incredible difference when the part went to the welding department. The welders had to bend the tubes and use hammers to smash certain tubes in place. I worked like a mad dog and increased production of these tubes and then mixed them up in the tube bins so nothing was in its right place. The foreman saw that the parts weren't working but couldn't figure out why. He consulted with various engineers and supervisors and they figured out that the tubes were being cut slightly shorter in an inconsistent manner. The foreman blamed everything on my saw, which was exactly what I wanted. I played dumb and went back to the inefficient saw without my invention. They never guessed that I cut all of the tubes short on purpose.

18 SEEING IS BELIEVING

Broadcasting

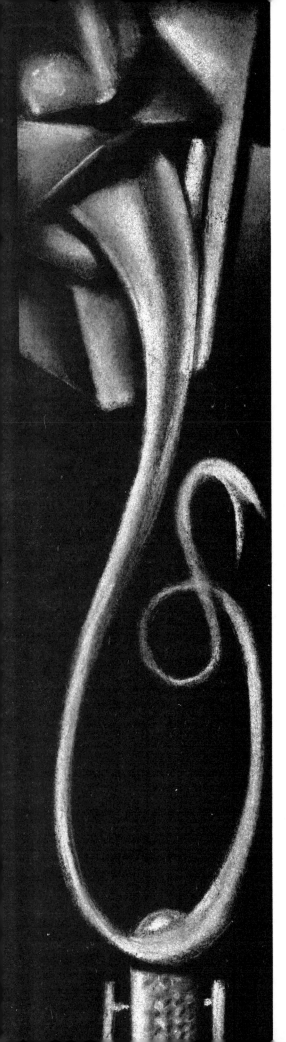

DISC JOCKEY • TICO

I was the sports director, the assistant news director and DJ for an adult contemporary FM station in Ohio. I was also the youngest person there. The people who worked there were these losers who were too ugly to get into TV, but who had great egos and loved to hear themselves talk. Everyone I worked with loved working in radio and had dreams of moving to a larger station and becoming radio stars. I didn't take things that seriously.

As part of being news director I had to do traffic reports each half hour during drive time in the morning and the afternoon. I was supposed to listen to a CB radio and switch back and forth among the police ban stations to listen for wrecks being reported. I did this for four or five days but it was so boring waiting for something to happen that instead, I listened to two other news stations' traffic reports and put what they said, verbatim, on the air. Sometimes the report I gave was an hour old; once I reported that I-75 was backed up but listeners called the station and explained that the road had been clear for the last forty minutes.

Some days, getting news stories was really hard. I had to go through the wire reports (AP and UPI) and find stories that would be of some interest to the listening audience, then edit them down. This took a long time and was tough to do, so sometimes I just made up news stories. I always incorporated my friends into the stories. For instance, I used a taped quote from a friend of mine to report how the state was going to start making people carry a voting license, much like a driver's license, which Ohio actually tried to pass a year earlier. We basically wanted to piss people off and get them involved.

Soon *all* of my friends wanted to be in stories. We kept getting away with it, even as the stories got wilder and wilder. One time our top news story was about a woman who caught her husband cheating on her and attacked him with an electric knife like you use to cut up turkeys. I worked it out with my engineer to play the sound of a Black and Decker saw and a man screaming on cue. I started the story and then the sound effects came in and somehow I didn't crack up. We immediately went to the next story and, sure enough, I noticed that the phone lights were all flashing. Not only were the call-in lines flashing, but also the special hot line that only the general manager at the station was allowed to use. It seems that every advertiser that had commercials during that news segment, and a couple who didn't, called in to complain. The general manager wanted to see me and the engineer in the office after our shifts. He told us that what we did was in bad taste. I got reprimanded pretty hard because a couple of advertisers dropped from the station.

I got in a lot of trouble at press conferences I had to report on. I would always ask the celebrity or politician real pointed questions. Most of the time I got kicked out of the press conference and the radio station got a bad reputation. Generally, the more important the person was, the more of a smart-ass I was. When Mohammed Ali was in town, I asked him what he had left upstairs and his manager came over to me and asked me to leave because Mohammed wasn't comfortable with me in the room. I couldn't handle these kiss-ass press conferences. I would do my research and grill the person until I was asked to leave.

A couple of my co-workers found out what I was doing and threatened me. Only two people at the station actually enjoyed what I did and they were friends of mine. I think I exploited the power of the mass media to help get over the boredom of the job, but I never did it to harm people, even though unconsciously I was acting true to the old saying, "the way the media interprets the news is the way people know it." I finally left the station because I realized I was starting to get serious about radio. I got a couple of offers from rock stations. I starting thinking about a career in radio and how depressing it would be, because I knew I would always have more fun making fun of it than working hard for it.

MASTER CONTROL OPERATOR • HAWLEY

Eight of my friends and I got jobs with a national cable company that had just opened up a new station. We had a enormous amount of responsibility and the pay was low, but the company knew people like us were burning to have access to the station's equipment so we had to take what they offered. We took our jobs really seriously because we all wanted a future in television. We took pride in our work, and wanted to make everything look like top quality television programming.

Because I was good with technical things, my job was to put all of the local programs on the air: turn on the tapes, cue them up and broadcast them at a certain time. I also produced Local Origination programs. The station put over a million dollars into their Local Origination facility. They had a five camera mobile unit, a van, edit suites, two studios, and the only ones working there were my friends and me. We had access to everything and produced a shitload of local programs — hockey, arts festivals, political events and the most phenomenal jazz concerts in Massachusetts. Our programming was seen nationally and we won countless local and national awards.

It was interesting when the company bigwigs had to ask me about what programs would fit where, and I told them what was going on. I had to tell this one guy what was happening because he couldn't operate any of the equipment right. He couldn't stand hearing it from a woman and he couldn't stand hearing it from me. This guy kept moving up in the company. It was phenomenal because he didn't have a skill in his pocket but kept finding another niche to fit into. As he moved up he started hiring people and created his own department. He came up with the ideas of Bingo for Dollars, Real Estate Buyers Guide and Auto Buyers Guide. He started taking up more and more channels because he was bringing in money. We only brought in awards.

There was a lot of excitement when the station started. After about a year, when the station started to get a lot of exposure and awards, the company realized it could do programming that made money. That's when we became aware that there was a mutiny on hand. All of a sudden this boss denied us access to equipment. He started bringing in older people who were smooth administrative types. They knew they were going to take over shortly. A dress code

The management of a radio station is one of the few areas where business and artistic creativity come together: the excitement of being able to implement your ideas, your feelings, and your knowledge.
— Radio Broadcasting,
Robert L. Hilliard [1]

Master control is the nerve center of a television station. Every second of programming you see on your home screen has gone through the master control room of the station to which you are tuned.
— Television Production Handbook,
Herbert Zettl [2]

Work is accomplished by those employees who have not yet reached their level of incompetence.
— Laurence J. Peters

was laid down, some people got their notices, and others resigned. The shit started to hit the fan.

Since I was in charge of the station's tapes, I started destroying the records of tapes we had given out to people. I began destroying certain computer programs that were essential for the station. Then I realized we ourselves wouldn't have access to the programs that we had made, so I started replacing the master tapes with lower quality dubs.

The company was scared shitless about me quitting. They needed me because I was the only one who knew how to use the master control equipment. When I finally did give my notice, it shocked them. I left them high and dry but that wasn't enough for me. I wanted to hurt them really bad.

On the night of the Fourth of July, a friend of ours who still worked at the station opened up the entire building for us. Once again, we had access to everything. Right away I knew this would be my last chance to do anything. Then it started to hit me that the company didn't deserve even dubs of the programs we made. So I made my way to where the taped programming was kept and proceeded to bulk erase the station's entire performance showcase library. Everything I felt they didn't deserve to have, I erased. After I was done, the station had not a shred of decent programming left. I felt very satisfied.

A smooth and harmonious relationship between the programming and engineering departments is important in matters dealing with the broadcast of a station's programs and local productions.
—Broadcast and Cable Management, Norman Marcus [3]

19

MAY I TAKE YOUR ORDER?

Restaurant

BUS BOY • CHUCK

I worked at a seafood restaurant in Fort Lauderdale, Florida, where we had to wear ridiculous outfits. They were these big, blue polyester sailor suits that had big, white bell-bottom pants and a French sailor hat that had a little red fuzzball on top. All the little old ladies who ate there thought we were cute. It was horrible: the suit made us sweat and we felt completely embarrassed.

I worked there with a lot of my friends and we were all bus boys. We were on the low end of the totem pole. The waitresses were cheesing us for the tips. We were supposed to get a certain percentage but we rarely got anything. The guy that ran the place had a horrible temper which he took out on us, so, needless to say, we had a lot of animosity towards the place.

The restaurant was famous for its desserts. The little old ladies liked to eat these massive napoleons and big cheesecakes. We had this game called "Search and Destroy." When the waitresses weren't looking or were turned away from the counter, we would run back into the kitchen, grab as many of these desserts as possible, take them back to the dishwashing area, and totally dig into them with our hands, filling our mouths and eating them as fast as we could. Then we'd throw the dish in the dishwasher to destroy the evidence.

I worked there for four months wearing that little hat. I used to take it off and hide it, but then the owner would ask me, "Where's your uniform?" I'd pull out the hat and put it back on. One time the owner wanted us to work on New Year's Eve and we were all at someone's house, saying how we were tired of it. We sat there burning our little hats and just being totally disgusted with the job. We all decided to quit at the same time, that same day, on New Year's Eve. We left him completely short-handed. That was the best thing, sticking it to that guy on one of the busiest days of the year. We had a permanent workers' strike!

PIZZA MAKER • DARRIN

I was in high school and the only job I could get was at Happy Joe's Pizza Parlor. It was really miserable. I had to work the big machine that rolled the dough, and of course, the dough would always get tangled in the machine, forcing it to a stop. Every time it fucked up, my asshole boss would scream at me. He was always screaming at me but he never quite got around to firing me because I did my job as best I could, even though the pizzas were bad and always fell apart.

I started to realize that I always worked the same shift as this girl who was constantly harassed by the boss. He always hit on her and she always turned him down. Then he started grabbing her, and I would be dealing with the dough, saying to myself, "Oh no...."

One night he did something completely outrageous to this girl like pinching her ass and I started yelling at him. Of course I was fired immediately. I finished my work for the night and left without fucking anything up, but before I came in the next day to pick up my paycheck, I made a copy of my key to the back door.

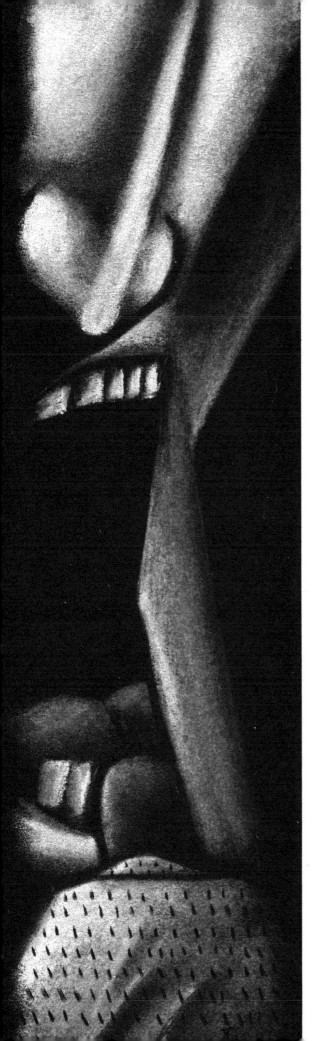

About a month later, me and a friend who also worked there started going in at night and stealing money. We knew where the boss put the cash, how to get into the safe, and on which days there would be the most money. We never took all of the money because we didn't want anybody to figure out what we were doing. We paced the hits apart so the boss wouldn't get suspicious and change the locks or the safe. Nobody ever caught on. There were never any reports in the newspapers or anything like that. After a while we got tired of being cautious and started taking all of the money. This went on for months.

It really hadn't been our intention, but it worked out that when all of the money started disappearing, the boss had no choice but to tell the owners about the problem. The regular bank deposits were always short money and because the boss was the last one to touch the money, the owners were suspicious of him. He got fired a couple of weeks later. The best part of it was that the owners charged him with embezzlement. Last I heard, the boss had to get a lawyer because the case was going to court. He was up shit creek.

So a fourteen-year-old kid fucked him up because he was an asshole.

WAITER • JOEY

I worked a job with two friends at a small café. The business did well enough, so we had no problem with feeding everybody we knew in the neighborhood. At the time we were all very social and knew lots of people. Often there were more people in the restaurant who weren't paying than were paying. What I found was that most of the people that we were working with were also giving away food. It was a thrill to recognize that other people were doing it. From then on, we just encouraged each other to go to greater heights by stealing more. It created a sensation of pleasure within the employees.

I worked there for a year and a half before I got fired. After I left, more friends were hired and the owner never caught on, so the restaurant served as a free food place for an extended community for close to five years.

I always steal from work because no matter how great the place is, they're always going to fuck you over at some point. It's just a question of when. I'm usually taking stuff way before the boss even starts yelling at me. It's like getting your revenge in advance, knowing that it's going to happen. I felt much better leaving the place knowing that I ripped them off.

DISHWASHER • STEVE

I was twenty-seven years old and had just graduated college. All I could get was a dishwasher job at a country-style French restaurant. I thought it would suit my needs because I was just looking for an easy job.

The boss was kind of a Charles Nelson Reilly meets Captain Kirk type, an incompetent leader who yelled when things were going wrong. He was the worst cook there, of course, and he loved to schmooze and waltz from table to table. Then he'd run back in the kitchen and start screaming, "Who put sauerkraut soup on the menu? No one's ordering it because they think they're going to fart. I knew that it was a bad idea." I know that everybody there must have thought he was an idiot. Everybody kissed this guy's ass, but the minute he was out the door, they would start opening the expensive bottles of wine and logging them in as if somebody had ordered them. We ripped him off blind. Everybody cared about the restaurant, but everybody also ate well and drank lots of wine.

The boss was the guy I was after, because he'd screwed over a friend of mine really good. She was a hostess and he replaced her but kept her on without telling her that she was replaced, so he could make her life a little shittier. It was so cruel that when I was ready to leave, I planned my revenge.

The restaurant had these little cassettes the boss had made up for the house music system. I think there were about thirty of them, really mundane stuff. The week before I was going to leave, I took five of the tapes over to a friend's house who had a really good cassette deck. I wound ten minutes into the tape, cranked the cassette deck to full volume and recorded a two-second noise burst off the radio; then, another five minutes further into the tape, an even shorter one, and ten more minutes in I recorded a really long gross one where I would rip down the dial. I did this to all five ninety-minute tapes of sleepy music. Then I put a really offensive song on one of the tapes as the ultimate bomb.

Very innocently, I came back the day that I was going to quit and put the tapes back in the pile. After the lunch rush was over, I explained to the boss that I couldn't work for him anymore. I walked out and never came back. For the next few months, sure enough, the customers would be sitting there in this quiet French restaurant, when all of a sudden blasts of noise would erupt and make them drop their forks.

This continued to happen over the months. They thought something was wrong with the sound system or that a CBer came by and cued his mike. When they finally figured it out, it was great because they didn't know how many tapes were ruined. They certainly couldn't afford to pay anyone to listen to all of the tapes, so they had to get rid of all of them.

I think that the rest of my life has been anti-climactic since then. It was a shining moment.

KITCHEN MANAGER • WEZ

I'd been working at a café called Pacific Desserts off and on for two years when the kitchen manager quit. I had seniority and was moved into the position, but neither the title nor the pay was offered to me, just the work.

High school kids waited tables at night there and often came in in the morning before the place was open for free coffee. I had been making myself breakfast before the manager got there and I decided to expand. For the last three months of school, I made omelettes and fried potatoes using the restaurant's eggs, cheese, milk, vegetables, potatoes, spices, etc., for what became the morning coffee club, at $1 per plate. Soon they started to bring their friends and one of them even made a plaque in his pottery class

that read "Wez's Underground Café." I usually made about $8 extra per day, which would about equal a raise. I was also spending an hour of the company's time for my own profit.

WAITRESS • CAROL

I've worked in the restaurant business my whole life. I've done all kinds of work: making sandwiches, cashiering, washing dishes and busing tables.

With restaurants, the way it works is managers want you to give 100 percent to the customer. In other words, they want you to be sweet as possible, no matter if the customer is grouchy or if you've had a bad day.

At one job I had, we were only making minimum wage. Our boss had promised us all raises but we didn't get them. This went on for a couple of months so three of us girls got together. There were these salads that were supposed to be kept refrigerated, but we purposely left them out for a couple of hours. Sure enough, about ten customers got food poisoning. They didn't get that sick. You get cramps, a stomach ache, and the runs for about four hours, but it wasn't bad enough to get them hospitalized or anything.

There was a lawsuit against the company. We lost our jobs because the guy had to finally close his business, just for that one incident. If the food's bad and people get sick, any restaurant will get a bad reputation. It didn't bother us that much that we did it; in fact, we were happy we did some damage.

I don't think I would do the same thing today. Now I have enough guts to go up to whoever is higher in authority and confront them about the pay. Today if I saw people doing what I did, I would probably try to stop them because it was kind of foolish. I think there are better ways of handling things like that.

20

AT NO EXTRA CHARGE

Shipping and Delivery

BICYCLE MESSENGER • KENNY

Being a bike messenger in Seattle is hellish, but we had it kind of cush. We had to work our butts off, but at least we got paid by the hour.

The company always let us wear shorts, but since we had to wear company T-shirts, we cut off the sleeves. All of a sudden the company decided to clean up its image because they were dealing with big businesses. They started making us wear long pants and shirts made of heavy material, which is insane. Try biking ten miles up hills, up massive hills with heavy packages as fast as you can, in long pants!

All of the messengers agreed there was no way this could continue. We all decided that we wouldn't wash our clothes at all and that we'd wear the same thing every day. We also realized that the intense heat you build up when you bike, mixed with the right food, means you're farting all the time. So we found the right type of food that caused the worst type of explosions, and whenever we were in a big office building, we farted. You can imagine what it was like when one of us was in an elevator with ten business people in suits. Our clothes were stinking, our bodies were stinking and within a month the company had enough complaints to let us wear shorts again.

LIQUOR COMPANY SHIPPING CLERK ROY

There was a time when I was a temp worker, an employee of Kelly Services. It was always amusing when I, obviously male, walked into a new assignment, when they'd called for a "Kelly Girl." I got to see a lot of people cutting slack for themselves in the world of work. As I moved around, one assignment in particular stands out as a hotbed of slacking off.

I did a stint as a shipping clerk at the Old Mr. Boston liquor warehouse. This was during the last six months the company was in Boston, before it moved to Louisville, having been bought out by another company. The previous shipping clerk quit when he found out the company was not going to transfer any of the workers to the new location. Everyone knew their job was ending, and for all the resume help and outplacement services, the bulk of them were going to end up unemployed. This completely destroyed morale in the entire plant. With even the plant manager about to go out on the streets, there was no one who cared to check up on the employees and keep them working hard.

So none of them did. Things were especially bad in shipping, since most of the warehouse employees were long-time alcoholics; I was one myself, encouraged by this job. One of my duties was to help my boss go around the warehouse once a week and pick up all the half empty bottles, and set the cases that had been broken aside so they could be refilled. The worst of the half-open bottles we would pour down the drains. The better stuff came into the office, where we drank it ourselves.

And we certainly had time to drink it. There were three people in the shipping office — with work for only one and a half, which declined rapidly as operations moved to Louisville. Whenever I was done typing up shipping papers for the day, I turned to reading. We also talked a lot about everything from auto repair to what was wrong with employers.

Meanwhile, in the warehouse, the half-drunk guys continued to knock over full cases of liquor with the forklifts, and more than once the stench of cinnamon schnapps filled the air. Every month we'd take inventory and track the "shrinkage," which should have been called "drinkage."

Things got worse and worse as the date for the final move came closer. Adding machines vanished from the offices all over the plant. Apparently a grand piano and a solid oak conference table did the same. Finally, the guys in the shipping department decided that we might as well arrange for our own severance bonuses as well. On the final day, we were supposed to load all of the remaining stock in a boxcar and send it down to Kentucky. We loaded about 200 cases of mixed liquor onto a panel truck instead, and drove it around town, stopping at the houses of all the workers. When it got back to the plant, the truck was empty.

I still have some of that booze...

OFFICE SUPPLY SHIPPING CLERK NORMAN

The family who ran the business treated their employees like second class citizens. The owners were really sloppy about running their business. They were responsible for most of the mistakes, but blame would always come down on the workers. Once I was blamed for a problem in accounting, but I worked in shipping and receiving. They would yell at me until I explained to them that I had nothing to do with the problem. Then they'd run off to yell at someone else.

Most of the paperwork came through me. I had to put copies of the invoices in slots for the different departments of the company. I purposely put the paperwork in the wrong slots. I knew that when people picked up the papers and found that they had the wrong ones, they would just throw them away; it was a reflection of the general attitude of the employees. At first, I did it discriminately. In time, I got more into doing it. Soon the owners couldn't figure out why no money was coming in when the computers stated that all of the bills were going out. As the confusion grew, the company brought in computer experts. At first they tried to blame a couple of innocent employees, until all of the focus shifted to the computers. They looked at every possible place where information could be getting lost, except the path the paperwork followed from department to department. They'd ask the accounting department why certain clients weren't getting billed. The accounting department would claim they didn't get the invoices. They asked me, and I claimed I put every piece of paperwork I got in the right slot. None of the workers would admit they had thrown away paperwork because they wanted to cover for the other employees. The buck would keep on getting passed but no answers could be found.

The company eventually ended up going out of business because the only thing they did was chase a problem around. I think they would have gone out of business on their own, but I helped them do it a little sooner. This gave the employees an excuse to get a new job — which everyone did — but it made most of the employees aware of how fucked-up bosses could be.

RECYCLING CENTER TRUCK DRIVER JOE

The recycling center that I work for has a board of directors that basically lives on another planet. It's funny; they consider themselves very progressive — some of them would even describe themselves as radicals. But they're not radical when it comes to dealing with workers fairly. Most of them don't think about the fact that we're running a recycling center and they don't think about the workers. Yet they're very happy deciding what to do with the money that we make.

Some of us were pretty disgusted about this and with the fact that the board decides where the money goes. We wanted a little more control over the money, so we did something to make sure that the money really went to people who need it.

I drive a truck for the center, making pickups from different apartment buildings and selling the full bags of aluminum to Reynolds. There's always homeless people out there at Reynolds, selling the cans they've collected on the streets. A few times, when me and another fellow were feeling particularly venomous towards the board, we played Santa Claus and handed out some bags. Each bag was probably worth about $15. We wouldn't say anything, just give the bags out. They'd be surprised. Sometimes we'd put bags around the yard at night for some of them to find.

I don't think the board would take too kindly to this, particularly since they're such a "moral" organization. But there's no way they could ever find out.

CHRISTMAS ORNAMENT SHIPPING CLERK EMMETT

At one time, the Bradley Novelty Company was the second largest maker of Christmas ornaments in the United States. They were very proud of it. They were in South Boston, which meant forty-nine percent of the people were Italian Catholic, forty-nine percent were Irish Catholic, and two percent were me and four black women. At lunchtime, an Italian matriarch would bring lunch for all the Italians, and an Irish matriarch would bring it for the Irish. The rest of us would just sit there. The black women and I wondered why there wasn't any child care, why we were only making $1.90 an hour and why everyone kissed ass to the factory. The Italian foreman offered me Italian girls from the assembly

Fred Harper testified he stole $1 million in parts from General Motors in eighteen years as a truck driver, most from Pontiac Motor plants where the company he drove for was making pick-ups.
— Automotive Industries Magazine[4]

line if I would do things for him. I really hated the place.

We were loading train cars with Christmas ornaments and there was this artificial snow stuff that was everywhere and it started caking in my lungs. I went to the supposed first-aid office to complain and it was locked with nobody there, as usual. I asked for a day off to go to the general hospital and they said no. "We've got to get these boxes out so people can celebrate Christmas; you wouldn't want to ruin their Christmas!"

I quickly got disillusioned with the place and started destroying all the Christmas ornaments I could get my hands on. I threw cases and cases of them against the brick walls. I just couldn't stop myself once I heard the sound of those delicate ornaments smashing into thousands of red pieces, green pieces, and pieces with snowflakes on them. When I reached my self-imposed quota, I packed the worthless ornaments up and sent them out to the hundreds of soon-to-be-irate customers. Since I was the last person to load them onto the trains, no one would find out til it got to its destination — and I knew I'd be long gone.

AIR FREIGHT TECHNICIAN • DIETER

We were called ground hammers. We'd guide airplanes in, park them, hook them up with the ground units, load them up with freight, then take them back out.

The work was insanely boring, but it was hard because everything was on a schedule. Each plane had to get to another state by a certain time and there's only a certain amount of time allotted for each one. Everyone who worked there had to bust their ass.

At times I enjoyed it because I worked with a lot of cool people. None of us liked the bosses because they were always giving us shit. We'd be doing our work and talking but they were constantly telling us to shut up and just work. They always expected optimum performance from us. We were always complaining about that because we could talk and work at the same time.

There was one asshole boss who would always come around to check on us. This guy was a total prick and constantly on our backs. We'd be working our asses off, drenched in sweat and he'd come over and yell at us, "Alright, put your shirts on and shut up. I'm tired of this shit!" He'd be throwing his clipboard around and telling us to speed up for no reason. Whenever he started acting like that, everyone thought, fuck it and slowed way down. There wasn't much he could do about it. It's not like he could fire everyone. Even the quiet people who always said they liked the job did it.

This boss really had it in for us. One of the guys I worked with got fired for some bullshit and another got suspended. I thought I was going to be next. So on a really busy night, I just quit. I waited until I saw the plane that I was supposed to guide in touch ground, and as soon as it did, I took off. The plane sat out on the taxiway waiting to be brought in. They were pretty pissed.

I think if we didn't do anything we'd have gone fuckin' nuts there. It was work, work, work and we were expected to leave our

personalities aside. What we did made us feel like we weren't owned.

MESSENGER • SAMMY

I delivered and picked up documents for the shipping industry. I had the hardest route, which included all the consulates. Documents for the shipping industry go from one place to another to another, so I always had to keep track of where they were at any one time. Some would be really strict about giving me documents unless I had some kind of proof that I was to pick them up. I couldn't walk in and get it. After I got to know the people on my route, they told me that I was the first person to last more than a month.

The company was really strict about time. The owners would pop in, yell at everybody, and leave. They had ex-messengers that they had set up to run things. I really hated the place — everybody hated it. The messengers were lowest on the totem pole in that company, and the company was the lowest in the hierarchy of messenger companies in the city. Nobody liked anybody. I don't even think the messengers liked each other.

One of the ex-messengers in charge stole my wallet from work, which shows you what management/employee relations were like. It was pretty obvious that no one made any money there, and the next day he took his girlfriend out to lunch at a really nice restaurant and showed up with a new pair of shoes. Everybody knew that he did it, but nobody would do anything about it. There was no attempt at an investigation or anything.

I decided to quit, and I said, "I'm going to fuck these people!"

I started dropping off documents and not keeping any records of what I was delivering. When anything had to be picked up, there'd be no record for it, nothing at all. I started leaving things at the consulates. If a customer said, "The ship's got to leave port. Where's the visa?" I'd say, "They said it would be delayed a couple of days, so next week." Of course I knew I was going to quit and I wasn't going to be there, and they wouldn't have a messenger to replace me. I did it to fifteen consulates representing about twenty shipping lines.

I believe the clerks at the shipping lines, who were responsible for getting the documents to the ships, started calling the company, saying "Where's my visa?" No one at my company could produce any paperwork and they couldn't find me. It was a major disaster, and it's a sure bet the company started losing accounts. That's all the consulates could do: not give them any more business.

I had a friend who was working there at the time. When I talked to him a couple of weeks later, he said the whole place was dying. I went by the place six months after that, and it wasn't there anymore. I don't know if it was because of me or not, since other people were in the same position. But it's safe to say that I did some serious damage, and I think I had something to do with them going out of business.

WAREHOUSE WORKER • AARON

I was the only white guy working for this furniture outlet store in Washington, D.C. I started out as just a grunt, but by the time I left I was the assistant manager. I just sort of fell into it because the owner and his white management weren't going to promote anybody that was black.

The owner would say "nigger" or "stupid nigger" when he thought he was alone with his white buddies. I also heard him say nasty things about me behind my back, but it was still really obvious that white people were the only ones getting the better jobs in the company.

There was one person who had worked there about three years longer than I had. He had the ability to do any of the jobs I did and was relatively loyal to the company. The only way I could explain why they didn't make him assistant manager was that he was black. Because I was pretty good friends with him, my promotion didn't create tension between us but it did create dissatisfaction all the way around.

Not too long after I started working there, I learned that the company's inventory was a joke and I figured out a variety of ways to steal from them. One day, the guy who should have gotten my position was talking about his money problems and I told him I knew a way to solve them. From then on, we worked together running this scam where we sold furniture for cash.

Customers would buy things at the store, then pick them up at the warehouse where we worked. We actually solicited among friends and acquaintances. If someone needed some furniture, they'd pull up to the warehouse like regular customers, we'd put what they wanted in their car and collect the cash later. We more or less had an understanding of what was going to be taken so nobody would get too greedy and get caught. In two years of doing it, the owner never caught on and we made at least $25,000 each in cash.

I didn't think of myself as Robin Hood helping his black brother. I just wanted to give him something because we were pretty good friends and it made me a lot more comfortable working there knowing that we'd shared the money.

The front defense line against thievery is its supervisors.
— *Supervision Magazine* [6]

Perhaps the most we can say is that theft by employees is a significant and pervasive part of the work experience with between one-half and one-quarter of the typical work force involved in taking company money or property sometime during their employment.
— *Theft by Employees, Richard C. Hollinger and John P. Clark* [7]

F.A.O. Schwartz, the 124-year old complement to Santa's workshop, has dismissed a mailroom employee for sending toys to himself, through various addresses, rather than to the children they were intended for.

The store said it could not determine just how many Petster Puppies, Lazer Tag games, microchip-controlled Yakity Yaks and Inhumanoids (this year's big sellers) were not sent to the correct addresses, but the company's director of stores, John G. Floor, said the "extent doesn't seem major." ... He said the case amounted to "more than just petty theft."

The man apparently took wrapped gifts, sent them to addresses of his own choosing, and then turned in altered freight slips so the store would not know that the packages had been sent improperly.
— *New York Times* [8]

21

PRIME INTEREST IN DOLLARS

Finance

BANK TELLER • JASON

I was sick of starving so I needed a job. I walked into the California Employment Development Department and this was posted on the wall: "Be a bank teller. We'll train you." I didn't have any experience at all. I just went in and took an aptitude and math test and aced them both. Then I went to a week of teller school that was run by Bank of America. They taught me how to count money, handle irate people, and what to do if someone pulled a gun on me.

The job was okay. It was just a job but I was getting paid more money than I had ever been paid before. I ended up working there for a little more than a year. There wasn't that much job pressure at first, but then there was this weird reorganization. I started out working part time, but then they had me doing other work and paid me at a lower rate for these extra hours. I was working full time but classified as part time so I wound up making less but working more. I got kind of tired of working full time but I was told that if I wanted to keep my job I would have to keep working those hours — they refused to hire me full time.

This is when I put the word out to my friends that I would cash any check, just come on down. So over the course of a couple of days, there was a stream of people who had forged checks, or had scammed them somehow and I cashed them. The next day was the busiest day of the year for that particular branch: a Friday, the first of October, payday for welfare, Social Security, San Francisco General, MUNI, the City, and private business. The line was out the door. I just didn't show up. My soon-to-be-wife, who also worked there with me, didn't show up either. We were the two best tellers at the bank and we were also the only ones who spoke English as our first language. It just wrecked that branch. I think that did more damage than all of the bad checks that I'd cashed. I never went back. They tried to call but we didn't answer the phone for a week.

Eventually all those checks came back as bad. I knew that if you steal from a bank from the inside, you'll never be prosecuted because it hurts the bank's reputation. So I didn't think twice about doing what I did. I did it to get even, which I don't think really happened, but it did make me feel better.

STOCK BROKER • P.J.K.

I worked for Smith Barney for two years. I got my job totally by accident. Headhunters love me. They see dollar signs when they read my resume. I don't make much effort to look the corporate part, since I have college up my ass and will do anything from the lowliest of word processing (I type 100 wpm and am literate in nine computer languages) to the highest level of analytical-type work Wall Street has to offer. I got into Wall Street because I'm a hustler. Six years ago I saw all the money those people were stealing, and I thought, "I want a slice."

When I was hired at Smith Barney, my new boss almost wouldn't let me leave — they wanted me to show up and start working the

next day. Of course, this is often a sign that the job has to be filled immediately because the company's a mess, but he wanted me to start the next day because he was a big-shot junk bond analyst and had no helper. He told me I was overqualified but that he'd consider himself fortunate to have me for a little while, doing analytical work at the low salary of $21,000 per year, less than half of what I was making at my previous job. Turns out that this guy is a really nice person and I respect him and like him a lot, but the rest of the shit I saw at that company was mind-bending.

Everything there is done shoddily. I've seen traders lose millions for the firm in minutes because they were hungover and mad at their bosses. You just pick up a phone on the trading floor and start hitting the keys. The touchtone phones are actually computer links to do block trades. One day I picked up some phones, pressed a bunch of buttons and then ran to a Telerate screen to watch the market plunge. I'll never know, but I may have caused a million shares of IBM to be sold that second. This became a big game and I enjoyed scrambling things in the trading department and then running to a screen to see the market fluctuate. It was funny because I'd ask traders if I could use their phones for a second, then get the computer on the line to just pound my fist on the keys.

Once this big, hot-shot analyst — these guys make millions, mind you — wrote this really uncool memo about how his secretaries had all been cocaine addicts and that's why he'd had to fire 'em, and personnel should get off his back for using up so many secretaries. I had six people photocopy this memo and send it around anonymously to hundreds of people inside and outside the firm, all at the company's expense. I sent "news releases" to Ray Brady, the CBS news correspondent, via rush messenger. This was before the big drug-testing shit and it must've really caused a stir. I sent copies to all his previous secretaries and all these other people, and a year later he left. This guy was a sadistic, arrogant fuck, and I sent this memo around to show everybody how he'd screwed himself through his indiscretion. After the way I'd seen him talk to female subordinates, I decided it had to be done. It was scary, but fun.

22 AT YOUR SERVICE

Community Assistance

PROBATION OFFICER • SAXON

As a kid, I was raised on probation, in foster care, and in the Department of Human Services, so I know what it's like to get through it all. When I turned eighteen, I couldn't read or write or do math. My probation officer asked me, "So what the hell can you do?" I said, "I can commit crimes." He then suggested that I become a probation officer because I'd be able to identify with the people I worked with. It sounded like a good idea so I eventually became an officer in a large East Coast city.

I try to think of the community's best interest, not the system's. The system just wants to perpetuate itself. If we were really good probation officers, no one would be on probation and there would be no crime! But then we'd all be out of jobs, and that's why I think the system perpetuates itself.

I'm told to try to keep as many people as possible out of jail, no matter how harmful they are to the community, which is preposterous. A first offender could get time; it all depends on what side of the bed the judge got up on in the morning. You can really work with a person and see them change, just to have the judge go and undermine you. All that work is down the drain because the judge wants to put the person away. I don't find it fair. An officer who works with clients every day and sees them regularly over a period of months should make the decision, not a judge.

I think anyone's lucky if they get me. When I'm working with my clients I try to put myself in their place. I know that I would want to be treated fairly and not put away. If I feel my clients have committed victimless crimes, or the judge is out to screw them, I'll do things in their best interest. I appoint myself as the judge of their case.

When one of these clients is arrested and brought to court, I'll hide their record so no one will ever find it. The judge has no verification so the charges are dropped and the client is off the hook. If a judge orders one of the clients to be drug-tested, it's up to me to make sure it gets done. I'll give the client advance warning so they can pass the test and get the judge off their back. When a client's on probation, they're supposed to have a minimal amount of supervision. For some people, that's five years or five weeks. All that can be done off the record, out of the judge's sight, enabling me to discharge a lot of people from probation before their time is up.

Unfortunately, I don't see any other officers doing what I do. I think that's because they're jaded and lazy. To them it's just a job and they never knew what it's like to come from the bottom.

GROUP HOME COUNSELOR • JESSE

When I was in college, I worked in a lot of group homes for the mentally disabled. These places become mini-institutions themselves, because the behavior programs are very repressive. It was very punitive and I hated that. I hated my boss and what the agency was doing to the clients.

In one job I had a good friend who felt the same way. We had

The probation officer's mission "to protect the community by rehabilitating the offender" is less than precise and provides a dual, sometimes conflicting objective. The focus is the good of the community and the well-being of the client, and within broad parameters established by the court, the officer must balance these interests. How the officer handles this balancing act is left largely to his good judgment in keeping with how he defines his role.
— Federal Probation Magazine [1]

A study by Shirley D. McCune of the job-interest patterns of social work students as compared with students in law, education, and business administration shows them as having a tendency to "avoid systematic-methodical methods for processing information and making decisions, evidencing a dislike for forceful exertion of leadership, and a dislike for the use of external controls to guide the behavior of others."
— Supervision in Social Work, Alfred Kadushin [2]

to work the overnight-awake shift and had this uptight, asshole supervisor who thought he knew everything. He didn't trust anybody, including the staff. He didn't think anyone knew how to do these behavioral programs, or how to work with the clients as well as he did. He and I always bantered back and forth where it was implied that he was trying to get me on something or I was trying to get him on something.

Of course, when he was gone we goofed off. We were supposed to stay up all night, but by the time we got in, the clients had been heavily sedated and were asleep anyway. We had to do these meaningless chores — the household laundry, housecleaning, and writing behavior programs. After we did all of our work we would go to sleep, and believe me, it wasn't like anybody's life was in danger.

One night the supervisor left instructions for us to write up a behavior program for cleaning the refrigerator. Basically you break it down into steps so you can teach a client how, through what's called "conditioning," to follow it. But the process was really intended for staff people, so they would know how to clean out a refrigerator step by step. I was terribly fucking pissed, so we sat down for three hours and wrote a program which had 243 steps to it. I submitted it to the supervisor and he almost had a fucking attack. He said, "Well, I guess you know how to write these up, but it isn't exactly what I was looking for."

When I worked during the day, we used to do stuff like take the van. This guy knew how to change the odometer, so we'd say we were going on a local field trip with the clients and then later turn back the mileage. We would write in the log, "We went to the park and flew kites today and the clients had fun and it was a swell, special day," but we'd really gone to Connecticut.

We saw the clients as adults. When we went out we were supposed to watch and restrict them, but we'd just say, "Go ahead, have fun!" and they were cool, they never got in any trouble. I told my boss he didn't know how independent these people could be if they didn't have to do all the stupid programs. For that reason, I was considered threatening. I had all these really great ideas I wanted to put into the program because I really cared about the people I worked with. Ultimately, I got out of that kind of work, because I couldn't deal with it.

YOUTH SHELTER COUNSELOR • HILARY

Hospitality House, a social service organization in San Francisco, hired me to be a shelter counselor for their youth program as a VISTA (Volunteers in Service to America) volunteer. My salary was $400 a month. The program had up to fourteen kids at one time, boys and girls, from thirteen to eighteen. It was a semi-long term program; they could stay for up to two months. The kids in the program were supposedly gearing themselves towards independent living: finding a job and learning how to live on their own. I was the monitor for the housing program while they were getting jobs or job counseling or education.

I worked there for just a year. During that time, I had very little say in anything. I came from a homeless youth background myself, and while working there I realized why I hadn't ever used services to help myself: most of the kids were treated as statistics. It's federal, state and county funded; there's a lot of competition for those grants. People's salaries, as well as development of the program, come from these grants.

After a year, the VISTA program is over and they have the option of hiring you at a regular salary for the same position. They went ahead and hired me as full-time staff. I worked the same hours, but my salary increased by 100 percent — to $800 a month. I had more say in things because I was a real staffperson. I started hooking into the other workers and the kids more, and started realizing that the kids weren't really learning "independent living" techniques. They weren't learning how to deal with landlords or how to live in a group situation. Certainly none of these kids would earn enough to get a studio apartment in San Francisco or Oakland. So I decided to take it upon myself to have group discussions about things I thought kids should know about living on the streets. The discussions were run by the kids but I facilitated. We talked about everything from how to avoid pimps to how to travel cheaply and safely to how to live in a group. This became very threatening to the hierarchy.

At the same time, I was starting to have more conflicts with the director over other issues, like how much input counselors were allowed to have at the meetings. The position of the counselors was that we spent more time with the kids than anyone else and knew everything about them. In staff meetings, we'd provide input but try to maintain confidentiality, like hinting about what they might need. It became apparent to the hierarchy that we were pulling more weight because we could really represent the kids. They didn't like this, especially the director, because it gave the kids power over the direction the program took. I took it a step further and said we should set up an independent living program the kids ran themselves. They pay the rent, they pay the bills, and you still have staff there involved with the whole program. It made everyone upset except the other workers, who thought it was a great idea. So I implemented meetings on the side, where we staff would go to restaurants to discuss it.

What I didn't realize at the time was that I was trying to collectivize the program and make the position of executive director obsolete. When the program got a grant, she'd always tell us where the money was going — and there was inevitably a portion for her. At the meetings I would say, "That's ridiculous. I don't need another raise. This money should go to this other program." It was gaining momentum; the kids were beginning to get involved and were very supportive of the changes that were happening. The director started to feel threatened by me, personally as well as politically, and decided that the shelter counselors could no longer attend staff meetings because our input — mine in particular — was damaging to the group process. She issued me a warning, which basically said I was disruptive to the group process. There was only one way I could fight it legally, and that was through paperwork. It took three months of going back and forth; it was this four-step process. We got to an impasse and it was sent to the executive director of all Hospitality House programs. He

Excellent organizations also prize autonomy and entrepreneurship among their employees. They allow workers to try new ideas and programs. They listen carefully to and are supportive of innovative ideas. Excellent organizations often are short on discipline and long on imagination and creativity. Managers in these organizations support the workers' search for new and better ways to serve clients. The workers may spend less time than their counterparts in more traditional organizations carrying out orders or following policy manuals or procedural guides.
— *New Management in Human Services*, Paul R. Keys and Leon H. Ginsberg, eds. [3]

Sabotage consists of the deliberate infliction of harm or damage to the employer's business with intent to cause him loss, and is therefore misconduct in the nature of disloyalty.
— *Penalties for Misconduct on the Job*, Alfred Avins [4]

sided with her and backed up the warning against me. I had been there for a year and a half.

The director called me into her office and said I was fired. She said I could stay if I said I was sorry, would never disrupt the group again and did everything her way. I said I was concerned for the program and that if the place wasn't open to different opinions, I couldn't stay.

I left that day. I came back four or five days later for my paycheck and was told by my friends who worked upstairs that if I went downstairs, they would have to call the police. I went downstairs. The six or seven kids down there asked why I hadn't been around, and I said, "Didn't you hear I was fired?" They said no and got upset. I said it wasn't a big thing and they could come visit me anytime, but they said, "This isn't the end." I left. Fifteen minutes later the kids went into the executive director's office and said "Why didn't you tell us that you fired Hilary, and why did you fire her?" She said, "It's none of your business," and they said, "Yes it is." They became very defiant with her, in the spirit of the process we'd been developing, where they are the program and have the right to decide some things. She said, "You'll have to come back later," hoping they'd go off and not come back. They went to this other program where kids hang out during the day and told the thirty to forty kids there, most of whom had been at the program, what happened. They came back — in full force — and demanded an explanation from her. They demanded that I get my job back. She refused. The next day they went upstairs to the art department and used the supplies to make picket signs. They held a picket line in my defense for a few hours to bring me back and in support of kids having the right to develop the program. I didn't get my job back.

Some of the kids made it. The ones I've seen around are doing fairly well. They come in and visit with me at my present job. I'm proud. I hope that everyone who works in the social service industry takes into account what I've done, what it means to be a worker in that industry, and what it means to be someone who is in a program.

WELFARE CASEWORKER • SHAWN

I worked in a large welfare department in Philadelphia. I had 300 cases and a lot of fucking paperwork. You don't work in social services because you care about money; you do it because you want to help people.

A lot of people who work at the welfare office are pissed off because of their own powerlessness. Any ideas we came up with to help the office operate better would get thrown out right away. One time I went to my supervisor with the suggestion of translating an important sign into Russian, since the office was located in a Russian neighborhood. She couldn't make up her mind so I went and did it myself. Later, I got written up for it because I put it up without approval. This was a perfect example of the supervisor's attitudes.

I wasn't protective of the welfare system. I just treated it like I had access to this money that people needed. I used to give welfare

The professional dedicated to serving people will understand that his or her most distinguishing attribute ought to be humility. The doctrine that "we know best" must be exorcised; there is simply no basis for the belief that we who have Masters of Social Work degrees or other similar credentials are better able to discern our clients' problems than they are, and better able to decide how to deal with these problems.
— *Radical Social Work, Roy Bailey and Mike Brake, eds.* [5]

There are signs of new stirrings of social conscience in the United States today, although it will probably be some time before substantial new funds are invested in the problems of common people. Meanwhile, how can the field of social work meet its historic challenge of responding to human need?
— Social Work Day to Day,
Carolyn Cressy Wells

away whether people were eligible or not. This saved me a lot of trouble because if you turned someone down, they'd bitch. We had access to the computer so it was really easy to add someone to the file. I would just overlook a few facts here and there.

About six months after you enter someone into the computer system you will sometimes get information claiming the person was working while they were collecting welfare, or that they have a bank account. The caseworker is supposed to write the person up and start the system of prosecution. Fuck that. If the person wasn't an asshole and wasn't eligible for welfare, I'd go into the computer, delete their files and claim that no fraud existed. Then I'd write a narrative about how good the person was. In that way, I felt that I was helping people out.

23

TIGHTENING THE BOLTS
AND LOOSENING THE SCREWS

Repair

INDUSTRIAL MAINTENANCE MACHINIST MAX

I was brought up with a strong work ethic. I work hard even when I don't think I'll get rewarded for it. In the same way, it's not a natural action for me to want to fuck up machines because I have a great respect for machinery.

I was on a maintenance crew at a big factory in Massachusetts that made plastics. There was a 900-ton hydraulic press which wasn't working right. They had it stamping out these cases for periscopes for the Department of Defense. We took the machine apart and as I was reassembling it, I found this steel protective ring that was supposed to protect the cast aluminum body of the machine from the bearings. It took me a while to figure out what side it was supposed to go on, and I realized that it would really fuck up the machine if I put it on the wrong side. At first I thought, "Wow, it's a good thing I figured that out; I could've wrecked the machine if I put this plate in on the wrong side." And then I thought, "Yeah, I could wreck this machine." It was a totally spur-of-the-moment thing. The machine would work, but the rollers would eventually wear through the aluminum and ruin the whole machine. These machines run at high speeds, twenty-four hours a day; I guessed it would take two weeks to a month to wear through.

I wouldn't have done it if I hadn't hated the place. Even by the standards of other factories I worked in, the work environment was grotesque. They were ultra-authoritarian. There was always some type of supervisor looking over my shoulder, watching my every move.

REFRIGERATION MECHANIC • ERNEST

I went to work for my father when he was doing maintenance construction for the Mark Restaurant chain, based in Akron, Ohio. I approached the company about doing their refrigeration, so they gave me eight of their stores to service on a trial basis. I had absolutely no experience. So when an ice machine was down, I would go to the manufacturer's, get brochures, and get the part I needed. The company would pay for the part and unknowingly pay for the brochure.

I'm really mechanically inclined, so I picked up on everything right away and I became really good at what I did. They gave me all of the restaurants in the chain and carte blanche on parts. I fixed the equipment with very few call-backs. Everybody liked me and I was very well trusted.

I would buy parts and charge the company for them as part of my labor. I bought all of my tools that way, electric meters and stuff like that. I think it was easily $3,000 worth of tools. Since I was sub-contracted, I wrote my own ticket. It was like a perk item.

I did this for about two years. To make a long story short, I quit the job and went to work for a private refrigeration company and I had a tool box loaded with tools. I didn't even use half of them.

I always covered my ass. I got a lot of tools but I did a lot of things

---

The importance of the maintenance function in industry has never been challenged. It certainly has had none of the glamor of the marketing or research functions, and it has not in the past enjoyed the close attention received by the production operations; but we have always been aware of the fact when the maintenance job was not being done.
— Modern Maintenance Management, Elmo J. Miller and Jerome W. Blood, eds. [1]

Last year some thoughtless workers neglected a machine and this year it's for sale as junk. This company cannot prosper unless each worker does his share to protect and care for valuable equipment.
— Labor poster from 1923

Marketers reported that service parts were taken by employees and sold; also vulnerable were the parts used to repair trucks and some tools.
— Fueloil and Oil Heat Magazine [2]

that somebody else would get paid a lot more for. I was always at peace with my conscience. I thought what I did was an equitable exchange. I felt I was worth what I got. I would never do it just to cause shit and I don't think I ever really did it to fuck them over.

CAR MECHANIC • SCOTT

I've been working solely on BMWs for ten years, but I've been working on cars ever since I can remember. I've always wanted to work on exotic cars, but in Rochester, New York, a BMW is as about as exotic as you can find. I pretty much service everything on them but I like to work on the higher tech stuff: fuel injection and things that require more knowledge of electronics and computer systems.

At my current job, my boss tries to overcharge the customers. Because of the kind of business he's in, he figures he can get away with it. He sees dollars flying away if he doesn't do it.

I get in arguments with him on how much time I spend on a car. Since I'm the most knowledgeable person in the shop, I'm constantly interrupted to help one of the other mechanics, answer the phone or talk to a customer. Every interruption takes away from my time of actually working on the car and it takes me a few minutes to get back into synch. The owner gets antsy about me spending five hours to do a two-hour job. He ignores the fact that I've only been working on the car for two hours and doing other things the rest of the time. Still, he wants to charge the customer for the full five hours. I'm like, "The hell you are," especially if I've talked to the customer on the phone and explained how long the job would take. I've threatened to get a stopwatch out and press the button only when I'm working on the car so we can bill the customer accurately. I actually started to do it for a couple of days, I was so pissed off.

COPIER REPAIR TECHNICIAN • C.J.

My job at Kodak in Denver, Colorado was repairing high speed copiers at customer offices, which I thought meant little supervision. Little did I know that "looking sharp and professional at all times" was most important. For the first five months there was little interference from my supervisor, Steve. Things went downhill quickly when the business climate changed and customers were buying and leasing fewer Kodak copiers.

Steve started evaluating my work by visiting where I was repairing the customer's copier. Then he would write me up, selectively noting bad things about my performance, like how I dressed in slacks that did not look "professional." One time he went out to lunch with my co-workers and me to see how I "interacted" with them.

When Steve fired me, he told me I had to sign a paper saying I left under my own free will. I told him he would have to wait a very long time before I did that. For sticking up for myself, I received two weeks of severance pay, medical benefits for two months, and unemployment benefits, none of which I would have gotten if I had just signed that agreement with Steve.

I moved out to California to work for a small company in the San Jose area that serviced Kodak copiers. They wanted someone right away and gave me the impression I was the one they wanted. I soon found that the service manager at this place wanted me to be even more "professional" than Kodak. A week after I was hired, I told my supervisor during lunch that I windsurfed and that I planned to keep my board on top of my car so I could sail after work. The supervisor told me that I would look "unprofessional." Needless to say, I only lasted two weeks and during my "de-interviewing" — firing — I was told how I didn't fit in. The supervisor insisted on insulting me and telling me about all his troubles, even though he didn't want to hear any of mine. So I asked for my check. After I got it, I "returned" the parts and tools that I carried in my car, throwing them all over the parking lot of the office complex and yelling, "If you don't give a shit about me, why should I care about you?"

My supervisor looked at me in this totally perplexed trance, like he was thinking: "This person looks mad and humiliated; gee whiz, I wonder why..." After I got into my car, I proceeded to run over the parts I had tossed onto the parking lot. Leaving like a flaming madman was not as humiliating as the supervisor would have liked to believe.

24

UNITS, LOTS AND PLOTS

Real Estate

REAL ESTATE SURVEYOR • SAM

A friend and I saw an ad for a job making $10 an hour. The ad said something about making maps, but it wasn't specific. So we checked it out. The place was on the nineteenth floor of a fancy office building in New York. It turned out that some woman in charge of some division of this huge conglomerate was hiring people to make maps of all ground-level retail stores in New York City, every single street in Manhattan, and eventually the other boroughs. All real estate companies do this kind of thing. I don't know exactly what they use the maps for, except for some kind of demographics of what sections of the city have what types of stores.

The job was pretty cool — we had to walk up and down the streets. We'd just draw a real crude diagram of where the store was and what level it was on the street, that's all. It was a pretty easy job even though it was time-consuming. Occasionally, some touchy property owner in Manhattan would tell us to get the hell away from his building, but that was expected.

A couple of weeks after we got the job, we realized that it was really stupid to be working for a large real-estate company. In New York City especially, there's a lot of really shitty stuff that goes on with real estate companies, like kicking people out of homes and demolishing affordable housing. This was one of the companies that did that. They had a lot of office buildings in places that were once residential buildings. At the same time, we worked out that no one at the company was about to go around verifying the information on the maps we drew, so we figured it wouldn't be a problem to start faking them.

At first we would sit in a restaurant and draw the maps; then we realized we could do it at home while watching TV. We'd check in with the office every morning then go back to my house and relax. At the end of the week we'd turn in the maps we made up. After a while, my partner stopped working altogether but still collected his paycheck. He told the boss he was working on a particularly difficult section of the city, like a part with a lot of stores.

Eventually I quit, which in retrospect was stupid because I could have gone on there for a long time that way. I would have made a lot of money. My friend kept going in to collect money without working to see how long he could do it. He did it for about a month and a half.

APARTMENT MANAGER • KENT

I like my job in many ways and one of the most significant is that I don't have a boss looking over my shoulder every minute of every day. That's rare in a job. This building is my own little forty unit kingdom. Although I don't own the building and don't get the rents that I collect, I've been delegated authority by the owner and that's how I treat the job — as if it were my building. I take care of things adequately and the owner's only wasting his time doing inspections. The bottom line is that as long as the rents keep coming in and the apartments rent easily, he really doesn't care.

The owner instructed me that every applicant should have a

One of the most remarkable feats in real estate is to acquire control of a potentially great site when it looks miserable. Perhaps it's out of the way or disfigured with decrepit buildings, or it may seem a poor bet because of land use restrictions. You need bold, contrary thinking to see beyond present realities and envision changes which will add value. Then you've got to back your convictions with cash.
— Risk, Ruin and Riches, Jim Powell [1]

Crime is a logical extension of the sort of behavior that is often considered perfectly respectable in legitimate business.
— The Business of Crime

Work, in short, can be a burden. And insofar as it is a burden, humans avoid it if they can; and if they cannot they need to have a reason for taking it up.
— Work, Inc.: A Philosophical Inquiry, Edmund F. Byrne [2]

The responsibility for liking your job and creating the conditions for job satisfaction is yours. Although you can enlist your employer's cooperation, your job satisfaction never becomes your employer's responsibility. That isn't to say that disliking your work is your fault. Doing something about it is your responsibility simply because no one else can do it.
— Working and Liking It, Richard Germann [3]

minimum net income of three times their rent, and that I'm to do a credit check on each applicant and base my decision on the credit check. I'm not supposed to rent to anybody who has been evicted by a previous manager or any previous residence. I basically throw these instructions right out the window. I rent the apartments to people I feel like renting them to. The entire application process is just a cover. I get a good understanding of the people through the application, but the actual figures on the piece of paper and the credit check have absolutely nothing to do with my decision. The owner has no idea of that because however I do it, it works.

The rent is due by the first of the month and then there's a five day grace period; if I don't get the rent by the night of the fifth I'm supposed to charge them a late fee. One of the things my tenants appreciate is that as long as I haven't delivered the rents to the owner, I count late rent as being on time. The concept of late fees is that the delay causes us trouble. But if they pay late and I haven't delivered the rest of the rents to the owner, then they really haven't caused any trouble and I don't charge them the $70 late fee. I've saved them a substantial amount of money by not being a dickhead.

When it comes to check-outs, the owner and the parting tenants end up splitting the cost of repairs, cleaning and other stuff that needs to be done, as opposed to places where managers use every trick in the book to get the maximum deduction. It's a question of what things I choose to include. An awful lot of managers make the most extreme judgment in favor of the owner. I'm very complete when I fill out the forms. With every little detail listed, it's hard for the owner to imagine that I would have missed something.

I'm still not compensated enough, but if it weren't for the fact that I like my job a lot, I wouldn't be doing it. I think that low technology jobs which deal with people, especially in their home-related life, are greatly undervalued. Garbagemen and babysitters have the lowest status, but when you think about it, they're providing the most vital functions. I think people's home lives are very important.

25 **YOUR TAX DOLLARS AT WORK**

Government

PAGE • MIKE

One of the main jobs of a page in the Montana House of Representatives is organizing these huge piles of papers outlining what's going to be talked about during the day. We had to manage a daily file for each representative. The system we were supposed to learn was very complex and based on all these strange numbers and bills. On my first day, it was really confusing. I was trying to go fast but I didn't really understand what was going on. All of the other pages were telling me to hurry up, so I stuffed the papers wherever I could.

At one point during the day, a bill was being discussed and the representative assigned to talk about it stood up and started talking about something completely different. Immediately there was chaos since no one had any idea what he was talking about. Nothing could really go on until everyone got things straight. It happened two more times that day and finally it got to the point where no one was listening to what anyone else was saying.

From then on I'd purposely put the papers in the wrong order. It was very entertaining.

SENIOR OFFICER • BRUCE

Federal employees are subjected to a wide range of management styles. The agencies and bureaus have widely different missions and very little training and development for their "professional" supervisors and managers. As a result, there is a wildly divergent set of standards among even adjoining offices.

The Federal Executive Board is a loose internal organization which establishes certain policies and procedures for federal agencies in a particular section of the U.S. — the "somebodies" who determine snow days and administrative leave. "Snow days" are reserved for worsening snow conditions, while "administrative leaves" are arbitrary employee leaves given around the Christmas holidays.

On a particularly slow Christmas Eve workday, I called the Regional Manager of all Northeast federal operations. I introduced myself to his secretary as "Steve Watkins" of the Federal Executive Board. The name was entirely fictitious, but the affiliation wasn't lost on the secretary. In a flash, she patched me through to the man who managed the entire Northeast.

Although I was a bit panicked, I plunged ahead and breezily introduced myself.

"Hello Ralph," I boomed. "This is Steve Watkins with the Federal Executive Board. How are you?"

This was the moment of truth. If he realized that he'd never heard of Steve Watkins, or had taken a similar phone call minutes earlier, the game would be up.

"Oh, hi Steve, how are *you?*"

This was fantastic! The Northeast Regional Manager was schmoozing away on the phone with a non-existent peer, at taxpayer expense.

"Ralph," I continued, "I thought I'd better call. We've decided that as of 3:00 pm you can let the chickens out of the coop."

"Great!" said Ralph. He thanked me for the call, and we exchanged hearty Christmas wishes.

It was a done deal and I was weak with relief. True to his word, Ralph called all his agency heads and, probably struggling into his own winter boots, passed on the good news. Within twenty minutes, all of the tiniest sub-offices across hundreds of miles in six different states had received the word. If news travels fast, good news goes out like a rocket.

I take pride in single-handedly affording hundreds of federal employees a crack at some last-minute Christmas shopping.

RECORDS CLERK • ZEKE

A long time ago, in the precomputerized days, I got a job with the records department of the Arizona Division of Motor Vehicles. I thought I'd be doing mindless filing from midnight to eight, but when I got there, I found that I was sitting there looking up vehicle registration numbers for cops who were investigating people. I said, "Oh Jesus, is this really what I want to do?" I couldn't afford to quit — I only had a hundred dollars — so I figured I could stand it for a while.

Four or five days after I started, I get this one cop who calls up and gives me half a dozen phone numbers and says, "Yeah, we got a pot party under observation and we're going to get these guys. Give me the information on them." I thought, "Oh, man!" and I just made up vehicle registration info: phony names and phony addresses for all of them. I never heard much more about it.

The following week, a narcotics agent calls and identifies himself as such. I gave him phony information too. This friend of mine was working there and started doing the same thing. Narcs would call in occasionally, and about seventy-five percent of the time, we'd give them bad information. This went on for about two and a half months, until we got word that detectives were coming around, talking to our supervisor. We called her the "peg woman" — she was absolutely awful. We got called in and she said, "Somebody is giving the police false information and we can't prove it's you, but if it happens again, we're going to fire everyone in the department."

My friend and I had both just gotten out of prison for dope dealing, and both of us were selling major quantities of pot at the time. I sort of felt like a Jew helping run a concentration camp. So at that point we both decided to quit rather than start giving the cops correct information. Fortunately, they were never able to pin it on us.

JUNIOR FEDERAL ASSISTANT • GLENN

My friend "Bob Francis" would never think of himself as a saboteur, but at one point he needed a job. Recently laid off from a retail sales job, with a new family to support, no education beyond a GED, a speech impediment and increasing New England unemployment, Bob was up against it. He was willing to work at a basic clerical job paying the equivalent of $15,000, and since I was with the Department of Defense, I stepped in.

Pretending to represent the local library, I conducted a bogus poll for them, inquiring about the education of every Robert Francis in the state. I came up with a Robert Francis who had an engineering degree from Northeastern University, but Jesus, Bob passing himself off as an ex-engineer now selling home appliances? He'd flunked high school math! Obviously, the wrong conversation in an interview would have him streaking for the parking lot with visions of the hounds on his desperate ass.

So Bob applied and replaced a two-year factory stint on the application with an associate degree from Calvin Coolidge Jr. College. CCJC was a defunct, unaccredited go-nowhere education that didn't look odd for a guy who'd spent three subsequent years hustling refrigerators.

The interview came and went. Bob nervously alluded to a diploma buried in a closet at home somewhere and made it through the ordeal without the hounds. The Department of Defense, however, merely needed a few men — or warm bodies — and he was hired as Junior Federal Assistant at thirty-four! Bob is no revolutionary figure though, and he half expects FBI agents in snap-brim hats to pay him a visit with a subpoena.

All went well and he received a few good promotions and he's still merrily shuffling papers for the Department of Defense. The kicker to the story, however, is that after two years they ran a security check on him and awarded him a secret clearance! Almost frightening, huh?

TYPIST • DUG

My bosses at the Pentagon were captains and colonels. They smoked stinky pipes and looked over my shoulder to make sure I was doing everything the way they wanted me to. It was a big drag and I got pretty bored and tried to find ways to add more excitement to the whole thing.

One day they gave me a letter to type asking permission to build fuel storage tanks in Europe for the Eighth Army. The letter described what the tanks were supposed to look like, what they held, and whatever. One of the numbers was for the volume of the tank: 1000 — or maybe it was 10,000 — gallons. Whatever it was, I just added a zero. What the hell, I didn't care.

Anything that left my office went to an office upstairs which consisted of three big desks with people who were even more uptight than the ones I worked for. I figured that if it got through them, it would really happen. If I got caught, I could just say, "It was my mistake."

But the letter didn't come back. For all I know, there are these tanks in Europe holding airplane fuel that are ten times bigger than they're supposed to be. If my bosses knew about this, they would shit in their pants and bleed through their stomachs for the next month. They're so into control that something like that would shatter their universe.

26 STRIKING A NERVE

Medicine

ATTENDANT NURSE • TOM

I spent four years working at a state psychiatric hospital in the Midwest. We had to go through orientation, and part of that was observing shock treatment: a bunch of us in a room watching some anonymous patient strapped onto a bed surrounded by a dozen or so attendants. Just standing there with this group of people and watching something like this I thought, "What are we? We're a bunch of Nazis." There wasn't a lot of electroshock going on at that institution but it was still was part of our orientation.

For a year and a half I worked on a geriatrics ward. We were the on-line staff: we fed, we bathed, we dealt with the day-to-day lives of everybody who was locked up on the ward. It was very degrading, this day-to-day existence. After working there, I promised myself that when I got old, nobody was going to put me in a place like that. I quit after that and went on unemployment.

I went back because I needed a job. My second stint was in a locked adult ward which was all male. I had a reputation as being a good and reliable worker, so I was trusted enough to work freely. I wasn't naive about the work or its implications. I always had some sort of a conscience and felt pretty torn up about some of the stuff going on.

Every morning we'd bring out the medication cart. People would be given doses up to four times a day. I knew all the drugs. You had to know what you were giving out because some people were getting medication for a heart condition or for seizures. After I'd worked there a while I started trying to monkeywrench the medication system. It was sort of a way to calm my conscience. The problem was that the other staff, especially the night staff, were doing exactly the opposite. They would snow the patients: give them larger drug doses than prescribed, and add on a couple of hundred milligrams of Thorazine or whatever, basically drug them so they'd have a quiet night. If someone is given Thorazine for a long time, it affects their central nervous system. Anybody coming to our ward would see lots of people shuffling around. They called it the Thorazine shuffle. You get facial spasms and all sorts of things. If you go out into the sun and you've been on Thorazine, you burn. It has all kinds of bad effects. So I'd give the patients straight orange juice, and not put the Thorazine in.

One of the few people I could talk to on our ward was Donald, a man in his forties. He was very quiet — psychiatrically, they'd probably call him a chronic depressive. They put him on Prolixin, a heavy duty tranquilizer which is administered in intramuscular shots that last two or three weeks. It's extremely powerful. I didn't like it when it was introduced in our ward, so I'd take Donald to the medication room and ask him, "Donald, do you want this shot?" Donald would never talk much, but he would shake his head. I'd then break the ampule and dump it down the sink, snap the needle and throw it in the needle box. It was just one small way of dealing with a really bad situation. The unfortunate thing is, you can do all the monkeywrenching you want, but it doesn't change anything. Donald's probably still in that institution, and there are still people administering those Prolixin shots.

Most people think that medical care is good for you. The fact is that some medical care is good for you, a great deal is irrelevant and, unfortunately, some of it is harmful.

— Dr. Lester Breslow

Perhaps the most we can say is that theft by employees is a significant and pervasive part of the work experience with between one-half and one-quarter of the typical work force involved in taking company money or property sometime during their employment.

— Theft by Employees, Richard C. Hollinger and John P. Clark [1]

When you work in an institution, one of the things you never escape is that you're basically a guard. If a doctor gives orders to put somebody in seclusion, whether right or wrong — I don't know if you could ever argue that it was right — you'd have to do that. If the person didn't go willingly, we were the people who had to take them to the seclusion room. If they were ordered to have a shot, we had to pull down their pants and stick them in the ass with this big needle. Sometimes it was because of the moods and the whims of the psychiatrists, who didn't want to listen to someone who was angry and maybe had something to say to that shrink. In the worst situations, they'd be thrown in the seclusion room, stripped down totally. There was nothing but a barred window with little holes in it. You'd look in there and you'd see this person stark naked in a corner, pacing around, spitting through the holes. It was pretty horrendous. After my second stint there, I decided that was it for me.

PHARMACY CLERK • ALBERT

Back when I was doing drugs, I had a friend who worked at this little pharmacy near where I lived. The guy who owned the pharmacy was this horrible, cantankerous, oppressive old man who treated my friend like shit and paid him as little as possible. He wasn't crazy, just really cheap. My friend wanted to get back at him, and me and two other friends wanted drugs. We were always trying to get him to steal us stuff but he couldn't do it. All the good stuff was locked up in the narcotics cabinet. If he got caught stealing, he'd get fired and busted.

We knew another guy that did occasional armed robberies to supplement his income. He was a strange person, a family man from out in the suburbs, with a wife and three kids. He was in his early thirties, had lots of mortgage payments, worked for Chevron, and didn't make enough money. Since they didn't know each other, we figured we'd put the two guys together.

We started planning something and my friend at the pharmacy was very amenable to it. He knew exactly when he and his boss were the only ones there. He chose a Saturday evening right before closing, when there would be lots of money in the register and nobody around. We drew up a list of the things we wanted and gave a copy to each person. We made a deal with the robber guy: he could keep any money he got from the register, and we'd get the drugs. We planned to use what we wanted and sell the rest. The pharmacy guy was going to get some of the money from the drugs. We even supplied the gun the guy used. Someone had left it at my house; it was a .22 target pistol that we didn't have any bullets for.

It went like clockwork. He went in about 5:00 pm and it was completely empty. The neighborhood was dead. He told the two of them to lie down on the floor. He had the list and two big paper shopping bags. They were worried about time, so our friend had already studied the list and knew what was on it. All he had to do was tell our other friend what he wanted. The clerk scurried around, emptied the drawer, and filled the order, while the robber guy kept the pharmacist on the floor. He was out of there in three minutes.

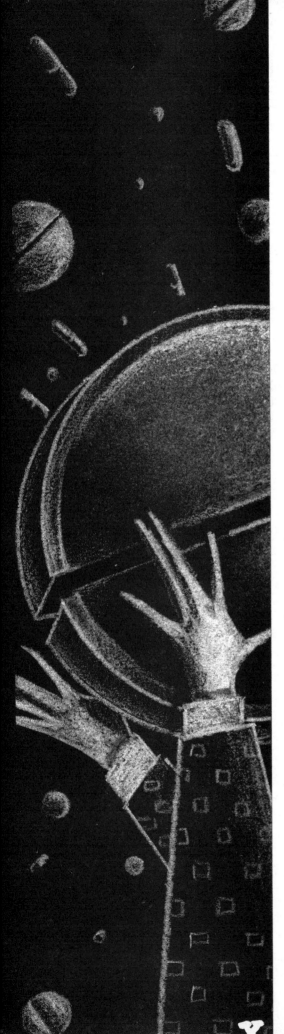

He came over to my apartment and gave us the stuff. For junkies, it was like Christmas. There was an insane amount of drugs, thousands of pills and two quart bottles of liquid morphine. We did an absurd amount of them and sold a lot of reds that we didn't want. We made several hundred dollars and gave most of it to the pharmacy guy. After all, we were junkies. We had drugs, so we didn't need the money.

It had been a busy Saturday and the robber guy got about $400 in cash. The insurance probably covered it, so ultimately it was the insurance company that got ripped off. The owner's premiums probably went up a bit. The owner called the cops and gave a description of the robber but it didn't make any difference; he was long gone.

My friend continued working at the pharmacy for a couple of months but finally got fed up. He didn't feel any remorse, he felt excited about it. He didn't care about the money. His main motivation was to fuck over this guy, who had been fucking him over for a long time.

AUTOPSY TECHNICIAN • FIONA

My job was to remove organs from dead bodies at George Washington University Hospital. A lot of the time we ended up just sitting around waiting for people to die. Two of us worked in the morgue there. We maintained and ordered supplies and assisted all the doctors.

I worked with this guy who drank two beers for breakfast. It made me kind of nervous. As it turned out, he managed to drink all the time without ever getting really out of it. He worked the system to his best advantage. When I started working there I would do tons of stuff and he'd say, "Sit down, what are you doing?" and I'd say, "Well I'm just sick of sitting around," and he'd say, "Don't knock yourself out on your job; how much are you getting paid to do this shit?" I was getting paid $8.50 an hour, which is ridiculous considering all the diseases I could have caught from all the dead people. After I'd worked there a month, I caught on and relaxed.

Not everyone who dies has to have an autopsy; it has to be requested by the physician and approved by the family. So we only had to do four or five a week. The rest of the time we'd sit around or sleep a lot. We'd get there, eat breakfast, read the paper and be ready to work at about 11:00 in the morning. It takes about two hours to do a complete autopsy. After that, feeling way overworked and underpaid, we'd take a long two hour lunch break.

The morgue is where they keep all the bodies; funeral homes come and pick them up. Usually just one funeral attendant would come and they would always need help — so we would help and they'd give us $5. If they didn't give us money, we would never help them again. We also used to sell them supplies, mainly towels or gowns. We'd make maybe $5 or $10 a day and go out for lunch.

I didn't really hate my boss that much; it didn't feel like I had one. The people who ran the department were actually across the street, so they were never around. One woman who didn't have anything to do with my job was always sticking her nose in to check

If 'conspicuous consumption' was the badge of a rising middle class, 'conspicuous loafing' is the hostile gesture of a tired working class.
— Work and Its Discontents: The Cult of Efficiency in America, Daniel Bell [2]

Robert Half of Robert Half International conducts annual surveys of time theft. He has estimated that employers lost $150 billion in 1984 to time theft. Coming to work late, taking excessive breaks, conducting personal business, taking long lunch breaks, and leaving early add up over a year's time.
— "Employee Theft: A $40 Billion Industry," American Journal of Political and Social Science [3]

The greater the power, the more dangerous the abuse.
— Edmund Burke

... not all sabotage involves aggressive or violent actions. It can be as simple as slowing down one's work output — and can be just as damaging in the long run as destroying expensive machinery.
— Supervisory Management Magazine [4]

us out, so we did whatever we could to screw her over. She'd ask us to set up the conference rooms and we wouldn't do it. She'd call and ask about it and we'd say, "We're up to our necks in work, we really can't do it." Other stuff was done out of convenience. I stole Clorox, soap, towels, tape, surgical blades, and scalpels. The biggest thing I ever took was a human brain.

I never got caught. The guy I worked with got caught stealing from the cafeteria, but he's still working there. I finally left after a year and a half because I got bored sitting around and not doing anything.

BIOLOGIST • MORT

I was a research assistant in a group doing immunology. A company had given us money to develop an antibody detection test for HIV. The company wanted to market a kit to physicians that would actually speed up the process of HIV detection.

The problem was they were getting into the game a little too late, because people were already looking at other methods that were more sensitive and definitely more reliable. I felt the focus was really on making money. I knew the company was profit-oriented, but I saw the research program directors were even more concerned with making money than with the ramifications of the disease. To that end, they were even willing to shade the truth. They told the granting agencies that we had purified "x" amount of proteins when we hadn't. I didn't like that. It's not right and it's against the law.

They were erratic about their objectives, and squelched a lot of really good scientific ideas. I felt my immediate boss had some really interesting ideas, really pertinent, but they were often squelched by very irrational pressure shifts in the group.

We were interested in a basic science project that looked more closely at the proteins involved on the surface of the virus. It was a really fascinating project, but it received very little support. I thought that the project was very attractive and would get funded. But these people go for something that's big money, like a product that can be marketed.

Unreasonable requests would be placed on us. They'd want an evaluation of antibodies or proteins, and they'd want it yesterday. They'd ask, "Why haven't you done this?" I would put them off by saying, "I don't have the blots ready, and it's going to take me some time to finish them," when in fact it would have taken half of the time to do it.

Oftentimes it would just be a matter of putting it off a day. But there were times when I'd slow something down a week. It wasn't worth it to me to stay late doing something I was uncomfortable with. They were wound up so tight that they were going to blow, but it wasn't my fault. It was a matter of my personal priorities. All I had to do was think, "How much time do I need to do this? What else do I want to do and what else is more important?"

It was a very passive sort of resistance, although it ended up being an active one. I don't want to imply that it was only motivated by a feeling that they were unethical. It was primarily motivated by ethics, but also by anger.

It wasn't malicious; I felt what *they* were doing was malicious. I think they had other motivations that I couldn't agree with. In this day and age, when people are dying, you don't want to squander resources for the sake of making a quick profit.

HOSPITAL PERSONNEL • MALCOLM

One day the three hospital workers I lived with showed me a memo the hospital put out announcing a picnic for the staff. It said you had to bring your own food. The administration thought they were doing all the workers a great favor sending them this invitation to a bring-your-own-food picnic.

We took the memo and reworded it so it said the hospital would provide steaks and a bunch of other stuff. We sent it through inter-office mail so it went to every station in the hospital. Supervisors took it as a real message and posted it around their departments. Within a few days, the administration sent out a message saying, "Disregard all previous messages about the picnic. There is still going to be a picnic. The kitchen workers will be cooking up hamburgers and hot dogs." It went from bring-your-own-food to them providing it.

The hospital circulated another memo about everyone having to help cut labor costs. We replied to it by sending out one suggesting that the best way to cut costs was to move the hospital to Korea. We listed all the options for moving and some people read it and halfway believed it, then realized it just wasn't possible. It was one of those jokes that gets to the heart of the matter.

The hospital puts out two magazines, one called *Pulse* and one called *Pulsebeats*. The first is internal, for employees, and the other is for the community, although it probably never gets out of the hospital. Because the memos we put out were well-received, we took *Pulsebeats* and turned it into *Deadbeats*. It was a complete parody of the official magazine.

Deadbeats was circulated and quickly became popular at the hospital. "We don't care" buttons were made and proudly worn by workers. Other hospital workers contributed material and another issue came out. Unfortunately, there were only two issues. The administration got wind of *Deadbeats*. They seized the mail room and searched all the mail packets to stop its distribution. The second issue was the last issue but a lot of people at the hospital still flash their "We don't care" buttons.

The stuff we did was well received. We only got negative reactions from one or two people. One nurse who made a comment like, "They must have too much time on their hands." I think that nurse was administrative and her job wasn't on the line.

It was a way of gaining leverage in different employee situations that were going on. They were cost-cutting and when they started to see all the sarcasm, they tried to do something that wouldn't get as big of a rebellion going. Judging from the stuff that was coming out, they knew they had to do something.

Reward programs are a major factor in lowering morale.
— Barbara J. Andrews, Minneapolis consultant [5]

Being in the right does not depend on having a loud voice.
— Chinese proverb

PARAMEDIC • DANNY

I worked for a private ambulance service that employs well over a hundred people and covers an entire county in Florida. Every bit of service that we offered cost money. When we performed CPR we were supposed to charge people $25.

We were assigned to the low-income housing projects, so most of the time the people we were helping couldn't afford the services anyway. We never charged for bandages, working on wounds or for oxygen. We never charged anyone for anything. The company knew what we were doing but there was nothing they could really do about it. On every call we gave something away for free. The only thing we couldn't get away from was the mileage, the basic ambulance cost of driving to the call.

All this was a common practice among people that worked there. Fifty percent of the time I did it because the people couldn't afford to pay, and fifty percent because of resentment towards the company. They overworked us and we didn't get a raise in over a year. We were low paid and treated very badly.

One time I worked a twenty-four-hour shift twenty-one days in a row. I had some blood on one of my uniforms and I was told not to wear it again until I'd washed it. After about five days I wore that uniform again, and they fired me for doing so. About a week later they called me up because they needed the names of four patients they had transferred because they couldn't bill them unless they had their names. I said that if they gave me my job back I might tell them the names. They said, "No. If you tell us maybe you'll get your job back." I said, "You're out of your minds." Needless to say, we never talked again. They were very mad at me but they never found out who those people were. The company has since gone out of business.

The next private ambulance service I worked for paid us hardly any money and ran us into the dirt. We got $125 for each twenty-four-hour shift and there was no such thing as overtime. The job was very stressful and was like working in a sweatshop. Like the other job, my uniform had to look perfect all of the time but when you're working on people who have blood all over themselves and you're working four or five days a week, what are you going to do? Carry thirty clean uniforms with you?

The company had this very good contract for one of the cities in the county. There was a standing order with us that if any of the councilmen or special people that approved the company's contract got hurt or injured, we had to respond immediately. One day we got a call from one of these people and halfway there I quit. I stopped the ambulance, got on the radio and told them that I quit and that I was going home. They went nuts. I've never seen a group of people go so nuts before. All three owners of the company called me up on the radio but there was no way they could convince me to go to the call. They didn't care about the person who made the call as much as they cared about returning his favor. I think I really nailed them for that one.

NURSE • ED

I deal with patients who are near death. These people have one foot in the grave and one foot on a banana peel. Most of the patients die. My job is to get these people over each crisis. I follow doctors' orders but I do a lot of my own thinking too. I have to maintain a close watch because any change, good or bad, must be recorded, so my job is very important.

It's a rare thing for a nurse to come out and say, "This doesn't work," because no one wants to believe it. It's almost taboo. Bureaucracy is a good way to maintain the appearance of a stable environment, which is more important to the corporation that owns the hospital than the basic needs of the patients and workers. Hospitals are businesses and nothing else. They see patients as problems that need to be solved in order to gain profit. Hospitals help people, but profit always comes first. What they do with the profit makes me sick. Health is not something that you make a business of.

I look at our society which exalts what we do. To them we perform miracles with our technology because we help people. We don't solve problems, we create them. We cause undue suffering and pain. We're forcing patients to live beyond what is natural. I see pain being inflicted by brilliant people, doctors, because they're following rules which are insensitive to the human beings they treat.

The number one problem among elderly people is infection, which can cause death. When the elderly are in hospitals they need antibiotics or they'll die. It is common for nurses to have an ethical problem with giving elderly people antibiotics because it prolongs their suffering. It's better for these elderly people to die if they want to. It's their right. Our society denies death. We don't want to look at it, so consequently these people suffer. The nurses document on charts that the medication was given, even when it wasn't. The corporations that make the drugs and the ones involved with boarding people in hospitals are making millions of dollars keeping these people alive. Can you imagine the amount of money they would lose if they allowed people who want to die to do so naturally?

With the patients I deal with, the only thing that is really intact is their minds. They're still human beings but aren't being treated as such. Before people are put on life support the doctors explain to the patient their critical condition and how they will do their best to help them from getting worse. They ask the patient if they want to be on life support. Anyone and everyone says yes because it's a human urge to want to live and because they don't know what is involved with their medical situation. Because they sign papers saying they want to be kept alive at any cost, it takes a load of bureaucrats and specialists to find out if the patient is mentally capable of deciding if they want the machine turned off. They would also need a good lawyer. When you're gravely ill and you want to die, you're usually in no condition to deal with the bureaucracy. I've seen patients begging to die, and the doctor ordering their hands and legs restrained to prevent them from disconnecting the life support mechanism. Every day we would hear these people moan and scream and there's nothing we can do about it.

Let me tell you about some common forms of sabotage I know are widespread among nurses. I've seen these things happen in every hospital I've worked at, from Michigan to California.

Many times when a nurse is confronted with a person whose ventricular beats are leading toward death, they will pull the curtain around the patient's bed and shut off the monitor so it can't record any fibrillation. If the doctors try to resuscitate them, the chances of success are far less. These people are elderly, at the end of their ropes, and have multiple serious problems like kidney failures, lung problems, respiratory problems and congestive heart failures. A common situation is a patient's heart going into v-tach and v-fib and then they code. The patient will stop breathing. The nurse will wait a couple of minutes then turn the monitor back on, record the immediate information and call the code where doctors rush in to try and save the patient by various means. They have to do this by law, but it's usually too late.

Nurses do this all of the time out of mercy and compassion for the patient. Sabotage at this level is highly illegal but it's the only way to beat a health system that does more harm than good. The medical field is not what it should be.

Few of nursing's highs surpass the one you get from recognizing subtle changes in a patient's condition, relaying the information to the physician, and thereby averting a code. You'll achieve this rich satisfaction more frequently if you have a mental checklist of dangerous signs and symptoms. Some require a stat response while others are merely urgent, but all red flags demand some level of nursing intervention.

— RN Magazine [9]

Hospitals are the only place where people aren't plotting to get something from you, the only place where man sympathizes with his fellow man.

— Céline

NOTES AND BIBLIOGRAPHY

CHAPTER 1 TRANSPORTATION

1. Morris L. Cooke and Philip Murray, *Organized Labor and Production* (New York: Harper and Row, 1940), quoted in Glen U. Cleeton, *Making Work Human* (Antioch, Ohio: Antioch Press, 1949), 109—11.

2. Arlie Russell Hochschild, "Smile Wars," *Mother Jones*, Dec. 1983, 36.

3. Ann Hagedorn, "Defendant May Get Stiffer Sentence for Violating Employer's Trust," *Wall Street Journal*, 17 June 1991, p. B3.

4. Hochschild, 40.

5. Michael D. Crino and Terry L. Leap, "What HR Managers Must Know About Employee Sabotage," *Personnel*, vol. 66 no. 5 (May 1989), 32.

6. "Ex-Truck Worker Sought in Spill," *Atlanta Constitution*, 25 July 1990, sec. XJ p. 1.

7. Stanley B. Mathewson, *Restriction of Output Among Unorganized Workers* (Carbondale: Southern Illinois University Press, 1959), 127.

8. "MBTA Absenteeism Hits a 9-Year High," *Boston Globe*, 5 Apr. 1989, 24.

9. Herbert G. Gutman, *Work, Culture, and Society in Industrializing America* (New York: Vintage, 1977), 58.

10. Walker C. Smith, *Sabotage: Its History, Philosophy and Function* (Chicago: Black Swan Press, 1913), 16.

11. "Transit Workers Held in Theft," *New York Times*, 16 Mar. 1991, 26.

12. Michael Karol, "The Lows of Being High," *Graphic Arts Monthly*, Sept. 1990, 103.

CHAPTER 2 FOOD PROCESSING

Parts of the Date Pitter story reproduced with permission from Processed World #12.

1. Pierre Dubois, *Sabotage in Industry*, trans. R. Sheed (London: Pelican Books, 1976), 25.

2. David Halle, *America's Working Man* (Chicago: University of Chicago Press, 1984).

3. Jack Horn, *Supervisor's Factomatic* (Englewood Cliffs: Prentice-Hall, 1986), 53.

4. Robert Giacalone, "Employee Sabotage: The Enemy Within," *Supervisory Management*, vol. 35 no. 7 (July 1990), 7.

5. Walker C. Smith, *Sabotage: Its History, Philosophy & Function* (Chicago: Black Swan Press, 1913), 6.

CHAPTER 3 COMPUTER

1. Michael D. Crino and Terry L. Leap, "What HR Managers Must Know About Employee Sabotage," *Personnel*, vol. 66 no. 5 (May 1987), 35.

2. Ibid.

3. Jack Horn, *Supervisor's Factomatic* (Englewood Cliffs: Prentice-Hall, 1986), 125-126.

4. Peter H. Lewis, "When the Password is a Passkey," *New York Times*, 27 Sep. 1987, sec. 3 p. 12, quoted in Mark Lipman and W.R. McGraw, "Employee Theft: A $40 Billion Industry," *American Journal of Political and Social Science*, July 1988, 53.

5. Gerald Mars, *Cheats at Work: An Anthropology of Workplace Crime* (Boston: George Allen & Unwain, 1982), 75.

6. John M. Carroll, *Controlling White Collar Crime* (Boston: Butterworth Publishers, 1987), 10.

7. *New York Times*, 30 Jan. 1977.

8. Courtland Milloy, "Looking for a Job? Watch Out for the 'Integrity Test'," *Washington Post*, 11 Oct. 1990, D.C. sec. p. 1.

9. "Research Reviews" brochure, Muzak Limited Partnership, 1989.

10. Peter J. Ognibene, "Computer Saboteurs", *Science Digest*, July 1984, 61.

11. Crino and Leap, 32.

CHAPTER 4 ART AND DESIGN

1. G. Vassari, "Giotto," in *The Lives of the Painters, Sculptors and Architects*, Everyman's Library, ed. William Gaunt, vol. 1 (New York: Dutton, 1963), 85—86, quoted in André Chastél, "A Fly in the Pigment: Iconology of the Fly," *FMR* (English ed.), vol. IV no. 19 (April/May 1986), 63—66.

2. James C. Cooper and Kathleen Madigan, "Desperately Seeking a Dose of Productivity," *Business Week*, Feb. 19, 1990, 27.

3. Ron A. DiBattista, "Designing a Program to Manage the Risk of Sabotage," *Supervision*, vol. 50 no. 10 (Oct. 1989), 7.

4. Arnold Blanch and Doris Lee, *It's Fun to Paint* (New York: Tudor Publishing Company, 1947), 10.

CHAPTER 5 KNOWLEDGE AND INFORMATION

1. Quoted in "Academic Ambassador," *Newsweek*, 25 May 1970, 69.

2. Herbert G. Gutman, *Work, Culture, and Society in Industrializing America* (New York: Vintage, 1977), 5—6.

3. Jack Horn, *Supervisor's Factomatic* (Englewood Cliffs: Prentice-Hall, 1986), 24.

4. Jeremy Brecher and Tim Costello, *Common Sense for Hard Times* (New York: Two Continents Publishing Group, Ltd., 1976), 71.

5. Michael D. Crino and Terry L. Leap, "What HR Managers Must Know About Employee Sabotage," *Personnel*, vol. 66 no. 5 (May 1987), 34.

6. Banned Books Week '89: Celebrating the freedom to read, American Library Association, 1989.

CHAPTER 6 HOTEL

1. Lewis C. Forrest, Jr., *Training for the Hospitality Industry* (East Lansing, MI: Educational Institute of the American Hotel and Motel Association, 1990), 4.

2. Quoted in "Employee Theft Saps Many Firms," *LA Times*, 7 Sep. 1990, sec. D, p. 3.

3. Forrest, 289.

CHAPTER 7 NEWSPAPER

1. Jack Horn, *Supervisor's Factomatic* (Englewood Cliffs: Prentice-Hall, 1986), 167.

2. Elizabeth Gurley Flynn, *Sabotage* (Chicago: 1916), 5.

3. "Former Paradise Publisher's Revenge?" *Chico News and Review*, 19 Sept. 1991, 14.

CHAPTER 8 GROWING AND CUTTING

1. John Helyar, "The Bad Seed: How Dishonest Children Killed Growing Firm: Young Salesmen Kept Funds Owed to Seed Company; 'Part of the American Way'," *Wall Street Journal*, 30 Sept. 1981, 1.

2. William F. Cheek, *Black Resistance Before the Civil War* (Glencoe, IL: Glencoe Press, 1970), 17.

3. Walker C. Smith, *Sabotage: Its History, Philosophy and Function* (Chicago: Black Swan Press, 1913), 15.

4. Herbert Applesbaum, *Work In Market and Industrial Societies* (Albany: State University of NY Press, 1984), 168—169.

5. Harold Davidson and Ray Mecklenburg, *Nursery Management* (Englewood Cliffs: Prentice-Hall, 1981), 60.

CHAPTER 9 OFFICE

1. Harry Bacas, "To Stop A Thief," *Nation's Business*, June 1987, 16.

2. "Preventing Internal Theft: Encouraging Employees To Report Their Suspicions," *The Peter Berlin Report on Shrinkage Control*, Feb. 1991, 1—2.

3. Herbert Applesbaum, *Work in Market and Industrial Society* (Albany: State University of New York Press, 1984), 77.

4. Jim Cory, "Controlling Employee Theft," *Hardware Age*, Feb. 1988, 53.

5. Harvey J. McGeorge II and Christine C. Ketcham, "Sabotage: A Strategic Tool for Guerrilla Forces," *World Affairs*, vol. 146 (Winter 1983-1984), 255.

6. Roberta Goldberg, *Organizing Women Office Workers* (New York: Praeger Publishers, 1983), 91.

7. Walter Kiechel III, "How Important is Morale, Really?" *Fortune*, 13 Feb. 1989, 121—22.

8. Robert Half International, Inc., *Memorandum*, 20 July 1988.

9. "9 to 5," Dolly Parton, Velvet Apple Music and Fox Fanfare Music, 1980.

CHAPTER 10 MAINTENANCE

1. Harold L. Sheppard and Neal Q. Herrick, *Where Have All of the Robots Gone? Worker Dissatisfaction in the '70s* (New York: The Free Press, 1972), xii-xiii.

2. Harry Bacas, "To Stop A Thief," *Nation's Business*, June 1987, 17.

3. Pierre Dupont de Nemours, quoted in Eduardo Galeano, *Genesis* (New York: Pantheon, 1985).

4. Jack Horn, *Supervisor's Factomatic* (Englewood Cliffs: Prentice-Hall, 1986), 128.

CHAPTER 11 MILITARY

1. RITA (Resisters Inside the Armed Forces), ACT Newsletter #10, vol. 1 no. 3, p. 1.

2. John M. Carroll, *Controlling White Collar Crime* (Boston: Butterworth Publishers, 1987), 179.

3. "Pair Sentenced in Air Force Thefts," *LA Times*, 28 Jan. 1990, A17.

4. Gerald Mars, *Cheats at Work: An Anthropology of Workplace Crime* (Boston: George Allen and Unwain, 1982), 87.

CHAPTER 12 SEX

1. Studs Terkel, *Working* (New York: Pantheon, 1974), 59.

2. Quoted in James D. Walls, Jr., Senior Vice President of Stanton Corporation, "The Workplace: America's Hot Bed of Crime," delivered at seminar entitled "In Search of Management Rights," Nashville, Tennessee, 28 Jan. 1988, in *Vital Speeches of the Day*, vol. LIV no. 12, 1 Apr. 1988, 382.

3. Peggy Morgan, "Living on the Edge," in *Sex Work: Writings by Women in the Sex Industry*, eds. Frédérique Delacoste and Priscilla Alexander (San Francisco: Cleis Press, 1987), 25.

CHAPTER 13 CONSTRUCTION

1. Emile Pouget, *Sabotage*, trans. A. Giovannitti (Chicago: Charles H. Kerr Co., 1912), 101—102.

2. Mark Lipman and W.R. McGraw, "Employee Theft: A $40 Billion Industry," *American Journal of Political and Social Science*, July 1988, 53.

3. Tom Mann, "Tom Mann in the U.S.A.," *Daily Herald*, 16 Aug. 1913, quoted in Geoff Brown, *Sabotage: A Study in Industrial Conflict* (Nottingham: Spokesman Press, 1977).

4. Stephen and Janelle Diller, *How to Succeed With Your Own Construction Business* (Carlsbad, CA: Craftsman Book Co., 1990), 117.

5. Heron, Alexander Richard, *Why Men Work* (New York: Arno Press, 1977).

6. Jeremy Brecher and Tim Costello, *Common Sense for Hard Times* (New York, Two Continents Publishing Group Ltd., 1976), 69.

7. Robert M. Figlio, "The Risk Where We Live," *Security Management* , Nov. 1991, 88.

8. Robert A. Giacalone and Stephen B. Knouse, "Justifying Wrongful Employee Behavior: The Role of Personality in Organizational Sabotage," *Journal of Business Ethics*, vol. 9 no. 1 (Jan. 1990), 60.

9. Ernest Brod, "In the Layoff Era, the 'Get Even' Ethic," *New York Times*, 26 Jan. 1992, 13.

CHAPTER 14 MAIL

1. Adam Abruzzi, *Work, Workers and Work Measurement* (New York: Columbia University Press, 1956), 291.

2. Pierre Dubois, *Sabotage in Industry*, trans. R. Sheed (London: Pelican Books, 1976), 133.

3. Walker C. Smith, *Sabotage: Its History, Philosophy and Function* (Chicago: Black Swan Press, 1913), 24.

CHAPTER 15 ENTERTAINMENT

1. Harry Bacas, "To Stop A Thief," *Nation's Business*, June 1987, 16.

2. Charles Musser, "Work, Ideology & Chaplin's Tramp," in Robert Sklar and Charles Musser, eds., *Resisting Images; Essays on Cinema and History* (Philadelphia: Temple University Press, 1990), 124.

3. Jack Horn, *Supervisor's Factomatic* (Englewood Cliffs: Prentice-Hall, 1986), 390.

4. James Palmer, "The Psychology of Successful Gambling," *Gamblers World*, December/January 1974, 27.

5. Daniel Vasquez, "$700,000 In Cash Stolen From Coliseum," *San Francisco Chronicle*, 23 July 1991, A1.

CHAPTER 16 RETAIL

1. "Workers Out-Stealing Shoplifters," *San Francisco Chronicle*, 24 Nov. 1990, A15.

2. *The Peter Berlin Report on Shrinkage Control*, Feb. 1991, 8.

3. Richard C. Hollinger & John P. Clark, *Theft by Employees* (Lexington, MA: Lexington Books, 1983), 60—61.

4. Peter Block, *The Empowered Manager* (San Francisco: Jossey-Bass Publishers, 1988), 7.

5. Mark Lipman and W.R. McGraw, "Employee Theft: A $40 Billion Industry," *American Journal of Political and Social Science*, July 1988, 55.

6. "Some Customers Are Always Wrong," *New York Times Magazine*, 10 June 1990, 56.

7. Mark Fore, "Strategy For Industrial Struggle," *Solidarity* pamphlet no. 37.

8. James D. Walls, Jr., Senior Vice President of Stanton Corporation, "The Workplace: America's Hot Bed of Crime," delivered at seminar entitled "In Search of Management Rights," Nashville, Tennessee, 28 Jan. 1988, in *Vital Speeches of the Day*, vol. LIV no. 12, 1 Apr. 1988, 383.

9. Lipman and McGraw, 58.

10. Stephen C. Kilgo, "A Theft Control Approach," *Security Management*, Apr. 1989, 82.

11. "Giving Them The Gears," *Open Road*, Spring 1983.

12. Sensormatic Electronics Corporation brochure.

13. Harry Bacas, "To Stop A Thief," *Nation's Business*, June 1987, 20.

CHAPTER 17 MANUFACTURING

1. James Peter Warbasse, "The Ethics of Sabotage," *New York Call*, 29 June 1913, 10.

2. Polly Lane, "Wires Cut on 737 at Renton Plant; Boeing Investigates as Sabotage," *Seattle Times*, 3 Apr. 1990, A1.

3. Geoff Brown, *Sabotage: A Study in Industrial Conflict* (Nottingham: Spokesman Press, 1977), 376.

4. Richard Feldman and Michael Betzold, eds., *End of the Line: Autoworkers and the American Dream* (New York: Weidenfeld and Nicolson, 1988), 36.

5. Quoted in Al Nash, "Job Satisfaction: A Critique," in *Auto Work and Its Discontents*, ed. B.J. Widick (Baltimore: John Hopkins University Press, 1976), 67.

6. Pierre Dubois, *Sabotage in Industry* (London: Penguin Books, 1976), 52.

7. Richard Greene, "Money for Nothing," *Forbes*, 25 Jan. 1988, 48.

8. Emile Pouget, *Sabotage*, trans. A. Giovannitti (Chicago: Charles C. Kerr, 1912), 99.

CHAPTER 18 BROADCASTING
1. Robert L. Hilliard, *Radio Broadcasting* (New York: Longman, 1985), 33.
2. Herbert Zettl, *Television Production Handbook* (Belmont, CA: Wadsworth Publishing Company, 1984), 25.
3. Norman Marcus, *Broadcast and Cable Management* (Englewood Cliffs: Prentice-Hall, 1986), 66.

CHAPTER 19 RESTAURANT
1. John B. Knight and Lendal H. Kotschevar, *Quantity Food Production Planning and Management* (New York: Van Nostrand Reinhold Co., 1979), 7.
2. Harper's Index, *Harper's*, May 1991, 17.
3. James Peter Warbasse, "The Ethics of Sabotage," *New York Call*, 29 June 1913, 10.
4. "Employee Theft Saps Many Firms," *L.A. Times*, 7 Sep. 1990, sec. D p. 3.
5. Peter B. Barr and Phillip W. Balsmeier, "Losing Dough in Bakeries," *Security Management*, vol. 32 no. 3 (Mar. 1988), 88.
6. Craig Wolff, "Ice Cream Crime." *Reader's Digest*, June 1991, 4.
7. Emile Pouget, *Sabotage*, trans. A. Giovannitti (Chicago: Charles H. Kerr, 1912), 55.

CHAPTER 20 SHIPPING AND DELIVERY
1. "Some Customers Are Always Wrong," *New York Times Magazine*, 10 June 1990, 19.
2. "New York Times Blames Delivery Problems on 'Slowdown'," *Editor & Publisher*, vol. 121 no. 22 (28 May 1988), 32.
3. Victor Santoro, *Fighting Back on the Job* (Port Townsend, WA: Loompanics Unlimited, 1984), 106.
4. Douglas Williams, "Stolen Inventory: JIT's Advantage," *Automotive Industries*, Sept. 1986, 30.
5. Bill Johns, "Supervision in a Production Environment," in *Supervisory Handbook*, ed. Martin M. Broadwell (New York: John Wiley & Sons, 1985), 47.
6. Richard Bauman, "It Isn't Stealing ... Is It?" *Supervision*, Oct. 1988, 34.
7. Richard C. Hollinger and John P. Clark, *Theft by Employees* (Lexington, MA: Lexington Books, 1983), 6.
8. Sam Howe Verhovek, "Suspected Grinch at F.A.O. Schwartz," *New York Times*, 17 Dec. 1985, B3.

CHAPTER 21 FINANCE
1. Michael D. Crino and Terry L. Leap, "What HR Managers Must Know about Employee Sabotage," *Personnel* , vol. 66 no. 5 (May 1989), 32.
2. Jack Horn, *Supervisor's Factomatic* (Englewood Cliffs: Prentice-Hall, 1986), 149.
3. "Are Employees Robbing Your Bank?" *Bankers Monthly*, April 1989, 42.
4. Banning K. Lary, "Why Corporations Can't Lock the Rascals Out," *Management Review*, Oct. 1989, 54.
5. Seth Rosenfeld, "Trickle of Treasure Missing from Mint," *San Francisco Chronicle/Examiner*, 27 Apr. 1986, A1.

CHAPTER 22 COMMUNITY ASSISTANCE
1. Darrell K. Mills, "Career Issues for Probation Officers," *Federal Probation*, Sept. 1990, 3.
2. Alfred Kadushin, *Supervision in Social Work* (New York: Columbia University Press, 1976), 109.
3. Leon H. Ginsberg, "Applying Modern Management Concepts to Social Work," in *New Management in Human Services*, eds. Paul R. Keys and Leon H. Ginsberg (Silver Spring, MD: National Association of Social Workers, Inc., 1988), 36.
4. Alfred Avins, *Penalties for Misconduct on the Job* (New York: Oceana Publications, 1972), 94.
5. Richard A. Cloward and Frances Fox Piven, "Radical Social Work," in *Radical Social Work*, eds. Roy Bailey and Mike Brake (New York: Pantheon Books, 1975), xxvii.
6. Carolyn Cressy Wells, *Social Work Day to Day* (New York: Longman Press, 1989), 198.

CHAPTER 23 REPAIR
Parts of the Copier Machine Repairman story reproduced with permission from Processed World #25.
1. Elmo J. Miller and Jerome W. Blood, eds., *Modern Maintenance Management* (New York: American Management Association, Inc., 1963), 5.
2. "Marketers Report on Losses Due to Vandalism, *Fueloil and Oil Heat Magazine*, vol. 47 (Apr. 1988), 60—61.
3. Jimmy Breslin, "Evening News," NBC, 15 May 1974.
4. Robert Sikorsky, "Finding a Mechanic You Can Trust," *Reader's Digest*, Aug. 1991, 131.
5. Jay M. Shafritz, *Dictionary of Personnel Management and Labor Relations* (New York: Facts on File,1985), 378.
6. William Thourlby, *You Are What You Wear* (New York: Forbes/Wittingeburg & Brown, 1990), 44.

CHAPTER 24 REAL ESTATE

1. Jim Powell, *Risk, Ruin and Riches* (New York: MacMillan Publishing Co., 1986), 27.
2. Edmund F. Byrne, *Work, Inc.: A Philosophical Inquiry* (Philadelphia: Temple University Press, 1990), 70.
3. Richard Germann, *Working and Liking It* (New York: Ballantine Books, 1984), 13.

CHAPTER 25 GOVERNMENT

1. Pierre Dubois, *Sabotage in Industry,* trans. R. Sheed (London: Pelican Books, 1976), 54.
2. Sydney Shaw, "New Rule Would Crack Down on Federal Phone Abuse," UPI, 27 March 1987, quoted in Mark Lipman and W.R. McGraw, "Employee Theft: A $40 Billion Industry," *American Journal of Political and Social Science*, July 1988, 54.
3. Gerald Mars, *Cheats at Work: An Anthropology of Workplace Crime* (Boston: George Allen and Unwain, 1982), 87.
4. "Workers Stealing Silverware from U.S. Treasury," *San Francisco Chronicle*, 18 May 1991, A3.
5. Peter J. Ognibene, "Computer Saboteurs," *Science Digest*, July 1984, 60.
6. Jack Anderson, "Flying the Flag," *San Francisco Chronicle*, 4 July 1989, A21.
7. Thorstein Veblen, *On the Nature and Uses of Sabotage* (New York: Oriole Chapbooks 1919), 2.
8. Harvey J. McGeorge II and Christine C. Ketcham, "Sabotage: A Strategic Tool for Guerrilla Forces," *World Affairs*, vol. 146 (Winter 1983-1984), 253.

CHAPTER 26 MEDICINE

1. Richard C. Hollinger and John P. Clark, *Theft by Employees* (Lexington, MA: Lexington Books, 1983), 6.
2. Daniel Bell, *Work and Its Discontents: The Cult of Efficiency in America* (Boston: Beacon Press, 1956), 15.
3. Mark Lipman and W.R. McGraw, "Employee Theft: A $40 Billion Industry," *American Journal of Political and Social Science*, July 1988, 54.
4. Robert Giacalone, "Employee Sabotage: The Enemy Within," *Supervisory Management*, vol. 35 no. 7 (July 1990), 7.
5. "Some Customers Are Always Wrong," *New York Times Magazine*, 10 June 1990, 57.
6. Jack Bologna, *Corporate Fraud* (Boston: Butterworth Publishers, 1984), 89.
7. Jack Horn, *Supervisor's Factomatic* (Englewood Cliffs: Prentice-Hall, 1986), 117.
8. Richard I. Henderson, *Influencing Employee Behavior at Work* (Atlanta: Georgia State University, 1982), 2.
9. Ellie Green, "Clues to a Code: Subtle Signs Can Help You Save a Life," *RN*, vol. 53 no. 7 (July 1990), 26.

- Abruzzi, Adam. *Work, Workers and Work Measurement.* New York: Columbia University Press, 1956.
- "Academic Ambassador," *Newsweek,* 25 May 1970.
- Anderson, Jack. "Flying the Flag." *San Francisco Chronicle,* 4 July 1989.
- Applesbaum, Herbert. *Work in Market and Industrial Society.* Albany: State University of New York Press, 1984.
- "Are Employees Robbing Your Bank?" *Bankers Monthly,* April 1989.
- Avins, Alfred. *Penalties for Misconduct on the Job.* New York: Oceana Publications, 1972.
- Bacas, Harry. "To Stop A Thief." *Nation's Business,* June 1987.
- Barr, Peter B., and Phillip W. Balsmeier. "Losing Dough in Bakeries." *Security Management,* vol. 32 no. 3 (Mar. 1988).
- Bauman, Richard. "It Isn't Stealing ... Is It?" *Supervision,* Oct. 1988.
- Bell, Daniel. *Work and Its Discontents: The Cult of Efficiency in America.* Boston: Beacon Press, 1956.
- Blanch, Arnold, and Doris Lee. *It's Fun to Paint.* New York: Tudor Publishing Company, 1947.
- Block, Peter. *The Empowered Manager.* San Francisco: Jossey-Bass Publishers, 1988.
- Bologna, Jack. *Corporate Fraud.* Boston: Butterworth Publishers, 1984.
- Brecher, Jeremy, and Tim Costello. *Common Sense for Hard Times.* New York: Two Continents Publishing Group, Ltd., 1976.
- Brod, Ernest. "In the Layoff Era, the 'Get Even' Ethic." *New York Times,* 26 Jan. 1992.
- Brown, Geoff. *Sabotage: A Study in Industrial Conflict.* Nottingham: Spokesman Press, 1977.
- Byrne, Edmund F. *Work, Inc.: A Philosophical Inquiry.* Philadelphia: Temple University Press, 1990.
- Carroll, John M. *Controlling White Collar Crime.* Boston: Butterworth Publishers, 1987.
- Chastél, André. "A Fly in the Pigment: Iconology of the Fly." *FMR* (English ed.), vol. IV no.19 (April/May 1986).
- Cheek, William F. *Black Resistance Before the Civil War.* Glencoe, IL: Glencoe Press, 1970.
- Cleeton, Glen U. *Making Work Human.* Antioch, Ohio: Antioch Press, 1949.
- Cloward, Richard A., and Frances Fox Piven. "Radical Social Work." In *Radical Social Work.* Edited by Roy Bailey and Mike Brake. New York: Pantheon Books, 1975.
- Cooke, Morris L., and Philip Murray. *Organized Labor and Production.* New York: Harper and Row, 1940.
- Cooper, James C., and Kathleen Madigan. "Desperately Seeking a Dose of Productivity." *Business Week,* 19 Feb. 1990.
- Cory, Jim. "Controlling Employee Theft." *Hardware Age,* Feb. 1988.
- Crino, Michael D., and Terry L. Leap. "What HR Managers Must Know About Employee Sabotage." *Personnel,* vol. 66 no. 5 (May 1989).
- Davidson, Harold, and Ray Mecklenburg. *Nursery Management.* Englewood Cliffs: Prentice-Hall, 1981.
- DiBattista, Ron A. "Designing a Program to Manage the Risk of Sabotage." *Supervision,* vol. 50 no. 10 (Oct. 1989).
- Diller, Stephen and Janelle. *How to Succeed With Your Own Construction Business.* Carlsbad, CA: Craftsman Book Co., 1990.
- Dubois, Pierre. *Sabotage in Industry.* Translated by R. Sheed. London: Pelican Books, 1976.
- "Employee Theft Saps Many Firms." *LA Times,* 7 Sep. 1990.
- "Ex-Truck Worker Sought in Spill." *Atlanta Constitution,* 25 July 1990.
- Feldman, Richard, and Michael Betzold, eds. *End of the Line: Autoworkers and the American Dream.* New York: Weidenfeld and Nicolson, 1988.
- Figlio, Robert M. "The Risk Where We Live." *Security Management,* Nov. 1991.
- Flynn, Elizabeth Gurley. *Sabotage.* Chicago: 1916.
- "Former Paradise Publisher's Revenge?" *Chico News and Review,* 19 Sept. 1991.
- Forrest, Lewis C., Jr. *Training for the Hospitality Industry.* East Lansing, MI: Educational Institute of the American Hotel and Motel Association, 1990.
- Galeano, Eduardo. *Genesis.* New York: Pantheon, 1985.
- Giacalone, Robert. "Employee Sabotage: The Enemy Within." *Supervisory Management,* vol. 35 no. 7 (July 1990).
- Giacalone, Robert and Stephen B. Knouse. "Justifying Wrongful Employee Behavior: The Role of Personality in Organizational Sabotage." *Journal of Business Ethics,* vol. 9 no. 1 (Jan. 1990).
- "Giving Them The Gears." *Open Road,* Spring 1983.
- Goldberg, Roberta. *Organizing Women Office Workers.* New York: Praeger Publishers, 1983.
- Green, Ellie. "Clues to a Code: Subtle Signs Can Help You Save a Life." *RN,* vol. 53 no. 7 (July 1990).
- Greene, Richard. "Money for Nothing." *Forbes,* 25 Jan. 1988.
- Gutman, Herbert G. *Work, Culture, and Society in Industrializing America.* New York: Vintage, 1977.
- Hagedorn, Ann. "Defendant May Get Stiffer Sentence for Violating Employer's Trust." *Wall Street Journal,* 17 June 1991.
- Halle, David. *America's Working Man.* Chicago: University of Chicago Press, 1984.
- *Harper's,* May 1991.
- Helyar, John. "The Bad Seed: How Dishonest Children Killed Growing Firm: Young Salesmen Kept Funds Owed to Seed Company; 'Part of the American Way'."*Wall Street Journal,* 30 Sept. 1981.
- Henderson, Richard I. *Influencing Employee Behavior at Work.* Atlanta: Georgia State University, 1982.
- Heron, Alexander Richard. *Why Men Work.* New York: Arno Press, 1977.
- Hilliard, Robert L. *Radio Broadcasting.* New York: Longman, 1985.
- Hochschild, Arlie Russell. "Smile Wars." *Mother Jones,* Dec. 1983.

- Hollinger, Richard C., and John P. Clark. *Theft by Employees.* Lexington, MA: Lexington Books, 1983.
- Horn, Jack. *Supervisor's Factomatic.* Englewood Cliffs: Prentice-Hall, 1986.
- Johns, Bill. "Supervision in a Production Environment." In *Supervisory Handbook,* Edited by Martin M. Broadwell. New York: John Wiley & Sons, 1985.
- Kadushin, Alfred. *Supervision in Social Work.* New York: Columbia University Press, 1976.
- Karol, Michael. "The Lows of Being High." *Graphic Arts Monthly,* Sept. 1990.
- Keys, Paul R., and Leon H. Ginsberg, eds. *New Management in Human Services.* Silver Spring, MD: National Association of Social Workers, Inc., 1988.
- Kiechel, Walter, III. "How Important is Morale, Really?" *Fortune,* 13 Feb. 1989.
- Kilgo, Stephen C. "A Theft Control Approach." *Security Management,* Apr. 1989.
- Knight, John B., and Lendal H. Kotschevar, *Quantity Food Production Planning and Management.* New York: Van Nostrand Reinhold Co., 1979.
- Lane, Polly. "Wires Cut on 737 at Renton Plant; Boeing Investigates as Sabotage." *Seattle Times,* 3 Apr. 1990.
- Lary, Banning K. "Why Corporations Can't Lock the Rascals Out." *Management Review,* Oct. 1989.
- Lipman, Mark, and W.R. McGraw. "Employee Theft: A $40 Billion Industry." *American Journal of Political and Social Science,* July 1988.
- Marcus, Norma. *Broadcast and Cable Management.* Englewood Cliffs: Prentice-Hall, 1986.
- "Marketers Report on Losses Due to Vandalism." *Fueloil and Oil Heat Magazine,* vol. 47 (Apr. 1988).
- Mars, Gerald. *Cheats at Work: An Anthropology of Workplace Crime.* Boston: George Allen & Unwain, 1982.
- Mathewson, Stanley B. *Restriction of Output Among Unorganized Workers.* Carbondale: Southern Illinois University Press, 1959.
- "MBTA Absenteeism Hits a 9-Year High." *Boston Globe,* 5 Apr. 1989.
- McGeorge, Harvey J., II, and Christine C. Ketcham. "Sabotage: A Strategic Tool for Guerrilla Forces." *World Affairs,* vol. 146 (Winter 1983-1984).
- Miller, Elmo J., and Jerome W. Blood, eds. *Modern Maintenance Management.* New York: American Management Association, Inc., 1963.
- Milloy, Courtland. "Looking for a Job? Watch Out for the 'Integrity Test'." *Washington Post,* 11 Oct. 1990.
- Mills, Darrell K. "Career Issues for Probation Officers." *Federal Probation,* Sept. 1990.
- Morgan, Peggy. "Living on the Edge." In *Sex Work: Writings by Women in the Sex Industry.* Edited by Frédérique Delacoste and Priscilla Alexander. San Francisco: Cleis Press, 1987.
- Musser, Charles. "Work, Ideology & Chaplin's Tramp." In *Resisting Images; Essays on Cinema and History.* Edited by Robert Sklar and Charles Musser. Philadelphia: Temple University Press, 1990.
- Nash, Al. "Job Satisfaction: A Critique." In *Auto Work and Its Discontents.* Edited by B.J. Widick. Baltimore: John Hopkins University Press, 1976.
- "New York Times Blames Delivery Problems on 'Slowdown'." *Editor & Publisher,* vol. 121 no. 22 (28 May 1988).
- *New York Times,* 30 Jan. 1977.
- "9 to 5." Dolly Parton. Velvet Apple Music and Fox Fanfare Music, 1980.
- Ognibene, Peter J. "Computer Saboteurs." *Science Digest,* July 1984.
- "Pair Sentenced in Air Force Thefts." *LA Times,* 28 Jan. 1990.
- Palmer, James. "The Psychology of Successful Gambling," *Gamblers World,* December/January 1974.
- Pouget, Emile. *Sabotage.* Translated by A. Giovannitti. Chicago: Charles H. Kerr Co., 1912.
- Powell, Jim. *Risk, Ruin and Riches.* New York: MacMillan Publishing Co., 1986.
- "Preventing Internal Theft: Encouraging Employees To Report Their Suspicions." *The Peter Berlin Report on Shrinkage Control.* Feb. 1991.
- "Research Reviews" brochure, Muzak Limited Partnership, 1989.
- RITA (Resisters Inside the Armed Forces). ACT Newsletter #10, vol. 1 no. 3.
- Robert Half International, Inc. *Memorandum,* 20 July 1988.
- Rosenfeld, Seth. "Trickle of Treasure Missing from Mint." *S.F. Chronicle/ Examiner,* 27 Apr. 1986.
- Santoro, Victor. *Fighting Back on the Job.* Port Townsend, WA: Loompanics Unlimited, 1984.
- Shafritz, Jay M. *Dictionary of Personnel Management and Labor Relations.* New York: Facts on File, 1985.
- Sheppard, Harold L., and Neal Q. Herrick. *Where Have All of the Robots Gone? Worker Dissatisfaction in the '70s.* New York: The Free Press, 1972.
- Sikorsky, Robert. "Finding a Mechanic You Can Trust." *Reader's Digest,* Aug. 1991.
- Smith, Walker C. *Sabotage: Its History, Philosophy and Function.* Chicago: Black Swan Press, 1913.
- "Some Customers Are Always Wrong." *New York Times Magazine,* 10 June 1990.
- Terkel, Studs. *Working.* New York: Pantheon, 1974.
- "Transit Workers Held in Theft." *New York Times,* 16 Mar. 1991.
- Veblen, Thorstein. *On the Nature and Uses of Sabotage.* New York: Oriole Chapbooks 1919.
- Verhovek, Sam Howe. "Suspected Grinch at F.A.O. Schwartz." *New York Times,* 17 Dec. 1985.
- Walls, James D., Jr. "The Workplace: America's Hot Bed of Crime," delivered at seminar entitled "In Search of Management Rights," Nashville, Tennessee, 28 Jan. 1988. In *Vital Speeches of the Day,* vol. LIV no. 12, 1 Apr. 1988.